At a time when some evangelical scholars question the centrality of the concept of Messiah in the Old Testament, Prof. Rydelnik courageously challenges fellow believers to re-evaluate the biblical evidence. With erudition he articulates clearly and convincingly the importance of the messianic hope, illustrating this by focusing on three often-disputed Old Testament passages. His book is a significant and timely contribution to a vitally important issue.

T. Desmond Alexander
Professor of Old Testament,
Union Theological College, Belfast, N. Ireland
author, *From Paradise to Promised Land*

When the Church seems increasingly to relish vagueness in its scholarship and spirituality, this book on messianic prophecy by Michael Rydelnik speaks with grace and clarity. It presents a solid exegetical case for the time-honored position that the Old Testament actually predicts the coming Messiah. The Bible is the story of God restoring and reconciling all that was lost in Eden. This grand work of restoration is bound up in the person of Messiah. It would be strange indeed if in the Old Testament God did not speak clearly, regularly, and precisely about this One. He does. Dr. Rydelnik's book is a wonderful explanation of what He has said. It will stimulate the mind and warm the heart of the reader.

Paul N. Benware
Professor of Biblical Studies,
Southwestern College, Phoenix, Arizona
author, *Understanding End Times Prophecy*

Michael Rydelnik's *Messianic Hope* is a well-crafted and timely refutation of the growing minimization of direct messianic prediction in evangelical scholarship. Using a cogent development of innerbiblical, canonical, and New Testament evidence, this study adduces text-critical evidence for reading the Hebrew Bible as messianic. Rydelnik persuasively argues that the centrality of the Messiah in the apologetic method of Jesus and the apostles is consistent with a canonical reading of the Hebrew Bible.

Kenneth Boa
President, Reflections Ministries, Atlanta, GA
President, Trinity House Publishers, Atlanta, GA

Michael Rydelnik's book on messianic prophecy will be of interest to all who wish they could have accompanied Jesus and the disciples on the Emmaus Road when "beginning with Moses and all the prophets, He explained to them the things concerning Himself in all the Scriptures" (Luke 24:27).

Thomas L. Constable
Senior Professor of Bible Exposition,
Dallas Theological Seminary
author, *Talking to God: What the Bible Teaches about Prayer*

This meticulous and readable defense of messianic prophecy is Michael Rydelnik's labor of love, and all who love to labor in the text of Scripture will take delight in it. Although not all will agree with all approaches the author takes and conclusions he reaches, all will respect his breadth of research, his irenic spirit, and his warm passion for Scripture, for the Messiah of whom it speaks, and for the people to whom He came. Michael's clarity of thought, argument, and language will surely cause a wide spectrum of readers to take delight reading this book, making his argument their own.

Stuart Dauermann
Senior Scholar,
Messianic Jewish Theological Institute

After hearing how Michael struggled with the prophecies of the Hebrew Scriptures before finally embracing Jesus as the Jewish Messiah ("My Search for Messiah"; *Day of Discovery*), I now find just as compelling the scholarly journey that has led him to maintain that the Bible is, not just in part, but as a whole, a messianic document.

Mart DeHaan
RBC Ministries and Host of *Day of Discovery*

When Jesus walked the road to Emmaus with two of His disciples, He focused on the messianic hope throughout the Bible. "And beginning with Moses and with all the prophets, He explained to them the things concerning Himself in all the Scriptures" (Luke 24:27). But what specifically did He share? Some today must think the lecture was quite brief because they find little in the Old Testament that points to the Messiah. And that is why this book is so important—and so necessary. Michael Rydelnik provides a sane, compelling case for discovering a consistent messianic hope on display throughout the pages of the Old Testament Scriptures. Interacting with two centuries of biblical scholarship, Michael presents an approach to the Hebrew Bible that is thoughtful, articulate, and refreshingly holistic. This book needs to be required reading for anyone who wants to understand the extent to which the Old Testament predicted the coming of the

Messiah. "You search the Scriptures, because you think that in them you have eternal life; and it is these that bear witness of Me" (John 5:39).

Charlie H. Dyer
Professor-at-large of Bible,
Moody Bible Institute
co-author, *The New Christian Traveler's Guide to the Holy Land*

It is not surprising that liberal theological scholarship claims there is no evidence of messianic prophecy in the Hebrew Bible, but the fact that even many evangelicals are also claiming the same is very disconcerting. As a messianic Jew, I have to ask: Was I tricked into believing in the messiahship of Yeshua (Jesus)? I and most messianic Jews came to faith through such messianic prophecy but if there is no such thing, then why did we believe? Did the New Testament falsely quote these prophecies as being messianic? If what these proponents claim is true, then we should renounce Yeshua's claim and return to Rabbinic Judaism. Dr. Rydelnik's book is timely and necessary to deal with this very issue and crisis within evangelicalism and he writes in both a scholarly and understandable format. This work is highly recommended.

Arnold G. Fruchtenbaum
Director of Ariel Ministries
author, *The Footsteps of the Messiah*

Jesus appealed to "Moses and all the Prophets" to explain His crucifixion and resurrection to the Emmaus disciples (Luke 24:25–27), but recently biblical scholars have questioned the messianic nature of the Old Testament. Michael Rydelnik provides a helpful analysis of what has brought about this change and gives a well-reasoned defense of the historic Jewish and Christian understanding. The messianic hope of the Old Testament is a vital issue, and this book is a welcome and timely defense of the traditional view that the Messiah was indeed anticipated by the authors of the Old Testament.

Kenneth G. Hanna
Senior Professor of Bible Exposition,
Dallas Theological Seminary

Michael Rydelnik has touched on something that is vital for Jewish evangelism—indeed for all evangelism. Much of evangelical scholarship is yet dry and sterile. Michael details a major reason why. It is allowing history to trump the transcendent power of God working in the biblical text. Thank you Michael for calling us back to the apostolic priority that transcends academia.

Barry Horner
Pastor, Christ's New Covenant Church, Sahuarita, Arizona
author, *Future Israel: Why Christian Anti-Judaism Must Be Challenged*

Although some evangelical scholars today seem to be retreating from the way the first Jewish apostles used direct messianic prophecies in their apologetic and evangelistic outreaches, Dr. Michael Rydelnik has written a book letting the Holy Scriptures speak for themselves. In doing so, he has led us back to God's proven strategy for Jewish and Gentile missions and discipleship: a direct messianic interpretation of the Hebrew Scriptures. Dr. Rydelnik's book, *The Messianic Hope: Is the Hebrew Bible Really Messianic?* answers this question in the affirmative: The Hebrew Bible is truly messianic, from beginning to end. Dr. Rydelnik proves to be erudite in his scholarship, irenic in his reasoning, and passionate in his approach to this most critical issue of our day. Thank God that we now have a biblically reliable resource to lead us back to the Messiah in the Old Testament. May God use this book to lead many Jewish women and men (like myself) back to Himself and to His messianic Son. And, of course, this goes for non-Jews as well.

Barry R. Leventhal
Provost and Distinguished Professor of Church Ministries
Director of the Graduate School of Ministry and Missions
Southern Evangelical Seminary, Matthews, NC

I can't think of a more able scholar to help us understand the controversial topic of messianic prophecy than Michael Rydelnik. This book should be read to help all of us understand messianic prophecy and also to give an answer to those who would deny that Jesus fulfills the Old Testament prophecies, or that these references should be interpreted nonliterally. The book takes us on an interesting journey showing how all the Scriptures coalesce around this central theme. To read this book is to tackle the most important theme in all the Bible.

Dr. Erwin Lutzer
Moody Church, Chicago

While the topic of this book may seem academic and theoretical, it is not. Rightly understanding the messianic message of the Old Testament has important practical ramifications for every serious student of God's Word. Dr.

Rydelnik tackles a difficult subject, but he presents his material in a manner that can be grasped by all. Read. Learn. Rejoice in the hope of the Messiah!

J. Paul Nyquist
President
Moody Bible Institute

Dr. Rydelnik has provided believers an invaluable service. Not only has the church been robbed of the original messianic interpretation of the Hebrew Scriptures, but so have the majority of the Jewish people. *The Messianic Hope: Is the Hebrew Bible Really Messianic?* answers the question with a resounding "yes" and recovers for readers the central message of the Old Testament. I have found Dr. Rydelnik's argument persuasive, his scholarship sound, and his passion more than justified. This book is packed with both fresh insights and ancient, but forgotten, truths.

Jim R. Sibley
Director, Pashe Institute of Jewish Studies,
Criswell College, Dallas, Texas

As trendy as it is to blur messianic prophecies in the Old Testament, Michael Rydelnik brings the issue back into focus with scholarly integrity in an impressively convincing way. Thanks to my friend Michael for bringing a much needed voice into the discussion. This book is a must if you are looking for Jesus in the Old Testament.

Joseph M. Stowell
President, Cornerstone University
author, *Simply Jesus and You*

Here's a clear and compelling case for the messianic prophecies. It's a well-reasoned and much-needed antidote to those who would water down their significance.

Lee Strobel
author, *The Case for the Real Jesus*

How messianic is the Old Testament? Many scholars say, "Not very!" Michael Rydelnik offers an insightful, irenic, and impressive discussion of the key issues and texts, and reaches a defensible conclusion. There is a lot about the Messiah in the Hebrew Scriptures. In *The Messianic Hope: Is the Hebrew Bible Really Messianic?* the author sifts through a bewildering amount of information and evaluates it with both a passionate and pastoral heart. This important book will help balance a minimalist approach to the topic of messianic prophecy.

Michael G. Vanlaningham
Professor of Bible
Moody Bible Institute

This volume by professor Rydelnik constitutes a rare offering to the Christian world and those who take Paul's challenge in 2 Tim 2:15 seriously—to wit: a lucid and well-reasoned methodological orientation to, survey of, and (very badly needed) *apologia* for the messianic hope as one of the Bible's central themes. Moreover, Rydelnik's emphasis on a canonical reading of the biblical text serves not only as a refreshing reminder of the early Christian and traditional Jewish perspective on Scripture, but also stands as a challenge to contemporary scholars who, while affirming the *doctrine* of biblical inspiration, yet diminish from the *fact* and *force* of it by overemphasizing the interpretive relevance of extrabiblical data concerning the writers and their world(s).

Michael Wechsler
Professor of Biblical Studies,
Moody Bible Institute, Chicago

To

Hilda Koser

now in eternity with her Messiah,

who showed me how Yeshua

fulfilled Messianic prophecy;

and to

Dan Rigney

who taught me how to follow Yeshua

and challenged me to persist in proclaiming

the Messianic hope to my people.

OTHER BOOKS IN THIS SERIES:

NAC STUDIES IN BIBLE & THEOLOGY

THE MESSIANIC HOPE:

IS THE HEBREW BIBLE

REALLY MESSIANIC?

MICHAEL RYDELNIK

SERIES EDITOR: E. RAY CLENDENEN

TABLE OF CONTENTS

LIST OF ABBREVIATIONS

AB	Anchor Bible
AThR	*Anglican Theological Review*
BDAG	Bauer, W., F. W. Danker, W. F. Arndt, and F. W. Gingrich, *Greek-English Lexicon of the New Testament and Other Early Christian Literature*. 3rd ed.
BDB	Brown, F., S. R. Driver, and C. A. Briggs, *A Hebrew and English Lexicon of the Old Testament*
BECNT	Baker Exegetical Commentary on the New Testament
BETS	*Bulletin of the Evangelical Theological Society*
BHS	*Biblia Hebraica Stuttgartensia*
Bib	*Biblica*
BJRL	*Bulletin of John Rylands Library*
BSac	*Bibliotheca Sacra*
CBQ	*Catholic Biblical Quarterly*
CC	Continental Commentaries
ChrT	*Christianity Today*
CRINT	Compendia Rerum Iudaicarum ad Novum Testamentum
DJD	Discoveries in the Judaean Desert
DJG	*Dictionary of Jesus and the Gospels*, ed. J. B. Green, S. McKnight, and I. H. Marshall
DOTP	*Dictionary of the Old Testament: Pentateuch*, ed. T. D. Alexander and D. W. Baker
EBC	*The Expositor's Bible Commentary*, ed. Frank E. Gaebelein
Eng.	English
ESV	English Standard Version
EvQ	*Evangelical Quarterly*
GKC	*Gesenius' Hebrew Grammar*. Edited by E. Kautzsch. Translated by A. E. Cowley. 2nd ed. Oxford, 1910.
HALOT	Koehler, L., W. Baumgartner, and J. J. Stamm. *The Hebrew and Aramaic Lexicon of the Old Testament*. Translated and edited under the supervision of M. E. J. Richardson. 4 vols. Leiden. 1994–1999.
Hb.	Hebrew
HBT	*Horizons in Biblical Theology*
HCSB	Holman Christian Standard Bible
IBC	*Interpretation: A Bible Commentary for Teaching and Preaching*
ICC	International Critical Commentary
JBL	*Journal of Biblical Literature*
JBR	*Journal of Bible and Religion*
JE	*The Jewish Encyclopedia*, ed. I. Singer. 12 vols.

JETS	*Journal of the Evangelical Theological Society*
JJS	*Journal of Jewish Studies*
JPS	Tanach: Jewish Publication Society, 1985
JSS	*Journal of Semitic Studies*
lit.	literal(ly)
LQ	*The Lutheran Quarterly*
LXX	Septuagint
MT	Masoretic Text
NA²⁷	*Novum Testamentum Graece*, Nestle-Aland. 27th ed.
NAC	New American Commentary
NACSBT	New American Commentary Studies in Bible and Theology
NASB	New American Standard Bible
NET	New English Translation
NICNT	New International Commentary on the New Testament
NICOT	New International Commentary on the Old Testament
NIDNTT	*New International Dictionary of New Testament Theology*, ed. Colin Brown
NIGTC	New International Greek Testament Commentary
NIV	New International Version
NIVAC	NIV Application Commentary
NKJV	New King James Version
NLT²	New Living Translation. 2nd ed.
NRSV	New Revised Standard Version
Presb	*Presbyterion: Covenant Seminary Review*
RB	*Revue Biblique*
RSV	Revised Standard Version
SBJT	*The Southern Baptist Journal of Theology*
Str-B	Strack, H. L., and P. Billerbeck, *Kommentar zum Neuen Testament aus Talmud und Midrasch*, 6 vols.
TDNT	*Theological Dictionary of the New Testament*, ed. G. Kittel and G. Friedrich, trans. G. W. Bromiley. 10 vols. (Grand Rapids: Eerdmans, 1964–74)
Them	*Themelios*
TNTC	Tyndale New Testament Commentaries
TOTC	Tyndale Old Testament Commentaries
TWOT	*Theological Wordbook of the Old Testament*, ed. R. L. Harris, G. L. Archer Jr., and B. K. Waltke. 2 vols.
TynBul	*Tyndale Bulletin*
VT	*Vetus Testamentum*
WBC	Word Biblical Commentary
WEC	Wycliffe Evangelical Commentary
WTJ	*Westminster Theological Journal*

SERIES PREFACE

We live in an exciting era of evangelical scholarship. Many fine educational institutions committed to the inerrancy of Scripture are training men and women to serve Christ in the church and to advance the gospel in the world. Many church leaders and professors are skillfully and fearlessly applying God's Word to critical issues, asking new questions, and developing new tools to answer those questions from Scripture. They are producing valuable new resources to thoroughly equip current and future generations of Christ's servants.

The Bible is an amazing source of truth and an amazing tool when wielded by God's Spirit for God's glory and our good. It is a bottomless well of living water, a treasure-house of endless proportions. Like an ancient tell, exciting discoveries can be made on the surface, but even more exciting are those to be found by digging. The books in this series, NAC Studies in Bible and Theology, often take a biblical difficulty as their point of entry, remembering B. F. Westcott's point that "unless all past experience is worthless, the difficulties of the Bible are the most fruitful guides to its divine depths."

This new series is to be a medium through which the work of evangelical scholars can effectively reach the church. It will include detailed exegetical-theological studies of key pericopes such as the Sermon on the Mount and also fresh examinations of topics in biblical theology and systematic theology. It is intended to supplement the New American Commentary, whose exegetical and theological discussions so many have found helpful. These resources are aimed primarily at church leaders and those who are preparing for such leadership. We trust that individual Christians will find them to be an encouragement to greater progress and joy in the faith. More important, our prayer is that they will help the church proclaim Christ more accurately and effectively and that they will bring praise and glory to our great God.

It is a tremendous privilege to be partners in God's grace with the fine scholars writing for this new series as well as with those who will be helped by it. When Christ returns, may He find us "standing firm in one spirit, with one mind, working side by side for the faith of the gospel" (Phil 1:27).

E. Ray Clendenen
B&H Publishing Group

AUTHOR'S PREFACE

How does one disagree without being disagreeable? That is the challenge of this book. I intend to differ with views taken by some of my teachers, colleagues, and friends. Regardless of my differences, I continue to have the highest regard for them as scholars and people. As scholars, they have taught me immensely and as friends they have modeled spiritual maturity and godly lives. As a result, I am confident that they will consider the positions I will take as a challenge to their thinking and consider this alternative approach I am offering.

It is also precarious to disagree about biblical interpretation and theology. It might lead some readers to conclude that I am alleging that those with whom I differ hold to some sort of suborthodox faith. I want to clarify, even before beginning, that this is not my opinion. Those with whom I disagree stand solidly in the mainstream of evangelical thought and sound theology. Frankly, we end up in the same place, with a firm commitment to Jesus as the Messiah and the advancement of His kingdom.

Biblical scholars come at the issue of interpretation from a variety of presuppositions and approaches. While critical scholarship has, by and large, abandoned biblical inspiration and adopted methodologies such as source criticism, form criticism, and tradition history, evangelical scholarship has maintained a commitment to the inspiration and authority of Scripture. In their struggle to determine the meaning of biblical texts, some evangelical scholars have adopted a historical reading of the text that often minimizes direct messianic prophecy.

In contrast to the historical interpretation of the Bible, there is a growing movement among some biblical scholars to approach the text of Scripture by focusing not upon how the text developed historically but rather upon its final canonical form. As a result of carefully examining the compositional strategies of the biblical authors themselves and reading the Scriptures according to their final form and in conjunction with innerbiblical interpretations, there is a growing tendency to see the Old Testament as an eschatological, messianic text. This is the approach I am attempting to adopt in this book.

I recognize that interpreting the Bible is a challenge. In this book, because of the methodology I have adopted, I will disagree pointedly with some other evangelical scholars. So here at the outset, I want to affirm that I believe those with whom I disagree are doing their best to interpret the Bible well. I believe they want to honor God's Word and serve God's people with their interpretation of Scripture. Their motives are pure, their scholarship is responsible, and their views are respectable. My concern in this book is to examine the shift in evangelical scholarship away from reading the Bible as a messianic text and to call for restoring the idea that the Messiah is a central feature of Old Testament biblical theology. In doing so, I am obviously disagreeing, though I hope I am not being disagreeable.

ACKNOWLEDGEMENTS

"If there's a book you really want to read, but it hasn't been written yet, then you must write it." Toni Morrison's words ring true, but my experience was slightly different. If there is a book my wife wants to read, but it hasn't been written yet, then I must write it. My wife Eva has wanted to read *The Messianic Hope* for years, and so my thanks go to her for all that she did to bring it to print. Her encouragement motivated me, her insights helped me re-evaluate my own thoughts, and her review of every word, several times, clarified my writing. Eva's influence is on every page of this book and I am forever grateful to her, not only for her help with this project, but for her acceptance of my request as a college student that we share love and life together, as long as we both shall live. Any faults with the book are my own, but anything good has Eva's fingerprints all over it.

Thanks also go to my teachers. I have tried to be meticulous in documenting, wherever possible, what they have taught me. Yet, so much is untraceable—from classes, discussions, and interactions over coffee or meals—that it was not always possible to find the citation. If I have failed in any way to give proper credit to them, let it be said now that I am indebted to those who taught me the Scriptures.

In particular, I am grateful to the late Dr. Louis Goldberg, my predecessor as Professor of Jewish Studies at Moody Bible Institute, who not only was my teacher but also a spiritual father to me. He always modeled absolute devotion to His Messiah Yeshua, unfailing commitment to God's Word, and sacrificial love for God's people, Israel.

Also, my thanks go to Dr. Edwin Blum, a true renaissance scholar, from whom I learned so much as his student and his grader at Dallas Seminary. His confidence in me led me to participate in writing projects that, apart from him, I would have never even considered doing. His sharp eye made any word of approval all the more meaningful and his wise suggestions, while adding more work, improved this book.

Likewise, my appreciation goes to Dr. John H. Sailhamer, who has deeply enriched my understanding of God's Word. His Messiah-centered approach to the Hebrew Bible in both classes and writings, has influenced my studies on this topic. My very first course with John was "Messiah in the Hebrew Bible," and it motivated me to persist in my study of the Messianic hope. It has been my great privilege to have studied with such an exceptional scholar and, greater still, to count him as my friend.

There are several others I must thank: Dr. E. Ray Clendenen, the editor of this series, for all the encouragement, support, and patience he has shown me throughout, and for his helpful editorial guidance—Ray's skill and wisdom are evident throughout the book; the administration and faculty of the Moody Bible Institute, which granted me a sabbatical, giving me time to write; my students at Moody Bible Institute, particularly those who have taken BI4452 Messianic Prophecy, whose questions and ideas constantly teach me; and my two sons, Zack and Seth, for their confidence in me as their Dad and their encouragement and expectation that I should write this book.

Above all, I thank God for His kindness and mercy, in allowing me to write this book. Blessed are You, O LORD our God, King of the universe, who has granted us life, sustained us, and allowed us to reach this day. Amen.

Chapter 1

INTRODUCTION: WHY MESSIANIC PROPHECY IS IMPORTANT

W hy write a book advocating the idea that the Hebrew Bible is messianic?[1] Since Jesus told his disciples, "These are my words that I spoke to you while I was still with you—that everything written about Me in the Law of Moses, the Prophets, and the Psalms must be fulfilled" (Luke 24:44), it would seem obvious to affirm the messianic nature of the Hebrew Bible. But this is not the case. Although few evangelicals[2] would deny that there are some direct messianic prophecies in the Old Testament, it is becoming increasingly popular to reject the idea that the Hebrew Bible has specific predictions of the Messiah. Instead, evangelical scholarship tends to affirm that the messianic prophecies are merely a form of general promise. Frank Thielman writes that "the difficulty in seeing such texts as references to the Messiah and the circumstances of his life seems to demand some other approach." He then goes on to endorse "promise" as opposed to prediction as the most valid.[3]

Thielman's is not a lone voice. There is a growing movement by evangelicals away from interpreting the Hebrew Bible as a messianic book. In this chapter, I will begin by defining some significant terms, such as what I mean by the word *Messiah* and the terms historical interpretation and literary interpretation. Then I will attempt to demonstrate the evangelical shift away from interpreting the Hebrew Scriptures as

---

[1] The terms "Hebrew Bible" and "Old Testament" are synonymous for me and will be so treated throughout this book.

[2] R. V. Pierard defines evangelicalism as a modern Christian movement that "emphasizes conformity to the basic tenets of the faith." He characterizes evangelicals as those who believe in the gospel, defined as "the message that Christ died for our sins, was buried, and rose again." He also notes that "evangelicals regard Scripture as the divinely inspired record of God's revelation, the infallible, authoritative guide for faith and practice." Other doctrines that Pierard associates with evangelicalism are the total depravity of humanity, the substitutionary atonement of Christ, justification by grace through faith alone, and the personal and visible return of Jesus Christ to this world (R. V. Pierard, "Evangelicalism," in *Evangelical Dictionary of Theology*, ed. W. A. Elwell [Grand Rapids: Baker, 1984], 379–80).

[3] F. Thielman, "Jesus B.C." (review of D. E. Holwerda, *Jesus and Israel: One Covenant or Two?*; C. J. H. Wright, *Knowing Jesus through the Old Testament*; and W. C. Kaiser Jr., *The Messiah in the Old Testament*), *ChrT*, March 4, 1996, 58–61. For an example of the view that supports messianic hope as promise rather than prediction, see Wright, *Knowing Jesus through the Old Testament* (London: Marshall Pickering, 1992).

messianic. Having done that, I will present the reasons that it remains crucial to maintain a messianic understanding of the Hebrew Bible.

The Definitions of Key Terms

Since this book is about messianic prophecy, it is imperative to understand the meaning of the word *Messiah*. Further, since it is about how messianic texts should be interpreted, it is also essential to define the terms *historical interpretation* and *literary interpretation*.

The Meaning of "Messiah"

The Hebrew word *māšîaḥ* (*mashiach*) is commonly and accurately translated as "anointed." It is used 39 times in the Hebrew Bible, generally with another noun, such as "the anointed priest." The word also has a technical meaning, commonly translated as "the Messiah" and defined by W. H. Rose as "a future royal figure sent by God who will bring salvation to God's people and the world and establish a kingdom characterized by features such as peace and justice."[4] It has become somewhat of an accepted scholarly opinion that the technical term "Messiah" (the Anointed One) did not develop until the period of the Second Temple.[5] Even if this is correct, as Rose points out, it is unnecessary "to conclude on this basis that one can speak of messianic expectations properly only after a particular word was used to refer to the person at the center of these expectations."[6]

Alternatively, Walter C. Kaiser Jr. correctly asserts that the Old Testament does indeed use the word "anointed" in its technical sense of "Messiah" at least nine times out of its thirty-nine usages, citing 1 Sam 2:10,35; Ps 2:2; 20:6; 28:8; 84:9; Hab 3:13; Dan 9:25,26.[7] I would also add 2 Sam 22:51; 23:1; and Ps 89:51 to Kaiser's list. Moreover, "Messiah" is not the only or most common designation for this future royal figure. Some of the other terms used for this king include "the Branch," "the Holy One," and "the Servant of the Lord." In this work, I am not limiting the discussion of the Messiah only to those passages that use the exact Hebrew term *māšîaḥ*, but I include all terms and passages relating to that future royal figure as "messianic."

---

[4] W. H. Rose, "Messiah," *DOTP*, 566.
[5] Ibid.
[6] Ibid.
[7] W. C. Kaiser Jr., *The Messiah in the Old Testament* (Grand Rapids: Zondervan, 1995), 16.

The Meaning of Historical and Literary Interpretation

Biblical scholars come at the issue of interpretation from a variety of presuppositions and approaches. While critical scholarship has, by and large, abandoned biblical inspiration and adopted methodologies such as source criticism, form criticism, and tradition history, evangelical scholarship has maintained a commitment to the inspiration and authority of Scripture. In their struggle to determine the meaning of biblical texts, some evangelical scholars have adopted a historical reading of the text that often minimizes direct messianic prophecy. In rejecting this sort of historical interpretation, I do not mean to indicate that there is no historical dimension to a biblical text or that the historical events did not happen. I fully affirm the historicity of Scripture. Rather, throughout this book, what I mean by a historical reading or historical interpretation is biblical interpretation that is constrained to find the referents of Old Testament prophecy within the historical confines of the prophet's own time.

In contrast to the historical interpretation of the Bible, there is a growing movement among some biblical scholars to approach the text of Scripture by focusing not upon how the text developed historically but rather upon its final canonical form. As a result of carefully examining the compositional strategies of the biblical authors themselves and reading Scripture according to its final form and in conjunction with its innerbiblical interpretations, there is a growing tendency to see the Old Testament as an eschatological, messianic text. In my judgment, this method takes a far more literary approach to a text, looking for the meaning of the author's words. As a result, biblical prophetic texts finds their referents in the distant future, with a messianic or eschatological fulfillment. This method of literary interpretation is the approach I am attempting to adopt in this book.[8]

The Shift Away from Messianic Interpretation

Although evangelical scholarship still recognizes that there is something messianic about the Hebrew Bible, for the most part it sees it as

---

[8] Additionally, I affirm the Reformation principle of historical, grammatical, and lexical interpretation. However, what the Reformers meant by historical interpretation was not the use of ancient Near Eastern backgrounds to explain biblical texts, simply because they did not have access to those backgrounds. Rather, what they meant by historical interpretation was to use the historical texts of the Bible as background for other texts of Scripture. As such, historical interpretation in this sense, is essentially an exercise in innerbiblical interpretation.

a story that finds its climax in Jesus, not as predictions that Jesus of Nazareth fulfilled. As such, it is becoming quite common to state that biblical authors did not have an intentional messianic meaning. For example, noted evangelical Old Testament scholar Tremper Longman III writes, "It is impossible to establish that any passage in its original literary and historical context must or even should be understood as portending a future messianic figure."[9]

Klyne Snodgrass, in his explanation of the New Testament's use of the Old writes, "The early church applied such texts to Jesus because of their conviction about his identity. The conviction about his identity did *not* derive from the Old Testament. They found Jesus and then saw how the Scriptures fit with him." He goes on to say that it would be better to view Jesus as the *climax* rather than the *fulfillment* of the Scriptures.[10]

Larry W. Hurtado posits that out of the postexilic biblical hope for a renewed Davidic monarchy, Jews began to look for "a future agent ('messiah') to be sent by God, usually to restore Israel's independence and righteousness." This expectation did not derive from the predictions of the Hebrew Bible but rather grew out of the hopes of the post-biblical Hellenistic age. He maintains that "recent research suggests, however, that ancient Jewish eschatological expectations of deliverance and sanctification of the elect did not always include the explicit or prominent anticipation of a 'messiah.'"[11]

The minimization of direct prediction is reflected not only by such general statements, but also specific expositions of texts that were previously viewed as directly messianic. For example, evangelical scholar John H. Walton rejects the messianic interpretation of Genesis 3:15, which speaks of the woman's seed striking the head of the serpent and the serpent striking the woman's seed. Although this has long been thought to speak of the Messiah's defeat of the enemy and thus has been considered the first messianic prediction, Walton maintains that the verse only affirms a struggle between good and evil that will "continue unabated."[12] While recognizing that this is not the "traditional

---

[9] T. Longman III, "The Messiah: Explorations in the Law and Writings," in *The Messiah in the Old and New Testaments*, ed. S. E. Porter (Grand Rapids: Eerdmans, 2007), 13.

[10] K. Snodgrass, "The Use of the Old Testament in the New," in *The Right Doctrine from the Wrong Texts?* ed. G. K. Beale (Grand Rapids: Baker, 1994), 39, 41.

[11] L. W. Hurtado, "Christ," *DJG* 107.

[12] J. H. Walton, *Genesis*, NIVAC (Grand Rapids: Zondervan, 2001), 233.

interpretation of the passage,"[13] he proceeds to ask, "How can we identify a passage as messianic if the Old Testament context offers no such support for such an interpretation either conceptually or textually, and the New Testament suggests no fulfillment connections?"[14]

Deuteronomy 18:15–19, a passage which speaks of a future prophet like Moses, is another example of a passage that has long been held to be directly, or at least progressively messianic, but that in recent years has been rejected as such by evangelical scholars. Daniel I. Block argues that "the literary context of Deut. 18:15 provides no hint whatsoever that Moses' original hearers should have understood his prediction of a prophet like himself either eschatologically or messianically." Nor does he find any support for the messianic interpretation in Moses' epitaph written in Deut 34:10–12 or in the New Testament. Instead, he maintains, "It is preferable to interpret this text primarily as a prediction of either the continued existence of the institution of prophecy or a succession of prophets, rather than as a prediction of an eschatological messianic prophet."[15] Longman concurs with this opinion when he writes, "Deuteronomy 18 understood within its ancient context may be perfectly explainable in terms of the rise of the prophetic movement and prophets like Samuel, Elijah, Elisha, Isaiah, and so on."[16]

Another case where evangelical scholarship seems to have shifted is with Psalm 110, in which David announces, "This is the declaration of the Lord to my Lord: 'Sit at my right hand until I make Your enemies Your footstool,'" and that "the Lord has sworn an oath [to "my Lord"] and will not take it back: 'Forever, You are a priest like Melchizedek'" (Ps 110:4). In times past, Delitzsch called this psalm "prophetico-Messianic" and affirmed that "the future Messiah stands

---

[13] Ibid.

[14] Ibid., 235. T. D. Alexander disputes the substance of Walton's interpretation when he writes, "Viewed solely within the context of ch. 3, it is virtually impossible to sustain a messianic interpretation of 3:15. Considered, however, in the light of Genesis as a whole, a messianic reading of this verse is not only possible but highly probable." ("Messianic Ideology in Genesis," in *The Lord's Anointed*, ed. P. E. Satterthwaite, R. S. Hess, and G. J. Wenham [Grand Rapids: Baker, 1995], 32). Although Walton sees no possible messianic interpretation, G. Wenham maintains that in interpreting Genesis 3:15 "it would perhaps be wrong to suggest that this (i.e., the messianic interpretation) was the narrator's own understanding" but that it is possible to see it messianically through "subsequent revelation" (*Genesis*, WBC [Waco, TX: Word, 1987], 1:80).

[15] D. I. Block, "My Servant David," in *Israel's Messiah in the Bible and the Dead Sea Scrolls*, ed. R. S. Hess and M. D. Carroll R. (Grand Rapids: Baker, 2003), 29–31.

[16] Longman, "The Messiah: Explorations in the Law and Writings," 28.

objectively before the mind of David."[17] However, evangelical scholar
Herbert W. Bateman IV has rejected the idea that David spoke of the
future Messiah as his Lord but instead has argued that the psalm is
directed to David's son Solomon. He writes, "Thus it seems reasonable that Psalm 110 refers to Solomon's second coronation in 971 B.C.
when David abdicated his throne to his son Solomon" and that "David
did not speak the psalm to the Messiah, the divine Lord."[18]

Just one more example will suffice to demonstrate this trend of
interpretation. One of the most well-known passages about the birth
of the divine Messiah is Isa 9:6–7. It describes the birth of the Son of
David, announces his throne titles as "Wonderful Counselor, Mighty
God, Eternal Father, Prince of Peace," and promises that he will rule
from the throne of David over an eternal kingdom of justice and
peace. Evangelical scholar Paul D. Wegner understands this not as referring to the divine titles of the Son of David but rather as indicating
a theophoric name. He states, "The name would then be translated as
'a wonderful planner [is] the mighty God; the Father of eternity [is]
a prince of peace [or well-being].'" Although Wegner recognizes that
Isaiah is speaking of a future deliverer, he nonetheless alleges that,
"This deliverer does not correspond exactly to the later concept of the
Messiah which included a restoration of the Davidic dynasty and an
eschatological perspective."[19]

Many more examples could have been presented because evangelical scholarship has so readily rejected direct predictions of the Messiah in the Hebrew Bible. In a thoughtful essay, Gordon McConville
has articulated the issue at hand. According to McConville, "Modern
Old Testament scholarship has been largely informed by the belief
that traditional Christian messianic interpretations of Old Testament
passages have been exegetically indefensible."[20] He traces this to S.
Mowinckel, the Old Testament scholar who argued that the "original meanings had nothing to do with the hope of deliverance by an
eschatological Messiah."[21] Mowinckel posited that there was no preexilic messianism in Israel, a claim rejected by some but accepted

---

[17] F. Delitzsch, *Psalms: Biblical Commentary on the Old Testament,* trans. A. Harper (Grand Rapids: Eerdmans, 1982), 5:183–88.

[18] H. W. Bateman, "Psalm 110:1 and the New Testament," *BSac* 149 (1992): 452–53.

[19] P. D. Wegner, "A Re-examination of Isaiah IX 1–6," *VT* 42 (1992): 111–12.

[20] J. G. McConville, "Messianic Interpretation in Modern Context," in *The Lord's Anointed,* ed. Satterthwaite, Hess, and Wenham, 2.

[21] Ibid., 3. McConville cites Mowinckel, *He That Cometh* (Oxford: Blackwell, 1959) and

by many others, including evangelicals. But, as McConville has argued, canonical criticism has "brought new contextual possibilities into interpretation."[22] Could it be that ancient writers and interpreters approached the Scriptures in this canonical way as opposed to the atomistic, nonmessianic readings currently in vogue? If so, it would produce a more messianic approach to the Old Testament. This turn toward a canonical reading of the Hebrew Bible yielding a messianic understanding seems essential in order to remain consistent with the biblical data. Therefore, it is necessary to discuss the reasons a messianic interpretation is so important.

The Importance of Messianic Prediction

The foremost reason for seeing the Hebrew Bible as a messianic document is that this appears to be the best way to explain the evidence of the Scriptures themselves. James Hamilton observes that the extensive messianic speculation of the intertestamental period, Second Temple Judaism, and the New Testament would indicate that these speculations are rooted in the Hebrew Bible. He sets aside "the possibility that ancient people were stupid, which seems to be an implicit assumption of a good deal of modern scholarship." Instead he hypothesizes that the best explanation for the congruence of all these ancient sources citing the same biblical passages as messianic is that they were all indeed messianic in their intention and meaning. He is accurate in positing "that the OT is a messianic document, written from a messianic perspective, to sustain a messianic hope."[23] This is similar to John Sailhamer's conclusion, when he writes,

> The messianic thrust of the OT was the *whole* reason the books of the Hebrew Bible were written. In other words, the Hebrew Bible was not written as the national literature of Israel. It probably also was not written to the nation of Israel as such. It was rather written, in my opinion, as the expression of the deep-seated messianic hope of a small group of faithful prophets and their followers.[24]

---

includes the following texts as nonmessianic: Gen 3:15; the royal psalms; other psalms including Ps 22, Num 24:25–29, and Gen 49:8–12.
[22] Ibid., 16–17.
[23] J. Hamilton, "The Skull Crushing Seed of the Woman: Inner-biblical Interpretation of Genesis 3:15," *SBJT* 10 (2006): 44.
[24] J. H. Sailhamer, "The Messiah and the Hebrew Bible," *JETS* 44 (2001): 23.

To put it plainly, it appears that the best way of understanding the Bible as a whole is to see the Old Testament as predicting the coming of the Messiah and the New Testament revealing him to be Jesus of Nazareth. A commitment to faithful exegesis of the Hebrew Bible should yield a messianic interpretation.

A second reason for treating the Hebrew Bible as a messianic document is that it provides the most biblical apologetic for Jesus as the Messiah. Without the evidence of the Tanak,[25] it would be impossible to identify Jesus as the Promised One. Consistently, the apostles contended that Jesus of Nazareth was "the Messiah . . . the One Moses wrote about in the Law (and so did the prophets)" (John 1:41,45). This was the perspective that they learned from Jesus himself when he said that "everything written about Me in the Law of Moses, the Prophets, and the Psalms must be fulfilled" (Luke 24:44).[26] Affirming the messianic hope is the apologetic linchpin in the New Testament for proving that Jesus is indeed the promised Messiah. For this reason, the apostles, church fathers, the medieval churchmen, biblical theologians, apologists, and missionaries have all recognized the importance of messianic prophecy.[27]

Besides the importance of messianic prophecy as a biblical apologetic, a third reason it is crucial to treat the Hebrew Bible as messianic is that it enables followers of Jesus to have confidence in the Bible as God's inspired Word. The specific fulfillments of the messianic predictions confirm the Bible's claim for itself that it is an inspired book. The Hebrew prophets could not have foretold the life, ministry, death, and resurrection of Jesus apart from inspiration of the Holy Spirit. Therefore, recognizing the messianic predictions of the Hebrew Bible will strengthen confidence in the Bible as a unified, inspired book that reveals Jesus of Nazareth truly to be the promised Messiah of Israel and of the world.

---

[25] Tanak refers to the Hebrew Bible. The three Hebrew consonants comprising the word signify the Old Testament's three divisions: T for Torah (the Pentateuch); N for Nevi'im (Prophets); K for Ketuvim (Writings).

[26] This will be treated more extensively in chapter 6: "New Testament Perspectives on Messianic Prophecy."

[27] The evidence from messianic prophecy is significant enough that chapters on the subject were included in apologetic works by J. McDowell, *Evidence That Demands a Verdict* (San Bernadino: Campus Crusade for Christ, 1972), 147–84; J. W. Montgomery, ed., *Evidence for Faith* (Dallas: Probe Books 1991), 203–14; and T. Cabal et al., *The Apologetics Study Bible* (Nashville: B&H, 2007), xxviii–xxix.

A fourth reason messianic prophecy is so essential is that it is foundational for identifying Jesus as the true Messiah. When John the Baptist was in prison and struggled with doubts about Jesus, he sent his disciples to Jesus with a question. They asked, "Are you the One who is to come, or should we expect someone else?" (Matt 11:3). Jesus responded (Matt 11:4–5) by referring to His fulfillment of Isaiah's predictions of the Messiah (Isa 35:5–6 and 61:1–4). Foundational to our confidence and salvation in the person and work of Jesus the Messiah is that He indeed did fulfill the words of the prophets. Though contemporary evangelical scholarship continues to recognize Jesus as both Lord and Messiah, they fail to see the importance that Jesus Himself gave to messianic prophecy as proof of His own identity.

A Look Ahead

In this first chapter I have attempted to demonstrate why messianic prophecy is important to a sound interpretation of the Hebrew Bible and, in fact, the whole Bible. The content of the following chapters is as follows.

Chapter 2 addresses *how contemporary interpreters approach the messianic hope* in the Hebrew Bible. In order to place this book in context, it is vital to understand the varying attempts to explain how the Hebrew Bible is messianic. While most authors would affirm that the Old Testament is indeed messianic in some way, they would put very little stock in direct messianic prophecy. This chapter describes these differing approaches to interpretation.

Chapter 3 begins to make the case for reading the Hebrew Bible as messianic by adducing *text-critical evidence*. This is the first of five chapters defending the idea that the Hebrew Bible is indeed messianic and that the prophecies are frequently direct predictions. To begin, it is necessary for interpreters to examine textual criticism because in a number of places the messianic hope is clearer in the variant readings and often these variants with messianic nuances are indeed the better readings. This chapter evaluates eight different readings to show that the messianic reading is the better choice. Hence, biblical interpreters at times will more readily find the Messiah in the critical apparatus.

Chapter 4 examines the *innerbiblical evidence* for a messianic reading of the Hebrew Bible. It is frequently charged that only the New Testament reads the Old Testament messianically or even that the messianic hope only developed in the inter-testamental period. The purpose of this chapter is to show that even the Hebrew Bible reads itself in a messianic fashion. It accomplishes this by taking three passages from the Pentateuch and examining them innerbiblically. Upon examination, it will become clear that later biblical authors read earlier ones as messianic.

Chapter 5 gathers the *canonical evidence* for a messianic Old Testament. It shows that the final canonical shape of the Hebrew Bible reveals a messianic understanding of the Hebrew text. This is evident in the final shaping of the Old Testament canon as well as in the books that were included in the canon. It will be seen that the canon was designed to present the messianic hope.

Chapter 6 presents *New Testament evidence* for a messianic Hebrew Bible. It is frequently asserted that the New Testament teaches that the Old Testament writers did not know that they were writing about the Messiah. Hence, the New Testament writers were adding an inspired interpretation that added a fuller meaning to the Hebrew Scriptures. This chapter examines the words of Jesus and the apostles to show that they also believed that the Old Testament writers actually knew that they were writing about the Messiah.

Chapter 7, titled "Decoding the Hebrew Bible: How the New Testament Reads the Old," studies the variety of *ways the New Testament uses the Old*. The New Testament largely understands messianic hope in a direct fashion, but not exclusively. It is important to recognize the various methods the New Testament employs to explain the messianic hope of the Hebrew Scriptures. This chapter considers Matthew 2 and its fourfold use (direct, typical, applicational, and summary fulfillments) of the Old Testament as a prototype for the four ways the entire New Testament uses the Hebrew Bible.

Chapter 8 investigates *Rashi's influence on biblical interpretation*. If the Hebrew Bible is messianic, why have so many abandoned this idea? This chapter studies the great Jewish interpreter Rashi (Rabbi Shlomo Yitzchaki) and his influence on Christian interpretation of the Hebrew Bible. It explains why interpreters largely abandoned direct prophecy for double fulfillment, typical prophecy, and other nondirect interpretations.

Chapter 9, titled "An Example from the Law: Interpreting Genesis 3:15 as a Messianic Prophecy," is the first of three chapters that studies passages that were viewed as messianic in the past but now are rarely seen that way. Traditionally, Gen 3:15 has been understood as *the Protoevangelium* or "first gospel." Many now read this passage as a promise of a perpetual conflict between humanity and snakes or good and evil. This chapter makes the case that Gen 3:15 must not be read atomistically but rather within the context of the book of Genesis, the whole Torah, and the rest of the Hebrew Scriptures. This results in the messianic reading Moses intended.

Chapter 10 studies an example from the prophets, namely, Isa 7:14. Although Isa 52:13–53:12 is assuredly the most significant prophecy of Messiah in the Prophets, evangelical interpreters have generally not abandoned the messianic interpretation of this crucial passage to the degree that they have forsaken others. In contrast, Isaiah 7 has become one of the most controversial prophecies in the entire Hebrew Bible. The difficulties range from the meaning of the word *ʿalmāh* ("young woman" or "virgin") to its relationship to the context. The direct messianic interpretation has been virtually abandoned. This chapter makes the case for translating *ʿalmāh* as "virgin" or "maiden" and for a messianic interpretation of the passage.

Chapter 11 considers an example from the book of Psalms, namely, Psalm 110. This psalm is frequently considered an ode written to King David, or if written by him, as directed to some other non-messianic figure. However, reading it in its final canonical shape clearly shows it to be a royal oracle about the future Messiah.

Chapter 12, the final chapter, calls for a return to a messianic interpretation of the Hebrew Bible by reading it with a text-oriented and holistic approach that yields a messianic intent. An approach of this sort will strengthen our understanding of the entire Bible and reaffirm its use in the classical apologetic method of Jesus and the apostles.

A Personal Perspective

For the purpose of full disclosure, I need to reveal why this subject is so significant to me personally. Messianic prophecy was the means God used to bring me to faith in Jesus the Messiah. My parents were Holocaust survivors who raised me in a traditional Jewish home. We were Orthodox in our Jewish beliefs and practices and, as such, I did believe in the future coming of a personal Messiah. Even so, it was not a central issue of my life. However, that changed when my mother announced that she believed in Jesus. This led to my father divorcing her and a radical shift in my life.

I decided to study the messianic prophecies of the Hebrew Bible and prove my mother wrong in attributing their fulfillment to Jesus of Nazareth. Although I was initially quite confident of my opinion, in time I was surprised to see that there was far more credibility to the messiahship of Jesus than I had first anticipated. After dealing with my fears of ostracism from the Jewish community, based on my new conviction that the Scriptures foretold a suffering Messiah who would be rejected by His own people and provide forgiveness through his death and resurrection, I put my trust in Jesus as Messiah and Lord. I became convinced (and remain so) that my faith in the Jewish Messiah, Jesus, who fulfilled the predictions of the Hebrew Bible, is an intrinsically Jewish faith. I would never have made this decision apart from studying messianic prophecy. In fact, apart from messianic prediction and fulfillment, Jesus could not be identified as the Messiah of Israel, and if not that, then He could not be the Messiah of the world. It is for this reason, joined with my commitment to exegetical accuracy, that I believe it is essential to understand the Hebrew Bible as messianic.

Conclusion

Seeing the Old Testament as a messianic text is not merely an issue of differing interpretations. Rather, it is of crucial significance. How messianic prophecy is viewed will ultimately affect the evangelical understanding of the inspiration and interpretation of the Scriptures, the defense of the gospel, and the identification of Jesus as the promised Messiah. Walter Kaiser captured the critical importance of recognizing the messianic hope of the Hebrew Bible: "This issue of the interpretation of the Messiah in the OT could be a defining moment for evangelical scholarship and ultimately for the Church's view of the way we regard Scripture."[28] He adds the reason messianic prophecy is so pivotal: "But if it is not in the OT text, who cares how ingenious later writers are in their ability to reload the OT text with truths that it never claimed or revealed in the first place? The issue is more than hermeneutics; it is the authority and content of revelation itself!"[29]

---

[28] W. C. Kaiser, "The Lord's Anointed: Interpretation of Old Testament Messianic Texts," *JETS* 42 (1999): 102.

[29] Ibid., 101.

Chapter 2

THE NATURE OF PROPHECY AND FULFILLMENT: HOW OLD TESTAMENT SCHOLARSHIP VIEWS MESSIANIC PROPHECY

There is a vast amount of literature on messianic prophecy. Since New Testament times, those who have believed that Jesus is the Messiah have affirmed that He fulfilled the messianic expectations of the Hebrew Scriptures in some way. As a result, much has been written on messianic prophecy through the centuries. The purpose of this chapter is to survey the scholarly literature written in the modern period on messianic prophecy. Then this chapter will summarize the various approaches to interpreting messianic prophecy and fulfillment.

The Survey of Literature

From the New Testament period until the modern period, the church spoke unanimously that in some way Jesus of Nazareth fulfilled Old Testament messianic prophecies. However, a shift began to occur in the modern period. The traditional view was first challenged by Anthony Collins in his *Discourse of the Grounds and Reasons of the Christian Religion* (1724) and then in his *The Scheme of Literal Prophecy Considered*.[1] Both works deal with the use of messianic proof texts from the Old Testament. Collins argued that the literal meaning of the texts could not support the messianic interpretations given them by the New Testament. In a sense, Collins's approach stripped classical apologetics of one of its major features, namely, the argument from prophecy. Moreover, Collins's view that the Old Testament should be studied historically "became the dominant view not only in the universities but also in the Protestant Christian Church, right across the theological spectrum."[2]

---

[1] R. E. Clements, "Messianic Prophecy or Messianic History?" *HBT* 1 (1979): 87. (I am indebted to Ronald E. Clements for his excellent survey of messianic interpretation, particularly for his discussion of Collins.)

[2] I. W. Provan, "The Messiah in the Book of Kings," in *The Lord's Anointed: Interpretation of Old Testament Messianic Texts*, ed. P. E. Satterthwaite, R. S. Hess and G. J. Wenham (Grand Rapids: Baker, 1995), 68.

As a rebuttal to the criticisms that Collins raised, Thomas Sherlock wrote *The Use and Intent of Prophecy* (1732). Sherlock argued for a dual fulfillment of prophecy. First, there was the original meaning, which was determined from the text, context, and historical circumstances. Second, there was a later or fuller meaning, which was the typical or spiritual understanding, which upheld a broader messianic interpretation.[3] Although this tactic became and remains popular, as Kaiser states, it forfeited "most of the predictive value of the anticipations of the Messiah in their Old Testament context."[4]

By the end of the eighteenth century, with the emergence of the two giants of the critical approach to the Old Testament, J. G. Von Herder (1744–1803) and J. G. Eichhorn (1752–1827), the shift away from any concept of messianic predictions became pronounced. Herder maintained that it was a mistake to believe that the Hebrew prophets foretold the distant future. Eichhorn was even more decisive in his rejection of all messianic predictions. He saw this as a dogmatic and theological imposition on the biblical text. Eichhorn asserted that the meaning of the text could only be discerned from the time and circumstances of the biblical authors. This changed the focus of interpretation away from the study of the text to the study of the individual prophets and their historical circumstances. As a result, Eichhorn rejected the approach that interpreted the prophetic text as revealing a long series of messianic predictions. In 1793, he boasted, "The last three decades have erased the Messiah from the Old Testament."[5] Herder's and Eichhorn's works caused the traditional understanding of messianic prophecy—as a series of predictions fulfilled at a remote later period by a particular individual—to be almost entirely repudiated.

In an attempt to reaffirm the messianic predictions and arrest the critical attacks on predictive prophecy, E. W. von Hengstenberg produced his massive *Christology of the Old Testament and Commentary*

---

[3] Clements, "Messianic Prophecy or Messianic History?" 88.

[4] W. C. Kaiser Jr., *Messiah in the Old Testament* (Grand Rapids: Zondervan, 1995), 19. Kaiser acknowledges the legitimacy of types, including messianic ones, in the Old Testament (p. 34). The New Testament, on occasion, authorizes some typological interpretation as demonstrated in L. Goppelt, *Typos*, trans. D. H. Madvig (Grand Rapids: Eerdmans, 1982). Moreover, the Old Testament often intends its readers to understand its narrative as a form of typology. See J. Sailhamer's discussion of narrative typology in *The Pentateuch as Narrative* (Grand Rapids: Zondervan, 1992), 37–44.

[5] As quoted in Clements, "Messianic Prophecy or Messianic History?" 88–89.

on the Messianic Predictions (1835).[6] Hengstenberg's interpretation allowed the New Testament to be the final arbiter of the Old Testament prophecies. This was essentially a confessional/dogmatic approach which paid scant attention to the historical setting or context of the given messianic predictions. It was decidedly antirationalist in tone and content. Despite the impressive work of Hengstenberg, it did not put an end to the critical approach to messianic prophecy.

In 1879, Paton J. Gloag published *Messianic Prophecies*, which was also a rejection of the rationalist approach.[7] At the outset, he "proposed to direct attention to Jesus as the Christ or the Messiah of ancient prophecy."[8] In general, this work was an attack on the critical and antisupernatural approaches to prophecy taking hold in the nineteenth century. He affirms the approach of Hengstenberg, stating, "This work must always occupy a high position in theology, as being perhaps the most complete investigation of the subject."[9] Gloag's book is a strongly evidentialist and polemical argument for supernatural, predictive messianic prophecy.

From 1880 through 1884, Alfred Edersheim delivered the Warburton Lectures in the chapel of Lincoln's Inn. These lectures were published as *Prophecy and History in Relation to the Messiah* (1901, reprinted 1955 and 1980).[10] Following the method of Hengstenberg, Edersheim asserts, "To say that Jesus is the Christ means that He is the Messiah promised and predicted in the Old Testament."[11] In addition to contending for the messianic nature of the Old Testament, Edersheim also attempted to show the weaknesses of the rationalistic approaches to prophecy and to the Old Testament as a whole.

In 1900, G. S. Goodspeed published *Israel's Messianic Hope to the Time of Jesus*, which affirmed so broad a view of messianic prophecy that it was hardly recognizable compared to the traditional view.[12] Goodspeed accepted the extreme literary and historical criticism of Wellhausen, Graf, and Keunen and as a result rejected any confidence

---

[6] It was published in three volumes in 1835 and then a revised edition with four volumes was published in 1858. It was republished in 1970 in an abridged edition. E. W. Hengstenberg, *Christology of the Old Testament*, trans. Reuel Keith (London: Francis and John Rivington, 1847; repr., Grand Rapids: Kregel, 1970).

[7] P. J. Gloag, *Messianic Prophecies* (Edinburgh: T&T Clark, 1879).

[8] Ibid., 1.

[9] Ibid., 34.

[10] A. Edersheim, *Prophecy and History in Relation to the Messiah* (London: Longmans, 1901).

[11] Ibid., x.

[12] G. S. Goodspeed, *Israel's Messianic Hope to the Time of Jesus* (New York: MacMillan, 1900).

in a supernaturally inspired text. He adopted "the historical method" of investigation.[13] Hence, his study of messianic prophecy shifted away from examining the prophecies of the person and work of the future redeemer of Israel to studying the progress of moral insight in the history of Israel. The messianic hope was no longer viewed as the outcome of various predictions of a future person but the logical outcome of Israel's history.[14] Jesus was the natural fulfillment of Israel's history, not the supernatural fulfillment of Israelite prophecy.

Several writers sought to bridge the gap between the historical and the confessional/dogmatic approaches to messianic prophecy. They did so by taking a developmental view of prophecy. First, Edward Rhiem published *Messianic Prophecy: Its Origin, Historical Growth, and Relation to New Testament Fulfillment* (1884 and revised in 1891).[15] Rhiem argued that the Old Testament must be understood in light of the prophet's immediate knowledge, which did not include direct prophecies of the Messiah. However, all the prophets did speak of the saving purpose of God that found its ultimate fulfillment in Christ. This fulfillment transcended their previous conception.[16] Thus, the prophets had an immediate fulfillment in view, whereas God's view included an ultimate fulfillment in the Messiah.

A second scholar, Franz Delitzsch, published *Messianic Prophecies in Historical Succession* (1891).[17] This book affirmed that the prophets' words only had a single sense and that there were no dual prophecies. He also argued that the prophecies should be understood according to their historical and literary context, though he did allow for the supernatural element of prophecy.[18] He maintained that the prophecies pertained to redemption, and as such they did not speak clearly to messianic fulfillment. However, they did indeed point to the Messiah who would ultimately fulfill them by providing redemption. He stated,

> Since the idea of the God-man is first announced in single rays of light, the Mediator of salvation, in general, does not yet stand in the centre of Old

---

[13] Ibid., 4–5.

[14] Ibid., 8–9.

[15] E. Rhiem, *Messianic Prophecy: Its Origin, Historical Growth, and Relation to New Testament Fulfilment*, trans. L. A. Muirhead, 2nd ed. (Edinburgh: T&T Clark, 1891).

[16] Ibid., 322.

[17] F. Delitzsch, *Messianic Prophecies in Historical Succession*, trans. S. I. Curtiss (Edinburgh: T&T Clark, 1891).

[18] Ibid., 12.

Testament faith, but the completion of the kingdom of God appears mostly as the work of the God of salvation Himself with the recession of human mediation. But we also classify these prophecies under the general conception of Messianic, because indeed in the history of fulfillment it is God in Christ who from Israel works out and secures for mankind the highest spiritual blessings. . . . Therefore, from a historical point of view, we regard the prophecies concerning ultimate salvation, which are even silent concerning the Messiah, as Christological.[19]

Walter Kaiser's assessment is correct when he writes of Delitzsch's developmental view: "This allowed Delitzsch to have the Old Testament say *less* than its fulfillment in Jesus required, but to provide for the Old Testament to say *more* when the original prophecy was filled out by later doctrine and Christian experience."[20] Nevertheless, Delitzsch did allow for explicit predictions about the coming Redeemer, specifically fulfilled by Jesus. He says, "These passages of Scripture are, indeed, like isolated points without connecting lines."[21] Additionally, he describes the Christological development of the Old Testament messianic predictions as "rays of light proceeding from single points of light."[22] Thus, Delitzsch viewed messianic fulfillment as the outcome of the progress of redemption while allowing for individual messianic predictions.

Charles A. Briggs was a third Old Testament scholar to adopt a developmental view. In his work *Messianic Prophecy: The Prediction of the Fulfillment of Redemption through the Messiah* (1886), Briggs argued for a single sense of prophetic writings and that they pertain to the messianic ideal.[23] However, he believed that history provided foreshadowings of the coming Messiah. His explanation of prophecy and fulfillment is as follows:

History constantly approximates to the Messianic ideal. It seems to fulfil the prediction as it advances, and to give ground for the theory of a double sense or a progressive fulfillment. But this is only the preparation of history for the real fulfillment which awaits it at the end of the course in the Messiah of history, the suffering, reigning, and glorified Redeemer.[24]

---

[19] Ibid., 21.

[20] Kaiser, *Messiah in the Old Testament*, 21.

[21] Delitzsch, *Messianic Prophecies in Historical Succession*, 10.

[22] Ibid., 11.

[23] C. A. Briggs, *Messianic Prophecy: The Prediction of the Fulfillment of Redemption through the Messiah* (New York: Scribner, 1886).

[24] Ibid., 63.

Thus, according to Briggs, the apparent historical fulfillments of prophecy were merely historical preparation for their ultimate and actual fulfillment in the promised Messiah.

In 1905, Willis J. Beecher published *The Prophets and the Promise*, which argued for a view of prophecy that distinguished between *promise* and *prediction*.[25] In his view, the prophets' message pertained to the promise made to Abraham that would ultimately culminate in the Messiah. Yet Beecher did not isolate individual predictions. He affirmed that the promise had but one meaning which included a progression of historical fulfillments, culminating in the Messiah. Beecher argued for an eternally operative promise that must necessarily imply a cumulative fulfillment. Hence, throughout history God fulfilled His promise through a long line of fulfillments that could vary in different ages and that found their ultimate fulfillment in Jesus.

Beecher maintained that "the idea of a long line of fulfillment is not a hypothesis offered for the solution of difficulties, but a part of the primary conception of a promise that is for eternity."[26] Thus, Beecher asserted that the promise had but one meaning. However, that single meaning included a series of mini-fulfillments culminating in the ultimate fulfillment in the Messiah.

The developmental views of Rhiem, Delitzsch, Briggs, and Beecher found followers among some of the more conservative biblical interpreters. Nevertheless, for the most part this approach failed to resolve the tension of prophecy and fulfillment as it pertains to the Messiah.

Still the critical, historical view prevailed. It did allow for some messianic hope, but it was a far cry from the traditional understanding of prediction and fulfillment. For example, W. Robertson Smith in *The Prophets of Israel and Their Place in History* (1882) and A. F. Kirkpatrick in *The Doctrine of the Prophets* (1901) reduced the messianic hope to a vague hope in the love of God and an assurance of the future.[27] Essentially, Jesus was viewed as the fulfillment of the prophets' moral goal but not their predictions.

In 1908, W. O. E. Oesterley wrote *The Evolution of the Messianic Idea: A Study in Comparative Religion*, which presented a new way of

---

[25] W. J. Beecher, *The Prophets and the Promise* (New York: Crowell, 1905).

[26] Ibid., 376–77.

[27] Clements, "Messianic Prophecy or Messianic History?" 89.

looking at the messianic idea.[28] Oesterley argued that the Old Testament borrowed from ancient Near Eastern pagan literature and even preserved fragments of this literature in the biblical text. This called for the coming of a future divine savior figure to appear as a herald of the kingdom of God. H. Gressman developed much the same view in his work *Der Messias* (1929).[29] B. B. Warfield challenged Oesterley's evolutionary approach in 1916, publishing "The Divine Messiah of the Old Testament."[30] In this extended article he argued for an Old Testament expectation of a Messiah who would be God. Citing numerous texts to support his view, Warfield bluntly affirmed direct messianic prediction. He agreed with Hengstenberg's approach, calling him "one of the most searching expounders of the Scriptures that God has as yet given His church."[31] He disputed the idea that the Old Testament prophets borrowed from pagan literature, stating the Old Testament savior ideal bore no relationship to ancient Near Eastern pagan literature.[32]

Despite Warfield's rejection of the idea that Israel's prophets borrowed from pagan literature, the view continued to gain adherents among critical scholars for the decades that followed. The rise of several Scandinavian scholars who held to a divine kingship view derived from pagan sources led to new discussions of messianic expectation.

Ivan Engnell in his *Studies of Divine Kingship in the Near East* (1943) argued that Israel's prophets borrowed a divine-royal formula from pagan mythology.[33] He studied ancient Egyptian, Sumerian, Akkadian, Hittite, and Canaanite literature, in which the reigning king was considered divine, functioning as a god on earth. According to him, Israel borrowed such ideas, developed them into sacral kingship (the king as priest), and ultimately developed an eschatological kingship idea.

Helmer Ringgren held a similar view in his *The Messiah in the Old Testament* (1956).[34] He maintained that Psalms 2 and 110 fit the divine kingship model, concluding that "this picture of Israelite kingship

---

[28] W. O. E. Oesterley, *The Evolution of the Messianic Idea: A Study in Comparative Religion* (London: Pitman, 1908).

[29] H. Gressman, *Der Messias* (Göttingen: Vandenhoeck & Ruprecht, 1929).

[30] This was originally published in *Princeton Theological Review* (1916) and reprinted in the collection of Warfield writings entitled *Christology and Criticism* (New York: Oxford, 1921).

[31] Warfield, "The Divine Messiah of the Old Testament," in *Christology and Criticism*, 7.

[32] Ibid., 20.

[33] I. Engnell, *Studies in Divine Kingship in the Near East* (Oxford: Blackwell, 1943).

[34] H. Ringgren, *The Messiah in the Old Testament* (Chicago: Allenson, 1956).

agrees in an astonishing way with ancient Mesopotamian kingship ideology. The Babylonian and Assyrian king, too, is a son of a god, he is the god's messenger and rules with divine authority."[35] Ringgren asserted that there was a gradual evolution from king to Messiah but that it was impossible to date exactly when the transition took place. Thus, he states, "The divine kingship of ancient Israel is part of the preparations that were necessary for the realization of God's plan of salvation."[36] In essence, Ringgren's view is that there was a natural evolution from the ancient Near Eastern pagan divine king to the plan of salvation that included the belief in Christ as the Messiah.

Aage Bentzen held a similar view in *King and Messiah* (1955).[37] Bentzen's position was that just as ancient Mesopotamians viewed their king as the son of god by adoption, so ancient Israelites came to regard their kings in the same way. He states that "the king of Israel has been invested with the same divine qualities as elsewhere in the ancient East."[38] In his view, the king of Israel was not an eschatological figure but the anointed messenger of God who guaranteed Israel's happiness through the New Year ritual. After the fall of the two Israelite kingdoms, Bentzen asserted, kingship took on an eschatological interpretation. The king was no longer present—he was the Coming King.[39] Thus, the king messiah of Psalm 2, for example, is not to be considered the eschatological Messiah. Rather he was regarded as the king of Israel who served as a prefiguration (a type) of the eschatological Messiah.[40]

Sigmund Mowinckel developed this theme in his work entitled *He That Cometh* (1959).[41] He argued that Israel borrowed a divine kingship concept from pagan Canaanite neighbors. Then Israel expressed the divine kingship motif through enthronement festivals and rituals. The king was extolled in the Psalms as superhuman and divine, but this never became a historical reality. Eventually, the divine king of ancient Israel became the ideal for the future, eschatological, messianic king.

---

[35] Ibid., 20.

[36] Ibid., 24.

[37] A. Bentzen, *King and Messiah* (London: Lutterworth, 1955). This was originally published in German in 1948 and then translated by the author himself in 1955.

[38] Ibid., 19.

[39] Ibid., 73.

[40] Ibid., 75–76.

[41] S. Mowinckel, *He That Cometh*, trans. G. W. Anderson (Oxford: Blackwell, 1959). This was originally published in Norwegian in 1954.

These Scandinavian scholars, all operating with the presupposition of critical views of the Bible, failed to recognize that the prophets of Israel would have roundly condemned any ascription of deity to the king. Even so, as Van Groningen says, "Most twentieth-century Old Testament scholars who have paid attention to the messianic concept have followed the divine-royal formula."[42]

European scholar, Joachim Becker, influenced much of contemporary scholarship's view of the Messiah and messianic hope with his publication of *Messianic Expectation in the Old Testament* (1977).[43] His argument was that the figure of a savior of the Davidic house, which is essential to messianism, is indiscernible until the second century BC.[44] Thus, the Old Testament "messianic prophecies cannot be considered visionary predictions of a New Testament fulfillment."[45] He asserted that the New Testament's use of fulfillment should be understood as a first-century Jewish hermeneutic known as "pesher."[46] Pesher is an arbitrary reading of the text which identifies fulfillment with current events. The Christ event, according to Becker, was the fulfillment of sacral history, not Old Testament prophecy.[47]

Richard Longenecker argued for a view similar to Becker in his *Biblical Exegesis in the Apostolic Period* (1975), although without adopting Becker's critical approach to Scripture.[48] Longenecker maintained that the New Testament used "midrash" or "pesher" to identify Jesus as the promised Messiah. According to him, it was valid for Jesus and the apostles to use this method but not for modern interpreters.[49] The latter are to interpret the Old Testament only according to historico-grammatical exegesis.[50]

The "midrash" or "pesher" argument for messianic fulfillment was also advocated by Donald Juel, in his book *Messianic Exegesis* (1988).[51]

---

[42] G. Van Groningen, *Messianic Revelation in the Old Testament* (Grand Rapids: Baker, 1990), 88.

[43] J. Becker, *Messianic Expectation in the Old Testament*, trans. D. E. Green. (Philadelphia: Fortress, 1977).

[44] Ibid., 79.

[45] Ibid., 93.

[46] Ibid., 94.

[47] Ibid., 96.

[48] R. N. Longenecker, *Biblical Exegesis in the Apostolic Period* (Grand Rapids: Eerdmans, 1975).

[49] Ibid., 74.

[50] Ibid., 219.

[51] D. Juel, *Messianic Exegesis: Christological Interpretation of the Old Testament in Early Christianity* (Philadelphia: Fortress, 1988).

According to Juel, the Old Testament had no clear messianic hope. However, by New Testament times, the Messiah was conceived as an eschatological king. Since Jesus was presented as a crucified and risen Messiah, the apostles had to use "creative exegesis" to substantiate his messianic claim.[52]

While the "midrash" or "pesher" approach may possibly fit first-century Jewish hermeneutics, it does not genuinely trace the growth of the messianic hope in the Old Testament. R. E. Clements, in an article entitled "The Messianic Hope in the Old Testament" (1989), has proposed "relecture" (reading an earlier saying or prophecy in a new way) as a method for understanding messianic prophecy and fulfillment.[53] According to Clements, some biblical texts were considered by later editors to be messianic, and thus they reread them as messianic expectations. In his words, "new wine was being poured into old bottles."[54] Clements's method was applied by his student, Paul D. Wegner, in his *An Examination of Kingship and Messianic Expectation in Isaiah 1–35* (1992). However, by Clements's own admission, in the relecture method "some of the important features of the older belief in a 'dual meaning' in certain prophecies has come to re-assert itself."[55] While not adhering to the presuppositions of Thomas Sherlock, much of the outcome is the same.

Attempting to restore the traditional view, J. Barton Payne in his *Encyclopedia of Biblical Prophecy* (1973) maintained the single sense of Scripture as well as the predictive nature of prophecy.[56] He asserted that the Old Testament has a variety of ways in which it predicts the Messiah, from direct prediction to type. Still he cited 103 direct messianic prophecies,[57] leading Waltke to classify Payne with Hengstenberg as "non-critical." According to Waltke, "non-critical scholars by their prooftexting actually discredit the claims of Jesus in the eyes of literary and historical critics."[58]

Along the same lines as Payne, Gerard Van Groningen wrote *Messianic Revelation in the Old Testament* (1990). This work is massive,

---

[52] Ibid., 13.
[53] R. E. Clements, "The Messianic Hope in the Old Testament," *JSOT* 43 (1989): 3–19.
[54] Ibid., 14.
[55] Clements, "Messianic Prophecy or Messianic History?" 96.
[56] J. B. Payne, *Encyclopedia of Biblical Prophecy* (Grand Rapids: Baker, 1973).
[57] Ibid., 665–68.
[58] B. K. Waltke, "A Canonical Process Approach to the Psalms," in *Tradition and Testament*, ed. J. Feinberg and P. Feinberg (Chicago: Moody, 1981), 5.

thoroughly evangelical, and reflective of the state of Old Testament studies up to the time it was written. Van Groningen allows for a dual meaning in some cases, such as Psalm 16, where he alleges that the divine author had a deeper meaning than the human author.[59] Van Groningen is eclectic in his understanding of messianic prophecy, affirming direct fulfillment, dual fulfillment, and typological fulfillment.

Chris Wright in his *Jesus in the Old Testament* (1992) views the Old Testament more as a book of promise than prediction.[60] In his view, unlike prediction, promises can be fulfilled in ways that people alive at the time of the promise may never have imagined. Thus, the promises of the Old Testament have a "transformable quality" that allows them to be fulfilled in ways different from those in which they were originally understood.[61]

In 1993, James E. Smith published *What the Bible Teaches about the Promised Messiah*, which takes the old prooftexting method and presents little in the way of new ideas or approaches. It is essentially a chronological look at 73 messianic prophecies, with little regard for historical or literary context.

Walter C. Kaiser Jr. in his *The Messiah in the Old Testament* (1995) presents a reworking of Beecher's *The Prophets and the Promise*. Arguing for the single meaning of Scripture, Kaiser maintained that the biblical prophecies had an epigenetic meaning.[62] Kaiser applied this biological concept to prophetic literature:

> The fixed core of ideas connected with the promise-plan of God and the representative of that promise remained constant. But as time went on, the content of that given word of blessing, promise, or judgment grew in accordance with seed thoughts that were contained within its earliest statements, much as a seed is uniquely related to the plant that it will become if it has life at all.[63]

Thus, according to Kaiser, the promise had a single meaning which could find expression in multiple lesser fulfillments, ultimately culminating in the Messiah.[64] This approach, which is basically a form of

---

[59] Van Groningen, *Messianic Revelation in the Old Testament*, 347–48.

[60] C. J. H. Wright, *Knowing Jesus through the Old Testament* (London: Marshall Pickering, 1992).

[61] Ibid., 70–77.

[62] This is a term borrowed from biology, and is "the theory that an individual is developed by successive differentiation of an unstructured egg rather than by a simple enlarging of a preformed entity." *American Heritage Dictionary of the English Language*, 3rd ed., s. v. "epigenesis."

[63] Kaiser, *Messiah in the Old Testament*, 27.

[64] Ibid., 24–25.

progressive fulfillment, was significantly influenced by the previous work of Beecher.

In 1997 Antti Laato, Professor at the Abo Academy in Turku, Finland, published *A Star Is Rising: The Historical Development of the Old Testament Royal Ideology and the Rise of the Jewish Messianic Expectations.*[65] His stated purpose was "to examine how certain historical circumstances have provided the impulse for the birth and the development of the Old Testament royal ideology and how this ideology generated different messianic expectations in Judaism(s) of late antiquity."[66] Laato takes a historical-redactional approach, extensively using the Bible to recreate the history of Israel. Nevertheless, he maintains that messianic ideology arose in the tenth century BC with the Davidic covenant (2 Sam 7) rather than as a result of the Babylonian exile or disillusionment with the Hasmonean dynasty in the intertestamental period.[67] Taking a maximalist approach, Laato sees the prophets progressively developing the royal messianic ideal that Nathan gave to David. While affirming messianic hope, Laato's historical rather than textual approach weakened his book. In using this historical method, Laato sees each prophet speaking independently of each other. A literary approach would recognize that these are works that interact with and build upon each other. Moreover, in the final canonical redaction, there are literary glosses to link messianic passages with those that came before and those that follow.

In recent years, John Sailhamer proposed understanding the Old Testament as a holistic book with one overriding purpose, namely, to reveal the hope of the coming Messiah. He affirms direct messianic prediction but with a fresh approach, eschewing the old prooftexting methods. His view is found in his *Introduction to Old Testament Theology* (1995), a work that discusses messianic prophecy but is not solely about that subject.[68] Using a compositional/canonical approach to the Old Testament,[69] Sailhamer's basic premise is that study of the text of

---

[65] A. Laato, *A Star Is Rising: The Historical Development of the Old Testament Royal Ideology and the Rise of the Jewish Messianic Expectations* (Atlanta: Scholars Press, 1997).

[66] Ibid., 1.

[67] Ibid., 33–47.

[68] J. Sailhamer, *Introduction to Old Testament Theology: A Canonical Approach* (Grand Rapids: Zondervan, 1995).

[69] Sailhamer is very careful to distinguish his method from B. Childs's canon criticism when he states, "Our use of the word *canonical* should not be understood in light of the particular focus of *canon criticism*. Though there are surface similarities between canon criticism and the canonical theology of the Old Testament that we are proposing here, there are, as well,

Scripture itself (and not the historical events behind it), at both the compositional and canonical levels, will yield a messianic meaning.[70]

Sailhamer's understanding of messianic prophecy has two significant elements. First, he asserts that the Masoretic Text should be viewed *not* as the original Hebrew text but as its final stage.[71] As such, the Masoretic Text is a consolidation of the Hebrew text and reflects postbiblical interpretation. In a variety of places, the Masoretic Text reveals a historical interpretation of texts that are messianic in other ancient versions.[72] Hence, the first task of the interpreter of the Hebrew Bible, particularly in messianic passages, is to establish the text through textual criticism.

Second, Sailhamer builds on the well-established fact that the medieval Jewish "peshat" (simple) interpretations of the text were designed as an answer to the Christian messianic interpretation of the Tanak. Through the rise and influence of Christian Hebraism,[73] Jewish non-messianic interpretations slipped into the Protestant understanding of the Old Testament. As a result, Protestant interpretation either denied messianic prophecy altogether or adopted alternative interpretations, such as dual, typological, and progressive fulfillment.[74]

Sailhamer concludes his discussion of messianic prophecy by suggesting that the Tanak does indeed point directly to the Messiah. He contends that the New Testament's use of the Old does reflect the Old Testament author's intent. He states:

> We strongly urge the consideration of a return to the notion that the literal meaning of the Old Testament may, in fact, be linked to the messianic hope of the pre-Christian, Israelite prophets. By paying careful attention to the compositional strategies of the biblical books themselves, we believe in them can be found many essential clues to the meaning intended by their authors—clues that point beyond their immediate historical referent to a future, messianic age. By looking at the works of the scriptural authors, rather than at the events that lie behind their accounts of them, we can find appropriate textual clues to the meaning of these biblical books. Those clues, we also suggest, point to an essentially messianic and eschatological focus of the biblical texts.[75]

---

fundamental differences. Chief among those differences are the understanding of the historicity of the biblical narratives and the nature of the composition of the biblical books." Ibid., 198.

[70] Ibid., 154.

[71] Ibid., 224.

[72] Ibid., 220–21.

[73] The post-Reformation movement of Christian scholars studying Hebrew and Rabbinics.

[74] Sailhamer, *Introduction to Old Testament Theology: A Canonical Approach*, 132–54.

[75] Ibid., 154.

Sailhamer summarized his view of messianic prophecy in his article "The Messiah and the Hebrew Bible." There he argued that the shape of the Hebrew Bible and its compositional strategies were "motivated primarily by a hope in the soon coming of the promised Messiah."[76] Thus Sailhamer makes the case that "the OT does not only *predict* the coming of a Messiah. It also *describes* and *identifies* that Messiah." Furthermore, the New Testament writers accepted the Old Testament's preinterpretation and "were in fundamental agreement with its interpretation."[77]

Shortly after the publication of Sailhamer's *Introduction to Old Testament Theology*, William Horbury offered a similar understanding of messianic hope in his *Jewish Messianism and the Cult of Christ*.[78] He maintained that the messianic hope of the preexilic prophets was clarified in the editing and collecting of the Old Testament books, thus explaining the presence of the messianic idea in the intertestamental period, the New Testament, and in the rabbinic writings. Responding to much of contemporary critical scholarship on messianism, which argues that the messianic idea did not develop until the intertestamental period,[79] Horbury states:

> Messianism grew up in Old Testament times; the Old Testament books, especially in their edited and collected form, offered what were understood in the postexilic age and later as a series of messianic prophecies; and this series formed the heart of a coherent set of expectations, which profoundly influenced ancient Judaism and early Christianity.[80]

Old Testament scholarship is now divided: The majority takes a more historical approach to the Old Testament, resulting in a minimalist view of the Messiah in the Hebrew Bible. The minority embraces a more holistic reading of the Old Testament in its final form, resulting in an affirmation that messianism is present in the Hebrew Scriptures. As a reflection of this divide, a group of Old Testament scholars

---

[76] J. H. Sailhamer, "The Messiah and the Hebrew Bible," *JETS* 44 (2001): 12.

[77] Ibid., 12–13.

[78] W. Horbury, *Jewish Messianism and the Cult of Christ* (London: SCM, 1998). He is professor of Jewish and Early Christian Studies and Fellow of Corpus Christi College, Cambridge University.

[79] Horbury cites J. Becker as a representative of current critical scholarship that find a "messianological vacuum" in the Old Testament. He says, "What may be called a 'no hope list'—a list of books wherein it is thought that no messianic hope can be found—has long been a standard item in writings on messianism." Ibid., 5.

[80] Ibid., 6.

released a collection of essays on the interpretation of Old Testament messianic texts, *The Lord's Anointed* (1995).[81] This compendium of interpretations of messianic texts reflects the varied perspectives of the different authors. A few fully embrace messianic prediction in the Old Testament while most see little messianic expectation there. This book is a reflection of where Old Testament scholarship on messianic prophecy stands at the present time.[82]

Kaiser finds the book's inconsistency and frequently minimalist messianic interpretations to be "disturbing." Although recognizing that a number of the chapters present a strong emphasis on messianic prediction, still Kaiser objects that "a number of the essays take a much too cautious and minimalistic approach to the question as to whether the messiah was predicted in the portion they wrote on or not. This muting of the messianic presence in the OT began with Anthony Collins' two volumes published in 1724 and 1727 and has continued to the present moment."[83]

The Summary of Positions

In surveying all these works on messianic prophecy, it is evident that they present a maze of approaches to the Old Testament and messianic hope. In order to clarify the differing interpretations just enumerated, it would be helpful to summarize them systematically. So, what follows is a summary of the basic approaches.

One of the ways to deal with the Old Testament and the messianic hope is to deny that the Tanak has any such hope (see Figure 2.1). This approach understands the Scriptures to be referring to events in the time of the writers. Therefore, it refers all the biblical author's words to historical figures. For example, in Psalms, passages that Christian interpreters have traditionally understood as messianic are thought to refer to David or to other Davidic kings. This view is generally held by those who approach the Scriptures from a critical viewpoint, as well as many medieval and modern Jewish interpreters. Liberal Christian

---

[81] P. E. Satterthwaite, R. S. Hess and G. J. Wenham, eds., *The Lord's Anointed: Interpretation of Old Testament Messianic Texts* (Grand Rapids: Baker, 1995).

[82] Two other recent compilations that reflect the same inconsistent approach, predominated by messianic minimalists are R. S. Hess and M. D. Carroll R., eds., *Israel's Messiah in the Bible and the Dead Sea Scrolls* (Grand Rapids: Baker, 2003); and S. E. Porter, ed., *The Messiah in the Old and New Testaments* (Grand Rapids: Eerdmans, 2007).

[83] W. C. Kaiser Jr., review of P. E. Satterthwaite, R. S. Hess, and G. J. Wenham, eds., *The Lord's Anointed: Interpretation of Old Testament Messianic Texts*, *JETS* 42 (1999): 101–2.

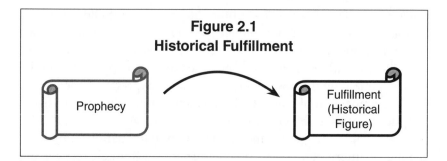

Figure 2.1
Historical Fulfillment

Prophecy → Fulfillment (Historical Figure)

(Anthony Collins, Critical Scholars)

- All prophecies refer to events in the time of the prophets.
- Prophecies refer to historical figures.
- Old Testament messianic prophecy teaches that Christianity is the *outgrowth of history* not the *fulfillment of prophecy*.

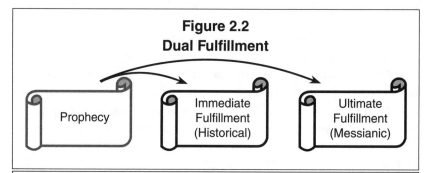

Figure 2.2
Dual Fulfillment

Prophecy → Immediate Fulfillment (Historical) → Ultimate Fulfillment (Messianic)

(Thomas Sherlock)

- Also known as "*Sensus Plenior*" (fuller sense).
- There are two fulfillments, one referring to an immediate historical figure and the second referring to the Messiah.
- The Divine author may have an added meaning that the human author did not intend.

interpreters who adopt this view see Christianity not as a fulfillment of prophecy but as the natural outgrowth of history.

Another way interpreters view the Old Testament is to see dual or even multiple fulfillments (see Figure 2.2). This system is sometimes called *sensus plenior*. It affirms that the divine author of the sacred text may have had a meaning that the human author did not intend. Thus there are two fulfillments. One refers to an immediate historical figure existing during the time of the human author, and a second ultimately refers to the Messiah. This view has been held by evangelicals and Roman Catholic interpreters.

Some interpreters understand Old Testament messianic fulfillment by means of types (see Figure 2.3). In this approach, the literal sense of a given Old Testament passage is taken to refer to a historical person. This person then becomes a type for the future Messiah who is the antitype. For example, in the Psalms, it is commonly asserted that David or a Davidic descendant was the literal subject. However, he formed a type of the future Son of David, the Messiah. This view is also commonly held by those who want to respect the historical context of a passage and do justice to the New Testament contention that Jesus fulfilled Old Testament prophecies.

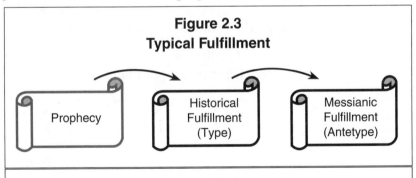

Figure 2.3
Typical Fulfillment

Prophecy → Historical Fulfillment (Type) → Messianic Fulfillment (Antetype)

(Aage Bentzen)

- The literal meaning refers to a historical figure.
- The historical figure is a type of the Messiah (or something related to his life).
- The type/antitype is the messianic sense of the Hebrew Bible seen in the New Testament

An alternative approach to the question of Old Testament messianic fulfillment views the prophecies as predictions that grow to their ultimate fulfillment (see Figure 2.4). According to this system, the biblical prophecy was given in seed form and developed progressively until it culminated in the Messiah. This view is frequently held by conservatives who want to retain the messianic hope as well as respect the biblical historical context.

Yet another method of interpreting messianic prophecy and fulfillment is relecture or rereading (see Figure 2.5). According to this view, earlier prophecies were read in a new ways so that they were filled with new meanings. This view has been adopted mainly by those who hold to critical views of the Bible, although some evangelicals have espoused it as well.

A hermeneutic that is growing in popularity is the midrash or pesher approach, which asserts that the New Testament understood the Old Testament messianic hope using the interpretive methods of early Judaism (see Figure 2.6). According to this view, the Old Testament prophecies commonly referred to historical figures present in the prophets' own days. Then, the New Testament interpreted these passages according to the intertestamental Jewish method called midrash or pesher. The New Testament cited these ancient passages in creative ways to show their fulfillment in contemporary events.

Figure 2.4
Progressive (Epigenetic) Fulfillment

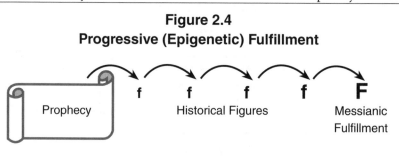

Prophecy	**f** **f** **f** **f** **F**
	Historical Figures Messianic Fulfillment

(Willis Beecher, Walter Kaiser)

- There is but one, single meaning of the passage and it is the meaning the author intended.

- The prophecy is given in seed form and grows progressively, with various historical figures, into the ultimate intended Messianic fulfillment.

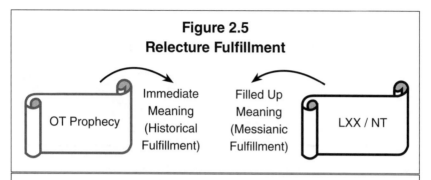

Figure 2.5
Relecture Fulfillment

OT Prophecy — Immediate Meaning (Historical Fulfillment) — Filled Up Meaning (Messianic Fulfillment) — LXX / NT

(R. E. Clements, P. D. Wegner)

- The literal prophecies refer to historical figures in the prophet's own day.
- Prophecies were re-read later (LXX translators, New Testament authors) in new ways so they have new meanings.
- The new readings "fill up" the original meaning with a messianic sense.

Adherents of this view hold that this method of interpretation should be rejected by modern exegetes. They believe that New Testament writers could use it because they wrote under the inspiration of the Holy Spirit. This approach has been adopted by critical as well as evangelical scholars.

The most traditional approach to messianic prophecy is to view it as predictions which refer directly to the Messiah (see Figure 2.7). That is not to say that all Old Testament messianic prophecy must refer directly and exclusively to the Messiah.[84] The traditional approach simply affirms that much of messianic prophecy is direct. There are two basic systems to this approach.

---

[84] There are clearly several other forms of messianic prophecy in the Old Testament. In addition to (1) direct fulfillment, at least three more categories should be recognized. I would add (2) typical fulfillment, which identifies the authorially intended patterns of certain Old Testament persons, events, or objects and finds corresponding fulfillment in the New Testament; (3) applicational fulfillment, which seeks to demonstrate the practical contemporary relevance of an Old Testament principle in a New Testament setting; and (4) summary fulfillment, which summarizes the teaching of several Old Testament passages while not directly quoting any of them. See Chapter 7. For another inventory of Old Testament fulfillment types, including typical, typico-messianic, eschatologico-messianic, divine parousia, messianic by extension, and messianic by way of preparation, see R. D. Culver, "The Old Testament as Messianic Prophecy," *BETS* 7 (1964): 91–97.

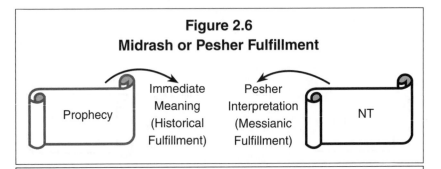

Figure 2.6
Midrash or Pesher Fulfillment

Prophecy — Immediate Meaning (Historical Fulfillment) — Pesher Interpretation (Messianic Fulfillment) — NT

(R.L. Longnecker, Donald Juel)

- The literal prophecies refer to historical figures in the prophet's own day.
- Prophecies were interpreted according to the intertestamental Jewish method called Midrash or Pesher.
- Midrash or Pesher interprets ancient passages in a creative way to show their fulfillment in contemporary events.
- New Testament writers can do this under the inspiration of the Holy Spirit.

The first is the confessional/dogmatic approach, which Hengstenberg defended. This method allows the New Testament to be the final arbiter as to the meaning of messianic prophecy and fulfillment and does not show much concern for the original audience or literary context.

The second is the compositional/canonical approach, which Sailhamer has proposed. This view maintains that when the Old Testament books were composed the authors had a messianic intention. Further, it observes a canonical shaping which recognizes the messianic nature of the text. This view asserts that, having established the Hebrew text through textual criticism, a close reading of that Hebrew text will result in a messianic interpretation.

Conclusion

The relationship between Old Testament prophecy and messianic fulfillment is essential to a theological defense of the messiahship of Jesus of Nazareth. It is so central to understanding the Old Testament's relationship to the New that it has produced a vast literature proposing various interpretive schemes. This book argues that reading the Old Testament according to its compositional strategies and canonical shape will yield a clear messianic intent, with far more direct messianic prediction than is commonly held. The next chapter will begin to make the case for this kind of direct fulfillment.

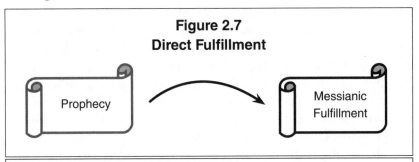

Figure 2.7
Direct Fulfillment

Prophecy

Messianic
Fulfillment

Dogmatic/Confessional Approach (E. W. von Hengstenberg)

- The prophecies of the Hebrew Bible are read through the New Testament.
- The New Testament is the final arbiter for the meaning of messianic prophecy and fulfillment.
- There is not much concern for the literary context or the original audience.

Compositional/Canonical Approach (John Sailhamer, William Horbury)

- The books of the Hebrew Bible were composed with a messianic intent.
- The final canonical shape highlighted the original messianic intent.
- The New Testament is read through the Hebrew Bible.

Chapter 3

TEXT-CRITICAL PERSPECTIVES ON MESSIANIC PROPHECY

J esus taught that the Law, the Prophets, and the Psalms all spoke of Him (Luke 24:44). As was seen in the previous chapter, for the last three centuries interpreters have struggled with discovering in precisely what sense the Hebrew Bible spoke of the Messiah. As has already been demonstrated, direct messianic prediction is but one method offered as a possible explanation, and at the present time it is certainly not the view most scholars accept, even among evangelicals. The purpose of this chapter is to begin to present the biblical evidence for interpreting many messianic prophecies as direct messianic predictions. Although the next few chapters will examine several lines of evidence, the focus of this chapter is the contribution of textual criticism in reading the Hebrew Bible as a messianic work.

This is so because the Masoretic Text is frequently treated as a received text rather than a version of the biblical text. Yet the Masoretic Text, although generally sound and truly the best Old Testament text available, is a somewhat late version of the Hebrew Bible. Therefore, other versions, such as the Samaritan Pentateuch, and ancient translations, such as the Septuagint, should be consulted to determine the best possible readings of the Old Testament.

The first task in exegesis is to establish the original text of any given passage. This is just as true when studying the Old Testament as it is for the New Testament. Second, textual criticism is especially significant for studying messianic prophecy because a considerable number of textual variants are found in Old Testament passages commonly understood to be messianic. The critical apparatus of the Hebrew Bible (*Biblia Hebraica Stuttgartensia*) frequently expands, with more variants, in those passages that have been thought to be messianic. Thirdly, the Masoretic Text may at times interpret some messianic passages as referring merely to historical figures. On the other hand, other earlier versions may reflect a more eschatological/messianic reading. Therefore, what follows is a discussion of the role of the Masoretic Text and textual criticism as it applies to messianic prophecy.

The Masoretic Text and Other Versions

John H. Sailhamer clarifies the way interpreters should view the Masoretic Text by warning, "Evangelicals, in the desire to stress the verbal inspiration of the OT text, should be careful not to identify the 'original' Hebrew text with the MT."[1] Eminent textual criticism scholar Emmanuel Tov concurs, writing that "the Masoretic Text does *not* reflect the 'original text' of the biblical books in many details."[2] He further states that "it should not be postulated that 𝔐 reflects the original text of the biblical books better than other texts."[3] In light of this, the Masoretic Text should not be accorded a status comparable to a *textus receptus*. Although the Masoretic Text is generally accurate and Old Testament exegesis would be near to impossible without it, it would be unwise to consider it as fully valid as the autographa. In fact, as Sailhamer says, "The history of the Masoretic Text is of vital importance . . . because it is the starting point of textual criticism, not because it is the final destination."[4] How is this so?

The Masoretic Text reflects a consonantal text that was not clearly consolidated until the second century AD.[5] Furthermore, the pointings and accents were not recorded until the ninth and tenth centuries AD.[6] With so many centuries between the consonantal text and the addition of vowels and accents, Wurthwein wisely cautions: "The pointing does not possess the same authority as the consonantal text."[7] Therefore, it is best *not* to view the Masoretic Text as the received text of the Old Testament, regardless of its strength and importance. Rather, it should be seen as the top layer of a distinct postbiblical exegetical tradition. Although the Masoretic Text seeks to identify the original intent of the biblical autographs in a consistent fashion, and often does, it also has an interpretive tradition embedded in it. As Jewish scribes, the Masoretes faithfully transmitted the textual traditions that they had received them from rabbinic Judaism. Thus, there is significant

---

[1] J. H. Sailhamer, *Introduction to Old Testament Theology* (Grand Rapids: Zondervan, 1995), 224.

[2] E. Tov, *Textual Criticism of the Hebrew Bible* (Minneapolis: Fortress, 1992), 11.

[3] Ibid. "𝔐" is the *BHS* symbol for the Masoretic Text.

[4] Sailhamer, *Introduction to Old Testament Theology*, 224.

[5] E. Wurthwein, *The Text of the Old Testament*, trans. E. F. Rhodes (Grand Rapids: Eerdmans, 1979), 26.

[6] Ibid.

[7] Ibid., 27.

rabbinic theology embedded in the Masoretic Text's standardization of the consonantal text and its addition of accents and vowels.[8]

In light of this, the theological importance of other ancient versions becomes readily apparent. For example, the Septuagint is a Greek translation of the Old Testament that is derived from a text nearly 1,000 years older than the Masoretic Text.[9] The point here is not that the Masoretic Text always, or even frequently, has an inferior reading. Rather, the point is that the Septuagint and other ancient versions provide "a viable alternative witness to the meaning of the text of Scripture, and thus the potential for an alternative biblical theology."[10] Furthermore, the New Testament authors' frequent use of the Septuagint when quoting the Old Testament lends further importance to this version.[11]

The Masoretic Text and Messianic Prophecy

So what does all this about the Masoretic Text have to do with messianic prophecy? It is significant to messianic prophecy because it has been shown that the Masoretic Text is a post-Christian, Jewish version of the Old Testament. As such, it reflects the theological perspective of post-Christian, rabbinic Judaism. Thus, there are several significant examples of the Masoretic Text interpreting Old Testament messianic texts in a distinctly nonmessianic (or historical) fashion, whereas other ancient versions interpret the same texts as referring to the Messiah. This is not to say that the Masoretic Text is the product of some conspiracy to excise the Messiah from the Old Testament, as some medieval polemicists claimed.[12] If that were so, the Masoretic Text would not have retained as much about the Messiah as it did. However, it can be argued that in some places the Masoretic Text reflects a less messianic view than other ancient texts and versions. What follows will highlight several of these examples.[13]

---

[8] For a more in-depth discussion of rabbinic influence, see Sailhamer, *Introduction to Old Testament Theology*, 204–5, 218–21.

[9] Tov, *Textual Criticism of the Hebrew Bible*, 136–37.

[10] Sailhamer, *Introduction to Old Testament Theology*, 205.

[11] Ibid. The New Testament perception of messianic prophecy will be addressed in chap. 6.

[12] This was maintained by medieval disputants with Judaism, such as P. Christiani and R. Martini. For a more thorough historical discussion of their claims, see J. Cohen, *The Friars and the Jews* (Ithaca and London: Cornell, 1982), 148–52.

[13] Sailhamer (*Introduction to Old Testament Theology*, 204–5, 220–21) discusses a number of

Judges 18:30

This first example serves to demonstrate that rabbinic thought is embedded in the Masoretic Text but does not address the interpretation of a messianic text specifically. The theological perspective of the Masoretic Text is evident in the suspended *nun* in Judg 18:30, which reads, "The Danites set up the carved image for themselves. Jonathan son of Gershom, son of Manasseh, and his sons were priests for the Danite tribe until the time of the exile from the land."

This verse records the establishment of the first pagan priesthood in Israel. The consonantal text's original reading indicated that *mšh* (Mosheh or Moses) was the grandfather of Jonathan, the founder of this pagan priesthood. The Masoretes inserted the raised letter ‪נ‬ (*n* or *nun*) making the word read *mnšh* (*Měnaššeh* or Manasseh).[14] According to Tov, the suspended *nun* was a correction of "an earlier reading which ascribed the erecting of the idol in Dan to one of the descendants of Moses. . . . The addition can therefore be understood as a deliberate change of content."[15]

The motive for the change is critical. Keil and Delitzsch cite R. Tanchum, who said that the written "Moses" reading ought to be corrected with a suspended *nun*, so that it would read "Manasseh."[16] Keil and Delitzsch also quote Rabba bar bar Channa who argued for the "Manasseh" reading "because it would have been ignominious to Moses to have an ungodly son."[17] Therefore, the *nun* was suspended to protect the honor of Moses. It was unthinkable for the exalted lawgiver and prophet of Judaism to have been the grandfather of the founder of a pagan priesthood.[18] Although this example does not pertain directly to messianic prophecy, it is significant because it demonstrates that the Masoretic Text can reflect a later theological perspective.[19]

---

these passages, and I am indebted to him for pointing me in this direction. I will include some of the passages he cites as well as several others.

[14] These two forms are also reflected in Septuagintal variants, with codex Alexandrinus (A) reading "Moses" (Μωυσῆ) and codex Vaticanus (B) reading "Manasseh" (Μανασση) demonstrating that this variant is extremely ancient.

[15] Tov, *Textual Criticism of the Hebrew Bible*, 57.

[16] So, according to Rabbi Tanchum, this should be viewed as a Ketib/Qere, "Moses" being written and "Manasseh" being read.

[17] C. F. Keil and F. Delitzsch, *Joshua, Judges, Ruth: Commentary on the Old Testament*, trans. J. Martin (repr., Grand Rapids: Eerdmans, 1980), 2:438.

[18] Sailhamer, *Introduction to Old Testament Theology*, 220.

[19] Another example of embedded rabbinic theology in the MT is Hos 14:3 [Eng. 14:2], which adjusts the place of the word division between the two last words. This shift changes the meaning

Numbers 24:7

The Masoretic Text of Num 24:7 presents a prophecy that would find its fulfillment in Israel's history. However, the alternate versions of this verse look forward to an eschatological messianic fulfillment. The Masoretic Text of Num 24:7 literally reads:

> Water will flow from his buckets, and his seed will be in the many waters;
> His king will be higher *than Agag,* and his kingdom will be exalted.[20]

According to the Masoretic reading, the verse predicts that a king would arise from Jacob who was to be higher than Agag. This is a prediction of the king whom Saul failed to kill (1 Sam 15:8–9). Thus, according to the Masoretic reading, the high king that Balaam foresaw is linked to the days of Saul's rejection and David's elevation. Based on the Masoretic reading, most interpreters understand the coming king to be King David.[21]

However, a variant reading substitutes "Gog" for "Agag." This reading has wide support, being found in the Septuagint, the Samaritan Pentateuch, Aquila, Symmachus, and Theodotion. According to this reading, Balaam foresees a king from Jacob who would be exalted over Gog, the end-time enemy of Israel (Ezek 38:3). Thus, the passage links this prophecy with Messiah's day, when He will have victory over the eschatological foes of Israel.

The "Gog" reading is supported by the context, in which Balaam says he is speaking of "the end of days" (Num 24:14).[22] Further, the

---

of the words from offering praise as "the fruit of our lips" to offering "our lips as bulls." The slight change makes a world of difference. In the LXX, praise is the result of being forgiven for sin. In the MT, prayers become a substitution for animal sacrifice, an important element in the restructuring of Judaism at Yavneh after the destruction of the temple in AD 70 (cf. *Avot of Rabbi Nathan,* 4). Hosea 14:3 is also cited in the daily prayer book as justification for the end of sacrifice as follows: "But thou hast said, that the prayers of our lips shall be accepted as the offering of steers." A. Th. Philips, *Daily Prayers with English Translation,* rev.ed. (New York: Hebrew Publishing, n.d.), 40–41.

[20] My translation.

[21] This is expressed well by M. Pickup, who cites several commentators holding to David or Davidic kingship as the future king envisioned here, including R. K. Harrison, *Numbers,* WEC (Chicago: Moody, 1990), 323; R. B. Allen, "The Theology of the Balaam Oracles," in *Tradition and Testament,* ed. J. Feinberg and P. Feinberg (Chicago: Moody, 1981), 118; R. D. Cole, *Numbers,* NAC (Nashville: Broadman and Holman, 2000), 420. Pickup writes: "The word 'king' in Num 24:7 (cf. v. 17) probably refers to the *state* of kingship in Israel's future history, yet David seems to be the primary referent due to his subjugation of Moab, Edom, and Amalek." M. Pickup, "New Testament Interpretation of the Old Testament: The Theological Rationale of Midrashic Exegesis," *JETS* 51 (2008): 375–76.

[22] The HCSB translates the Hebrew בְּאַחֲרִית הַיָּמִים as "in the future" but the literal "in the end of days" is preferable.

context identifies the king as the messianic royal figure of Genesis 49 when it says of Him "He crouches, he lies down as a lion" (Num 24:9) in a deliberate innertextual allusion to Gen 49:11. The prophecy also promises that this future king's "kingdom will be exalted" (Num 24:7), using more glorious terminology than what would be used of David or one of his nonmessianic descendants. Additionally, in Ezek 38:17, there is a recognition that Gog is known from earlier Scripture. There the Lord addresses Gog and asks, "Are you the one I spoke about in former times?" This is an obvious reference to the variant reading in Num 24:7.

Curiously, after recognizing the antiquity of the Septuagintal messianic reading and noting that the Masoretic Text on this verse is "difficult and obscure (and possibly corrupt)," Timothy Ashley still prefers the Masoretic Text reading. He dismisses the messianic rendering of the Septuagint as a mere reflection of the intense messianic speculations of the second century BC and not as an authentic reading that would yield a messianic prophecy.[23]

Ashley's approach, although common, seems ill advised. In light of broad witness to the "Gog" reading, the internal evidence, and the weaknesses of the Masoretic Text, it is better in this instance, as Albright suggested, to take the Septuagint as the original reading.[24] Thus, in an obscure verse in the Torah, it appears that the variant readings point to a future, glorious, Messiah with an exalted kingdom, not merely to King David.

2 Samuel 23:1

Second Samuel 23:1 provides another example of the Masoretic Text exhibiting a historical reading rather than the more messianic variant reading of the versions. In this verse, the Masoretic Text contains a seeming self-description of David, when it reads,

> These are the last words of David:
> the declaration of David son of Jesse,
> the declaration of the man raised on high,
> the one anointed by the God of Jacob,
> the favorite singer of Israel.

---

[23] T. R. Ashley, *The Book of Numbers*, NICOT (Grand Rapids: Eerdmans, 1993), 491.

[24] W. F. Albright, *Yahweh and the Gods of Canaan* (Garden City, NY: Doubleday, 1968), 16. See also Sailhamer, *Introduction to Old Testament Theology*, 220–21.

In the Masoretic Text, the passage contains five synonymous identifications of the author of these words. They come from David, who is the son of Jesse, who is "the man raised on high," who is "anointed by the God of Jacob," who is "the favorite singer [lit. "the delightful one of the songs"] of Israel." This translation and interpretation hinges on the Masoretic Text reading ʿāl, "on high." However, the Septuagint translates *epi* ("concerning"), apparently reading the same Hebrew consonants but a different Hebrew vowel: *pathah* (yielding ʿal) rather than *qamas* (yielding ʿāl). This slight vowel difference results in a substantial difference in translation:

> These are the last words of David:
> the declaration of David son of Jesse,
> and the declaration of the man raised up *concerning*
> the Messiah [Anointed One] of the God of Jacob,
> and the Delightful One of the songs of Israel.

Sailhamer aptly explains the significance of the different readings when he writes, "The effect of the difference in the length of the vowel is such that the title 'anointed one' in the Masoretic Text refers to King David, whereas in other, non-Masoretic versions of the text, David's words are taken as a reference to the Messiah (cf. 2 Sa 22:51)."[25]

The internal evidence is against the interpretation that David was writing about himself. In 2 Sam 23:3–4, David proceeds to describe the righteous reign of the king as "the one who rules the people with justice" (2 Sam 23:3–4). In v. 5 David makes a declarative statement (lit.): "For not so is my house with God" (*kî lōʾ kēn bêtî ʿim ʾēl*; 2 Sam 23:5). Most translations recognize the internal contradiction. In v. 1 David seems to be saying it is all about him, and then in v. 5 he plainly states it is not. Therefore, most English versions translate v. 5 as a question to avoid this internal contradiction with the first verse in the paragraph: "Is it not true that my house is with God?" (HCSB), "Truly is not my house so with God?" (NASB), "For does not my house stand so with God?" (ESV), "Is not my house right with God?" (NIV), or "Is it not my family God has chosen?" (NLT [2]). However, the problem with taking 2 Sam 23:5 as a question is that there is no interrogative particle (prefixed *h*), the Hebrew form normally found

---

[25] Sailhamer, *Introduction to Old Testament Theology*, 221.

in yes/no questions.[26] Hence, it is unlikely that the phrase should be understood as a question.

It makes far more sense to understand that, in his last words, David has said that the future Messiah was his favorite subject to write about in the Psalms, that David knew about the Messiah because the Spirit of God spoke to him (2 Sam 23:2), that the Messiah would be a righteous ruler (2 Sam 23:3–4), that readers ought not to confuse David with that future righteous ruler because David's "house is not so with God"; and finally, that David had assurance that the Messiah would come because God had "established an everlasting covenant" with him (2 Sam 23:5), namely, the Davidic covenant.

If the alternate, non-Masoretic reading is correct (and it must be remembered that the vocalization of the consonantal text occurred in the ninth through tenth century AD), then 2 Sam 23:1 gives a crucial interpretive clue to reading Davidic Psalms. By David the psalmist's own admission, he frequently wrote about the Messiah, the Delightful One of the songs of Israel, indicating that the Psalms should be understood to have an eschatological, messianic focus rather than merely a historical one.

Psalm 72:5

Psalm 72:5 is another example of a significant difference between the Masoretic Text and the Septuagint.[27] The Masoretic Text reads, "*They will* [or "May they"] *fear you* while the sun endures, and as long as the moon throughout all generations." On the other hand, the Septuagint reads, "*May he continue* while the sun endures, and as long as the moon, throughout all generations." The difference in the two versions is in the Masoretic Text *yîrā'ûkā*, "they will [may they] fear you," versus the Septuagintal reading *kai sumparamenei*, which is a translation of the Hebrew *wĕya'ărîk*, "and he will continue/endure."[28] The resulting meanings are quite different. The Masoretic Text refers

---

[26] GKC §150.2 states, "As a rule, however, the simple question is introduced by *He interrogative*." This does not include factual or Wh- questions (Who? What? Why? etc.), for which there are other particles or interrogative pronouns. See C. H. J. van der Merwe, J. A. Naudé, and J. H. Kroeze, *A Biblical Hebrew Reference Grammar* (Sheffield: Sheffield Academic Press, 1999), §43.

[27] Note that 72:17 has a similar difficulty between the MT and the LXX. The MT reads "may his name sprout forth before the sun shines," while the LXX reads, "his name shall remain continually before the sun." See R. E. Murphy, *A Study of Psalm 72* (Washington, DC: The Catholic University of America, 1948), 42–43.

[28] The MT reads a third-person plural qal imperfect of ירא, "fear," with a second-person

to a righteous king who would have such a significant impact on the nation that the people would fear God and submit to him forever. The Septuagint's meaning reflects the messianic interpretation inherent in the psalm, asking for the messianic king's life and reign to endure forever.

There are several reasons to prefer the Septuagintal reading over the Masoretic Text in Ps 72:5. First, there is no clear reason for the Masoretic Text to change pronominal subjects from the surrounding verses, which use the third person singular ("he will judge" in v. 2 and "may he vindicate" in v. 4), obviously describing the king/king's son introduced in v. 1, to a third person plural subject ("they") and a second person address to the Lord ("you"), resulting in the phrase "*they* will fear *you*." The second person pronoun cannot properly refer to the king (who is described in the third person singular), but would have to refer to God. Yet a second person address to God in v. 5 would be clearly out of place, especially since the next verse returns to the third person singular pronoun reference to the king ("may he be like rain").[29]

Second, the subject of *yîrā'ûkā* ("they will fear you") has no clear antecedent.[30] It would have to be "the people" (which is singular) from vv. 2–4, but the action of "fear" on the part of the king's people would be out of place here (the king's enemies kneel before him in vv. 9–11).[31]

Third, the verb *wĕya'ărîk* ("continue") fits better with the temporal allusions in vv. 5–7. There it speaks of the permanence of the sun, the moon continuing through all generations, and abundant peace "until the moon is no more." The context refers to time, not the fear of God.[32]

---

masculine singular accusative pronoun. The LXX reading reflects a third-person singular hiphil imperfect/jussive of אָרַךְ, "continue."

[29] According to H.-J. Kraus (*Psalms 60–150: A Continental Commentary,* trans. H. C. Oswald [Minneapolis: Fortress,1993], 75), "'may they fear you' is hardly possible in the context, for the suffix of the second person must refer to Yahweh. In a royal song such a relation is out of the question."

[30] See M. E. Tate, *Psalms 51–100*, WBC 20 (Dallas: Word, 1990), 220. Tate further explains that the MT reading "changes the focus of the psalm" from "the king and his subjects and other kings" to the people and God. Yet the LXX reading "fits easily into the context of the psalm."

[31] C. C. Broyles notes this shift in pronouns and the odd verb choice in the MT reading, concluding "The LXX probably points us to the original." See "The Redeeming King: Psalm 72's Contribution to the Messianic Ideal," in *Eschatology, Messianism, and the Dead Sea Scrolls,* ed. C. A. Evans and P. W. Flint (Grand Rapids: Eerdmans, 1997), 27n11.

[32] Murphy, *A Study of Psalm 72,* 21.

It might be argued that the Masoretic Text is the harder reading and therefore original. However, it would be necessary to demonstrate that there is a literary basis for the Masoretic Text reading somewhere in the context. However, a careful study of the psalm reveals no clear explanation.

Knut Heim has argued against the messianic rendering because the psalm is preexilic and "at this early stage in Israel's history a developed messianism or expectation of 'eternal life' is highly unlikely."[33] Nevertheless, this is nothing more than circular logic as he himself admits: "This argument could of course be accused of circular reasoning."[34] It is the same kind of logic that caused Duhm, who accepted the Septuagintal reading, to date the psalm as postexilic. He believed the messianic meaning could not have been present in the preexilic period.[35] Both of these writers seem to deny the possibility of supernatural revelation, which would allow the author to write of the Messiah prior to the exile. In light of all of the above evidence, it seems best to accept the Septuagintal reading for this verse, with all its messianic implications.

Isaiah 9:5[Eng. 6]

In this central messianic verse, the Masoretic Text's accentuation can produce a significantly different interpretation than the Hebrew words alone might express. The verse is commonly read, "He will be named Wonderful Counselor, Almighty God, Eternal Father, Prince of Peace." In this rendering, the title "Almighty God" is applied to the child who is to be born as Davidic king, seemingly indicating the deity of the king (cf. Isa 10:21).

However, the Masoretic Text inserts accents which divide the titles, resulting in this translation: "The Wonderful Counselor, the Mighty God, calls his name eternal father, prince of peace."[36] According to this translation, the first two couplets are names that refer to God himself, and the second two refer to the child that was born. The point

---

[33] K. Heim, "The Perfect King of Psalm 72: An Intertextual Enquiry," in *The Lord's Anointed: Interpretation of Old Testament Messianic Texts*, ed. P. E. Satterthwaite, R. S. Hess and G. J. Wenham (Grand Rapids: Baker, 1995), 241.

[34] Ibid.

[35] Duhm is cited by Heim, "The Perfect King of Psalm 72," 239.

[36] F. Delitzsch, *Isaiah: Commentary on the Old Testament in Ten Volumes*, trans. J. Martin (repr., Grand Rapids: Eerdmans, 1980), 249.

of this reading appears to be to negate any thought of considering the child whose birth is described as deity. Additionally, the Masoretic Text reading is decidedly different from the New Testament rendering in Luke 1:32–33.[37]

Hebrew scholar Franz Delitzsch objects to the Masoretic accents and their attendant translation for a number of reasons.[38] First, he contends that it is unlikely that there are two sets of names here, one for God and one for the child. Second, he finds it "impossible to conceive for what precise reason such a periphrastic description of God should be employed" when naming the child.[39] Third, he argues that a dual-name construction, as the Masoretic accents indicate, is not found elsewhere in Isaiah. Fourth, he conjectures that the first two titles would have been written with definite articles (*The* Wonderful Counselor and *the* Mighty God) had the author intended to distinguish God from the child. Thus, he concludes regarding the Masoretic accentuation: "We must necessarily reject it, as resting upon a misunderstanding and misinterpretation."[40] Once more, it appears to be an example of the Masoretic Text exhibiting an interpretive bias, advancing the perspective that a born child could not be the "Mighty God."

Psalm 22:17[Eng.16]

Psalm 22:17 (Hb.) is one of the most controversial verses in the Old Testament and the source of much contention. There are a multitude of variants but the basic difference is as follows: The Masoretic Text reads *kā'ărî*, ("as a lion") and the Septuagint reads *ōruxan*, from the verb *orussō*, "to dig/excavate" or "to perforate/pierce,"[41] apparently a translation of the Hebrew *k'rû* ("they pierced").[42] Thus, the verse in the Masoretic Text reads, "For dogs have surrounded me; a gang of evildoers has closed in on me; *as a lion* . . . my hands and my feet." However, the LXX, Syriac, and the Vulgate read, "For dogs have

---

[37] Sailhamer, *Introduction to Old Testament Theology*, 221.

[38] Delitzsch, *Isaiah*, 249–50.

[39] Ibid, 249.

[40] Ibid, 250.

[41] T. Muraoka, *A Greek-English Lexicon of the Septuagint* (Leuven: Peeters, 2009), 507.

[42] It is uncertain whether the verb rendered by the LXX was כאר or כור, both of which occur in a few Masoretic mss. R. L. Harris took it from כור, giving the meaning as "bore, dig, hew (meaning dubious)." He explains that it "occurs only in Ps 22:16 [H 17]," and "may be an hapax *kā'ar*. The meaning 'dig, wound, pierce' would derive from the context and LXX."

surrounded me; a gang of evildoers has closed in on me; *they pierced my hands and my feet.*"

Plainly, the Masoretic Text rendering avoids the Christological implications of predicting the crucifixion, thereby taking the less messianic rendering and making it more acceptable to Judaism.[43] The primary arguments for taking the Masoretic Text as the correct reading is that preference should always be given to the Masoretic Text and to the harder reading. The absence of the verb, making the phrase elliptical, yields not only the harder reading but a virtually unintelligible one. On the other hand, the Septuagintal reading has the older support and makes grammatical sense within the literary context.[44]

In the final analysis, it seems that the Septuagintal reading should be preferred for several reasons. First, although the Masoretic Text has the harder reading, there is a difference between a harder reading and an impossible one. One would have to assume incoherence on the part of the author, which is far more than the principle of taking the harder reading requires. As Peter Craigie has noted, the Masoretic Text reading "presents numerous problems and can scarcely be correct."[45] Second, defining the harder reading depends on the audience reading it. For a Masorete, "they pierced my hands and my feet," a seeming prediction of the Messiah's crucifixion, would certainly have been the harder reading. Third, the LXX reading fits the literary context, makes grammatical sense, and is supported by the other versions (and even some Masoretic traditions). Perhaps most important, in 1997, the translation of a textual discovery from Nahal Hever in the Judean Wilderness brought strong support to the Septuagintal reading.

The discovery of a fragment of the book of Psalms, dated between AD 50–68,[46] contains Ps 22:17 and reads, *kᵓrû* ("they pierced").[47] It

---

[43] The MT reading is also supported by the editors of the NET Bible. Although they recognize that the reading is "grammatically awkward" and characterized by "broken syntax," their apparent commitment to the MT above all motivates them to retain the Masoretic reading and to argue that "it is better not to interpret this particular verse as referring to Jesus' crucifixion in a specific or direct way." *The NET Bible* (Richardson, TX: Biblical Studies Press, 1997), 924n20.

[44] For a thorough analysis of the text-critical problem and a compelling argument for the LXX reading, see C. R. Gren, "Piercing the Ambiguities of Psalm 22:16 and the Messiah's Mission," *JETS* 48 (2005): 284–99.

[45] P. C. Craigie, *Psalms 1–50*, WBC (Waco, TX: Word, 1983), 196.

[46] P. Flint, "Biblical Scrolls from Nahal Hever and 'Wadi Seiyal': Introduction," in *Miscellaneous Texts from the Judaean Desert*, ed. J. Charlesworth, N. Cohen, H. Cotton, and E. Eshel, DJD 38 (Oxford: Clarendon, 2000), 143.

[47] M. Abegg Jr., P. Flint, E. Ulrich, *The Dead Sea Scrolls Bible* (New York: HarperSanFrancisco, 1999), 519; J. VanderKam and P. Flint, *The Meaning of the Dead Sea Scrolls* (New York:

might be objected that this was a Christian interpolation or contamination. But a Christian interpolation is unlikely because it would have been far too early in Christian history for a Christian corruption to make its way into this text. Moreover, it has strong support from the earlier Septuagintal reading.[48] Thus, the oldest extant Hebrew manuscript of Ps 22:17 reinforces the Septuagintal, Syriac, and Vulgate readings, supporting the translation "They pierced my hands and my feet." In this case, it is better to take the more messianic variant reading than the nonmessianic rendering of the Masoretic Text.

Conclusion

The above examples have shown the occasional tendency of the Masoretic Text to offer readings that find their fulfillment in historical figures rather than in eschatological times or a personal Messiah. The passages discussed are not unusual or unique. Even though there are others, these serve to demonstrate the tendency of the Masoretic tradition. As valuable as the Masoretic Text is, it should be viewed as the topmost strata of the interpretive layers of the Hebrew Bible. The careful interpreter of messianic prophecy should be aware of text-critical issues because these predictions may be buried in the Hebrew Bible's critical apparatus rather than in the Masoretic Text itself. Nevertheless, there is much in the Masoretic Text that reveals the Messiah. A careful, innerbiblical examination of the Scriptures themselves will reveal that the Hebrew Bible reads itself in a messianic way. This sort of innerbiblical interpretation will be addressed in the following chapter.

<hr>

HarperSanFrancisco, 2002), 125. The latter states, "Among the Dead Sea Scrolls, the reading in question is not preserved at Qumran, but in the Psalms scroll from Nahal Hever (5/6HevPs), which is textually very close to the Masoretic Text. In line 12 of column 10 we read: '*They have pierced* my hands and feet'! For the crucial word (כארו) the Hebrew form is grammatically difficult; but it is clearly a verb, not a noun and means *they have bored* or *they have dug* or *they have pierced.*"

[48] Gren, "Piercing the Ambiguities of Psalm 22:16 and the Messiah's Mission," 297.

Chapter 4

INNERBIBLICAL PERSPECTIVES ON MESSIANIC PROPHECY

I t is commonly believed in some scholarly circles that there was no clear messianic idea in Israel until the postexilic period[1] or even until the second century BC.[2] J. H. Charlesworth states, "I am convinced, Jewish messianology developed out of the crisis and hope of the non-messianic Maccabean wars of the second century B.C.E."[3] This would lead to the conclusion that Old Testament texts that have historically been interpreted as messianic, even by the New Testament, should not be viewed as messianic in their original intention. Thus, Donald Juel views the apostolic messianic identification of Old Testament texts as "a creative exegetical enterprise."[4]

However, this approach to messianic texts assumes that the Old Testament did not read itself in a messianic way. Having shown in the previous chapter that not treating the Masoretic Text as received text and practicing sound textual criticism may yield a more messianic perspective in various Old Testament texts, the point of this chapter is to show that the Old Testament, when reading itself innerbiblically, considers itself a messianic book. This chapter will explore three passages from the Torah (Gen 49:8–12, Num 24:14–19, and Deut 18:15–19) and demonstrate that later Old Testament writers viewed these earlier Old Testament texts as messianic.[5]

Genesis 49:8–12

The context of this prophecy is Jacob's blessing of his sons before he died. Jacob establishes an eschatological perspective in 49:1 when

---

[1] S. Mowinckel, *He That Cometh* (Oxford: Blackwell, 1959), 17.

[2] J. Becker, *Messianic Expectation in the Old Testament* (Philadelphia: Fortress, 1977), 50, 87.

[3] J. H. Charlesworth, "From Messianology to Christology," in *The Messiah*, ed. J. Charlesworth (Philadelphia: Fortress, 1992), 3.

[4] D. Juel, *Messianic Exegesis: Christological Interpretation of the Old Testament in Early Christianity* (Philadelphia: Fortress, 1988), 13.

[5] H. Wolf, *An Introduction to the Old Testament: The Pentateuch* (Chicago: Moody, 1991), 141–48; and G. L. Archer, *A Survey of Old Testament Introduction* (Chicago: Moody, 1964), 212–23, both defend Mosaic authorship and a mid-fifteenth century BC date for the exodus. This would require that the Pentateuch be dated by the end of the fifteenth century BC, which this chapter will presuppose.

he states that he will tell what will happen "in the last days" (*bě'aḥ ărît hayyāmîm*).[6] In 49:1–7, the three older brothers are described as unqualified to receive the birthright because of their previous sinful behavior. Reuben is disqualified because he lacked sexual control, sleeping with his father's concubine (Gen 35:22). Simeon and Levi are disqualified because they lacked control of their tempers, being overzealous in their vengeance for Dinah's rape (Gen 34:29–35).

The prophecy about Judah refers to his preeminence (v. 8), his power (v. 9), and the future king who is to come from his tribe (vv. 10–12). The most controversial aspect of this prophecy is the identification of "Shiloh" (*šîlōh*), for which there are four main views.

(1) Shiloh is a place name.[7] This position holds that Judah's conquest of Canaan is in view. It would translate the phrase, "until he comes to Shiloh," referring to the Israelite worship center. The problem with this interpretation is that the Masoretic Text consistently distinguishes the spelling of the place name "Shiloh" (שִׁלֹ [*šilô*], שִׁילוֹ [*šîlô*], or שִׁלֹה [*šilōh*]) with the word Shiloh (שִׁילֹה [*šîlōh*]) in Gen 49:10.[8]

(2) Shiloh is a proper name of the Messiah. This is the view of the Talmud in *Sanhedrin* 98b, which answers the question of what the Messiah's name is by saying, "Shiloh is his name, as it is said, 'Until Shiloh come.'" It is also the view of the *Targum Pseudo-Jonathan* ("until that time that King Messiah shall come")[9] and the Qumran community ("until the coming of the Messiah of Righteousness").[10] Some who hold this view understand this proper name to mean "peacemaker or pacifier" from the root of the Hebrew word *šālāh*, which means "to rest." They consider this similar to the word *šālôm* (peace) and relate the idea to Isa 9:6[Hb. 5], which calls the Messiah the Prince of

---

[6] Some English translations render this phrase "in (the) days to come" (NASB, NIV, HCSB) as if it refers to future events and not the end times. While this may be possible, the literal rendering "the end of days" or "the last days" is certainly more literal and more common. According to BDB, 31, it is "a prophetic phrase denoting the final period of the history so far as the speaker's perspective reaches; the sense thus varies with the context, but it often = the ideal or Messianic future."

[7] F. Delitzsch, *Messianic Prophecies in Historical Succession* (Edinburgh: T&T Clark, 1891), 51.

[8] BDB, 1017–18.

[9] S. H. Levey, *The Messiah: An Aramaic Interpretation* (Cincinnati: Hebrew Union College–Jewish Institute of Religion, 1974), 9.

[10] M. Burrows, *More Light on the Dead Sea Scrolls* (New York: Viking, 1958), 401.

peace, and Micah 5:5[Hb. 4], which says "He will be their peace."[11] Delitzsch rightly objects that this is not confirmed lexically or by the analogy of Scripture.[12]

(3) Shiloh means "his son." This was the view of Calvin who saw the derivation of the word as *šîl* (child) and *-ōh* for the possessive pronoun *-ô* (his). Thus, the scepter would not depart from Judah until Judah's son came. As desirable as this view may be, unfortunately *šîl* does not mean "son," making this view unacceptable.[13]

(4) Shiloh is a word meaning "which belongs to him" or "to whom it belongs." This view is sustained by accepting the variant reading *šelōh* (i.e., *šlh*) instead of *šîlōh* (i.e., *šylh*).[14] According to this view, *šelōh* is a word formed from *še,* an archaic relative pronoun like the more common *'ăšer* ("which, who"), plus *lě* ("belonging to"), and the suffix *-ōh* for *-ô* ("him"). The critical apparatus of *BHS* cites multiple Masoretic and Samaritan manuscripts which read *šlh*.[15] This is apparently the source of the Septuagint's translation *heōs an elthē ta apokeimena* ("until there should come the things stored up for him"). It is also supported by *Targum Onqelos*, Aquila, Symmachus, and Theodotion.[16] According to the Hebrew lexicon by Koehler and Baumgartner, the pronoun *še/ša* is archaic in Hebrew, its function eventually being taken over by the more common *'ăšer*. It occurs, for example, in Gen 6:3; Judg 5:7 (an especially important text since this is considered some of the oldest Hebrew in the Bible); 6:17; 7:12; 8:26; and Job 19:29.[17]

Although all four views have difficulties, the fourth has intertextual support from Ezek 21:27 [Hb. 21:32]. Barnes states that "perhaps the oldest extant reference to the שִׁילֹה [*šîlōh*] passage is the parallel phraseology to be found in the book of Ezekiel."[18] The passage

---

[11] E. W. Hengstenberg, *Christology of the Old Testament,* trans. R. Keith (repr., Grand Rapids: Kregel, 1970), 30–31; A. McCaul, *The Messiahship of Jesus* (London: Unwin, 1852), 144; H. C. Leupold, *Exposition of Genesis* (Grand Rapids: Baker, 1950), 2:1176–85; C. F. Keil, *The Pentateuch: Commentary on the Old Testament,* trans. J. Martin (repr., Grand Rapids: Eerdmans, 1980): 1:1:397.

[12] F. Delitzsch, *Messianic Prophecies: Lectures,* trans. S. I. Curtiss. (Edinburgh: T&T Clark, 1880), 34.

[13] G. Van Groningen, *Messianic Revelation in the Old Testament* (Grand Rapids: Baker, 1990), 173–74.

[14] W. C. Kaiser Jr., *Messiah in the Old Testament* (Grand Rapids: Zondervan, 1995), 51.

[15] Kaiser states that there are thirty-eight manuscripts supporting this reading. Ibid.

[16] Ibid.

[17] *HALOT* 4:1365. They point out that etymologically שֶׁ is comparable to Akkadian *šu/ša*.

[18] Ibid., 42. See also K. A. Mathews, *Genesis 11:27–50:26,* NAC (Nashville: B&H, 2005), 895.

in Ezekiel substantiates two ideas: First, it affirms the rendering of *šîlōh* as "to whom it belongs." Second, it confirms that Gen 49:10 is a messianic prophecy.[19]

In Ezek 21:24–27 [Hb. 29–32] God addresses Zedekiah typically (as head of the Davidic house) about his sins. God tells him to "remove the turban, and take off the crown" (Ezek 21:26 [31]) to picture the loss of his kingship and the overthrow of the kingly line.[20] Using a triple repetition ("a ruin, a ruin, . . . a ruin") to express a strong superlative, God announces the temporary overthrow of the Davidic line "until He comes whose right it is" (NASB; *ʿad bōʾ ʾăšer lô hammišpāṭ*, Ezek 21:27[32]).

There are essentially two interpretations of this phrase, one which views Nebuchadnezzar as the referent, and the other which identifies it as the Messiah. The interpretation hinges on the meaning of the word *mišpāṭ*. The first, nonmessianic view, takes *mišpāṭ* to mean "judgment/punishment." Therefore, the phrase refers to the one who will execute judgment on Judah, namely, Nebuchadnezzar, the king of Babylon. This position is supported in two ways. First, it is argued that the translation of the word *mišpāṭ* must be understood in light of its use in Ezek 23:24b where it plainly means judgment.[21] Second, the context of Ezek 21:27[32] is all judgment, and it would be unlikely for this verse to include a promise of restoration. Moran writes, "And finally, it seems most improbable that in a context in which everything speaks of ruin and destruction, both before and after, in one short phrase of two words we should have a promise of restoration: such a *volte face* is without parallel in Ezekiel."[22]

The second interpretation takes *mišpāṭ* to mean "justice/just" and views the phrase as a promise of restoration by the Messiah. The

---

[19] Numbers 24:7–9, in its variant reading, speaks of a future glorious King with an exalted kingdom who will defeat Gog (see chap. 3), the eschatological enemy of Israel. This messianic prophecy concludes by comparing the future king to a lion ("He crouches, he lies down like a lion or a lioness—who dares to rouse him?"). This is plainly an innertextual reference to Gen 49:11, giving further confirmation that the author viewed 49:10 as messianic.

[20] It is better to view the words "turban" and "crown" as synonymous parallels, referring to royalty, rather than to take the turban to refer to priesthood and the crown to refer to kingship. See J. H. Taylor, *Ezekiel: An Introduction and Commentary*, ed. D. J Wiseman, TOTC (Downers Grove, IL: InterVarsity, 1969), 164; C. H. Dyer, "Ezekiel," in *The Bible Knowledge Commentary: Old Testament*, ed. J. F. Walvoord and R. B. Zuck (Wheaton: Scripture Press, 1985), 1269.

[21] W. L. Moran, "Gen. 49:10 and Its Use in Ez. 21:32," *Bib* 39 (1958): 405–25; W. Zimmerli, *Ezekiel: A Commentary on the Prophet Ezekiel, Chapters 1–24* (Philadelphia: Fortress, 1979), 447.

[22] Moran, "Gen. 49:10 and Its Use in Ez. 21:32," 419.

supports for the messianic interpretation of Ezek 21:27[32] are as follows:

(1) Although *mišpāṭ* frequently means "judgment/punishment" in Ezekiel (Ezek 5:8; 16:38; 23:24,45; 39:21), it can also mean "justice/just" (Ezek 18:5,8;19,21,27; 22:29; 33:14,16,19; 45:9).[23]

(2) It is possible for Ezekiel to give a promise of restoration within an oracle of judgment, indeed, as he did in Ezek 17:22–24. In fact, a promise of restoration after judgment fits with the theology of the book of Ezekiel.[24]

(3) There is an intertextual allusion to Gen 49:10 in Ezek 21:27[32], which describes one who would defeat Israel's enemies and bring blessing to his people. However, since the last kings of Judah were evil and not qualified to fulfill this promise, the nation would have to wait for another one who had the right. Thus, von Rad writes, "Even the grievous harm done to the royal office by those who had last worn the crown did not vitiate the prophet's hope that Jaweh would redeem the promise attached to the throne of David, 'until he comes whose right it is'" (Ezek 21:32).[25]

In light of these arguments, it is best to view Ezek 21:27[32] as a prophecy of the messianic hope in the midst of judgment. Thus, Ezekiel's message was that "the line of David would not be restored till the righteous, God-appointed King would come."[26]

Since the phrase used in Ezekiel (*'ad bō' 'ăšer lô hammišpāṭ*) is, according to Ralph Alexander, "a definite reference to Genesis 49:10," Ezekiel was using the earlier messianic passage in his context to stress that "kingship . . . would be removed in judgment but returned ultimately in the Messiah's coming in accord with Genesis 49:10."[27]

This intertextual reference to Gen 49:10 demonstrates that *šîlōh* does indeed mean "which belongs to him." Furthermore, it establishes that Gen 49:10 is a messianic prophecy. As Barnes states, "That Ezekiel confirms the Messianic interpretation in his allusion to Gen

---

[23] C.-K. Lai, "Jacob's Blessing on Judah (Genesis 49:8–12) with the Hebrew Old Testament: A Study of In-Textual, Inner-Textual, and Inter-Textual Interpretation" (Ph.D. diss., Trinity Evangelical Divinity School, 1993), 309.

[24] Ibid., 309–10.

[25] G. Von Rad, *Old Testament Theology* (New York: Harper and Row, 1965), 2:235.

[26] C. H. Dyer, "Ezekiel," 1269.

[27] R. H. Alexander, "Ezekiel," in *EBC* 6:845. Mathews (*Genesis 11:27–50:26*, 895) interprets the one who is "coming" according to Ezek 21:27[32] as "the future, rightful successor to the wicked Zedekiah of Judah."

49:10 in Ezek. 21:32 alone should be sufficient to substantiate this view for anyone who holds to the Divine inspiration and unity of Scripture."[28]

Numbers 24:14–19

Numbers 24:14–19, the fourth and last of Balaam's oracles, foretells Israel's hegemony over both Moab and Edom. It begins with Balaam telling Balak, king of Moab, the subject of the oracle, namely, what Israel will do to Moab in the last days (*bě'aḥărît hayyāmîm*, 24:14). After affirming that this oracle is derived from a vision of God, Balaam places the fulfillment of the prophecy in the distant future, ("I see him but not now; I behold him but not near," Num 24:17a). After declaring that a star and scepter shall come from Israel that will crush Moab and take possession of Edom, Balaam states that Israel will perform valiantly and one from Jacob shall have dominion (24:17b–19).

At issue here is whether or not Balaam's oracle is a messianic prediction. After considering the interpretive options, the intertextual evidence will be examined.

The Interpretive Options

(1) The first option takes the star and scepter to refer corporately to the nation of Israel. This view is based on the context, in which Balaam declares that the oracle concerns what the people of Israel will do to Moab. Furthermore, it speaks of Israel (the nation) performing valiantly.[29]

Although the passage does describe the actions of Israel, it does so in conjunction with an individual at the nation's head. The terms star

---

[28] W. H. Barnes, "A Text-Critical and Historical Examination of the 'Shiloh' Reference," 96. M. Fishbane also sees Zech 9:9, "Behold your king will come to you [לך יבוא], triumphant, his victory won, humble, riding on an ass, the foal of a she-ass [בן־אתנות]," as an intertextual reference to Gen 49:10–11 (*Biblical Interpretation in Ancient Israel* [Oxford: Oxford University Press, 1988], 501–2). If he is correct, this would be another direct and clear messianic prophecy that interpreted Gen 49:8–12 messianically.

[29] According to T. R. Ashley, *The Book of Numbers*, NICOT (Grand Rapids: Eerdmans,1993), 500, this is the view of G. B. Gray, *A Critical and Exegetical Commentary on Numbers*, ICC (Edinburgh: T&T Clark, 1903), 369; A. H. McNeile, *The Book of Numbers in the Revised Version*, Cambridge Bible for Schools and Colleges (Cambridge: Cambridge University Press, 1911), 139; and L. E. Binns, *The Book of Numbers: With Introduction and Notes* (London: Methuen, 1927), 171–72.

and scepter are in synonymous parallel and refer to a royal figure.[30] This king is the leader of Israel and represents the whole nation. Therefore, the prophecy as a whole may be about the actions of Israel the nation, but it still refers to a royal figure at its helm.

(2) The second option takes the star and scepter to refer to the historical figure of David (or even his kingly line). Hengstenberg argues for this position as do others.[31] The view is substantiated by the victories of David over Moab (2 Sam 8:2) and Edom (2 Sam 9:14). Thus, it is maintained that the prophecy does indeed speak of a future king but that it is not the messianic king.[32]

Asserted against this view is that Moab and Edom later won their freedom, making David's victories only temporary.[33] Furthermore, prophets writing many years after David saw the subjugation of these nations as still future (Isa 11:14; 15:1–16:14; 34:5–17; Jer 48–49; Ezek 25:8–14; Amos 2:1–3; 9:11–12; Zeph 2:8–11; Obad 1–21).

(3) The third view is that the star and scepter refer directly to the Messiah. This is the view of the ancient Targumim,[34] the *Midrash Rabbah* (*Devarim* 1:20), and church fathers such as Justin Martyr and Athanasius.[35]

In support of the messianic view, it appears that the text itself calls for an eschatological reading. By declaring that the prophecy refers to "the last days" and by seeing the king in the far distant future ("but not now . . . but not near"; *wĕlō' 'attâ . . . wĕlō' qārôb*), the passage demands an eschatological reading. Keil states, "By the 'end of days,'

---

[30] Keil, *The Pentateuch*, 1:192.

[31] Hengstenberg, *Christology of the Old Testament*, 34–37; Ashley, *The Book of Numbers*, 500–503; Van Groningen, *Messianic Revelation in the Old Testament*, 244; J. H. Hertz, *The Pentateuch and Haftorahs* (London: Soncino, 1937), 244; Rashi, "Bamidbar," in *The Metsudah Chumash/Rashi* (Hoboken: KTAV, 1995), 4:338.

[32] G. Wenham agrees that David is spoken of here. Nevertheless, he also affirms that David foreshadows the Messiah as a type (*Numbers: An Introduction and Commentary*, TOTC [Downers Grove, IL: InterVarsity, 1981], 178–79).

[33] Keil, *The Pentateuch*, 1:194.

[34] Levey, *The Messiah: An Aramaic Interpretation*, 21–27.

[35] Cited in R. B. Allen, "Numbers," *EBC* 2:655–1008 (Grand Rapids: Zondervan, 1990), 911. Among modern commentators the messianic view is held by Allen, "Numbers," 908–11; Keil, *The Pentateuch*, 1:191–202; Kaiser, *Messiah in the Old Testament*, 53–57; Delitzsch, *Messianic Prophecies: Lectures*, 39–41; and J. Smith, *What the Bible Teaches about the Promised Messiah* (Nashville: Thomas Nelson, 1993), 59–64. According to R. D. Cole (*Numbers*, NAC [Nashville: B&H, 2000], 425), "One of the most remarkable prophecies of the Hebrew Bible, interpreted for centuries before the Christian era as portending and heralding the great Messianic king and kingdom, is here uttered by a pagan divination expert."

both here and everywhere else, we are to understand the Messianic era."[36]

Moreover, the prophecy refers not to temporary setbacks to Moab and Edom but to Israel's ultimate victory to be achieved under the Messiah. As Kaiser states, "This portion mainly depicts what will take place at the second advent of Messiah. He will literally clean house of all evil and all opposition to his rule and reign."[37]

It has been argued that the phrase *bĕʾaḥărît hayyāmîm,* "in the last days," is ambiguous and need not refer to eschatological times but merely to the future.[38] However, the phrase generally does refer to the end of days, and understanding it otherwise requires some reason within the text or context, not just a presupposition that it could not be so. The careful reading of the text itself indicates that the eschatological/messianic interpretation of Num 24:14–19 seems most appropriate.

The Intertextual Considerations

The key passage that sheds light on Num 24:14–19 is Amos 9:11–12. Amos's prophetic ministry took place in the middle of the eighth century BC.[39] If Moses wrote the Torah about 1400 BC, then Amos wrote about six and a half centuries later. His perspective was decidedly post-Davidic and his message was essentially judgment. At the close of the book, however, despite its overall message of judgment, a prophecy of hope is added (9:11–12). This offer of consolation looks ahead to the eschatological period (*bayyôm hahûʾ,* "in that day")[40] when the Davidic dynasty would no longer be functioning.

Amos promises that God will raise up the fallen booth of David. This is not just a promise of a restored dynasty but of the coming of the son of David, the messianic king. Kaiser correctly argues that the interpretation of this passage rests on the suffixes of three words in Amos 9:11, although they are not usually translated literally. The interpretation turns on the phrases "their broken places" (*pirṣêhen*) with its feminine plural suffix, "his ruins" (*waḥărisōtāyw*) with its

---

[36] Keil, *The Pentateuch,* 1:199.

[37] Kaiser, *Messiah in the Old Testament,* 57.

[38] Ashley, *The Book of Numbers,* 499.

[39] C. H. Bullock, *An Introduction to the Old Testament Prophetic Books* (Chicago: Moody, 1986), 59–60.

[40] Kaiser, *Messiah in the Old Testament,* 145.

masculine singular suffix, and "build it" (*ûběnîtîhā*) with its feminine singular suffix.[41]

The feminine plural suffix ("*their* broken places") refers to the two kingdoms that had been divided since the days of Rehoboam. God will unite the nation once again under their messianic king. The masculine singular suffix ("*his* ruins") refers to David (not his booth, which is feminine). Since David is dead, Kaiser points out that this "must refer to that 'second David,' mentioned in Hosea 3:5. God will raise up from the ashes of 'destruction' the new David, even Christ, the Messiah."[42] The feminine suffix ("build *it*") refers to the fallen booth, the Davidic dynasty that will be restored under the Messiah.[43] The messianic expectation of Amos 9:11 is clear.

Amos also declares God's purpose in raising up David's dilapidated booth, "so that they may possess the remnant of Edom, even all the nations that bear my name" (9:12). Sailhamer notes that the mention of possessing the remnant of Edom is a transparent intertextual reference to Num 24:18.[44] Kaiser concurs when he writes, "The verb 'to possess' is deliberately chosen, for it preserves the prophecy made by Balaam in Numbers 24:17–18."[45] Keil also notes the intertextual reference when he writes, "*yîrěšû*, to take possession of, is chosen with reference to the prophecy of Balaam (Num. xxiv. 18), that Edom should be the possession of Israel."[46]

The point of this intertextual reference is plain. As Sailhamer states, "The eschatology of Amos is the same as that of the Pentateuch. The future Davidic king will rule victoriously over Israel's enemies and establish his eternal kingdom."[47] The reference by this later prophet to the very words found in the Mosaic Torah confirms that Amos read the fourth Balaam oracle as a messianic prophecy.[48]

---

[41] Ibid., 145–46.

[42] Ibid., 146.

[43] Ibid.

[44] J. H. Sailhamer, *Introduction to Old Testament Theology* (Grand Rapids: Zondervan, 1995), 250–51.

[45] Kaiser, *Messiah in the Old Testament*, 148.

[46] C. F. Keil, *The Minor Prophets: Commentary on the Old Testament*, trans. J. Martin (repr., Grand Rapids: Eerdmans, 1980), 10:1:332.

[47] Sailhamer, *Introduction to Old Testament Theology*, 251.

[48] Acts 15:16–21 quotes Amos 9:12 to support the idea that Gentiles would share in God's Kingdom and therefore they need not convert to Judaism first. Acts quotes the Septuagint rendering, which reads Edom as "Adam" or "humanity," which reflects the meaning of Amos 9:12. For a more detailed discussion of this use of the Old Testament in the New as it relates to contextuality, see Sailhamer's discussion in *Introduction to Old Testament Theology*, 248–52.

Deuteronomy 18:15–19

Deuteronomy 18:15–19 contains God's promise that He will raise up a prophet like Moses that the people of Israel are to heed. The issue to be addressed here is whether or not this passage refers to the Messiah when it speaks of a prophet like Moses.[49] After surveying the common interpretive approaches to Deut 18:15–19, the innertextual interpretation of the passage will be examined to demonstrate the messianic nature of the passage.

The Interpretive Approaches

There are essentially four ways that interpreters have approached this text.

(1) The first interpretation is the direct nonmessianic view.[50] This approach, held by some medieval Jewish interpreters, takes the coming prophet to be a particular future prophet but not the Messiah. According to McCaul, Abarbanel held that Jeremiah was the prophet like Moses, while Ibn Ezra applied the prophecy to Joshua.[51]

Although these interpretations try to make good sense of the singular noun *nābî'*, McCaul rejects them both. He objects to Jeremiah being the referent since Moses was a prophet of deliverance, whereas Jeremiah was a prophet of doom. McCaul also rejects Joshua as the referent because Joshua was not like Moses in mediation nor direct revelation.[52] Additionally, it should be noted that in Deuteronomy 34, immediately after the description of Joshua (Deut 34:9), the writer says that no prophet had arisen like Moses (Deut 34:10), obviously disqualifying Joshua as the referent.

(2) The second interpretation is the collective nonmessianic view which holds that the institution of the office of prophet is in view.[53]

---

[49] Y.-H. Kim, "'The Prophet like Moses': Deut 18:15–22 Reexamined within the Context of the Pentateuch and in Light of the Final Shape of the TaNaK" (Ph.D. diss., Trinity Evangelical Divinity School, 1995). This is an outstanding dissertation that evaluates the various options and argues for the direct messianic interpretation.

[50] Despite her extensive research, Kim only interacts with the direct messianic, collective nonmessianic, and collective messianic views. She does not deal with the direct nonmessianic view.

[51] McCaul, *The Messiahship of Jesus*, 146.

[52] Ibid., 146–47.

[53] Adherents of this view are Rashi, "Deuteronomy," in *The Pentateuch and Rashi's Commentary*, trans. A. Ben Isaiah and B. Sharfman in collaboration with H. M. Orlinsky and M. Charner (Brooklyn: S. S. & R. Publishing, 1950), 173; S. Fisch, *The Book of Deuteronomy*, in *The Soncino Chumash*, ed. A. Cohen, The Soncino Books of the Bible (London: Soncino Press, 1947), 1086;

This position is based on taking the singular *nābî'* as a collective noun and is defended as follows:[54]

(a) The wider context (Deuteronomy 16–18) describes the offices of king and priest, so it is not likely that the prophet would be an individual but rather an order or office.

(b) The nearer context of Deut 18:9–14, which prohibits pagan divination, contrasts with 18:15–19, and thus the text's intent appears to be a prophetic order.

(c) The discussion of the false prophet in Deut 18:20–22, clearly a collective noun, assumes a reference to the preceding true prophet. Hence, they both must be collective.

In response to these arguments, the following may be stated:

(a) The wider context makes it most fitting for Deut 18:15–19 to refer to the Messiah, as the head of all offices and authorities spoken of in the surrounding passages.

(b) The nearer context of rejecting pagan divination would contrast with the Messiah who would be the perfect revelation of God.[55]

(c) The discussion of false prophets in 18:20–22 is indeed consistent with an individual prophet in 18:15–19. This is seen in two ways. First, the particle *'ak* in 18:20 is an adversative that is short of a full antithesis and can best be translated as *however*.[56] Thus, this paragraph is not intended "to show an equal antithetical relationship between the prophet in vv. 15–19 and the prophet in vv. 20–22." A close examination of the text demonstrates that what is being contrasted is that the prophet

Hertz, *The Pentateuch and Haftorahs*, 827; P. Heinisch, *Christ in Prophecy*, trans. W. G. Heidt, (Collegeville, MN: Liturgical Press, 1956), 46–48; A. Phillips, *Deuteronomy* (Cambridge: Cambridge University Press, 1973), 124–26; L. J. Hoppe, *Deuteronomy*, Collegeville Bible Commentary (Collegeville, MN: Liturgical Press, 1985), 59–60; G. Oehler, *Theology of the Old Testament* (New York: Funk & Wagnalls, 1883), 362–64; R. K. Harrison, *Introduction to the Old Testament* (Grand Rapids: Eerdmans, 1974), 656; C. Barth, *God with Us: A Theological Introduction to the Old Testament*, ed. G. W. Bromiley (Grand Rapids: Eerdmans, 1991), 306–7; R. Clifford, *Deuteronomy with an Excursus on Covenant and Law* (Wilmington: Glazier, 1982), 102.

[54] This is a summary of the arguments for and against this view as found in Kim, "'The Prophet like Moses,'" 89–94.

[55] Ibid., 91–92.

[56] F. I. Anderson, *The Sentence in Biblical Hebrew* (The Hague: Moulton, 1974), 173–74.

like Moses will speak in God's name, whereas false prophets
will only presume to do so.[57]

The second point about these two paragraphs is that the word *nābîʾ*
does not have the definite article in vv. 15–19, but it is used with the
article in vv. 20–22. This is a small but significant difference. When
nābîʾ is used without the article in vv. 15–19, it is a simple singular defined by being "like Moses,"[58] a category not normative for all
prophets (cf. Num 12:6–8). However, when *nābîʾ* is used with the
definite article in vv. 20–22, it is a "generic use of the article."[59] Thus,
the prophet in vv. 20–22 refers to a generic idea of any false prophet.
Kim accurately notes the significance of this minor difference in usage
when she states,

> By this slight change of form of the word, the text clearly wants to make a
> distinction between the two terms and does not present an antithetical rela-
> tionship between true prophets versus false prophets. Rather it focuses on the
> false prophets who would misuse either God's name or God's message.[60]

On the basis of the above discussion, the collective nonmessianic view
is not demanded by the context of the prophecy.

(3) The third interpretation is the collective messianic view. It
seeks to accommodate both the collective and the messianic views at
the same time. This position is generally maintained by those who feel
that the context argues for a collective idea in Deut 18:15–19 but also
recognize that the New Testament sees the Messiah as the fulfillment
of the prophecy (cf. Acts 3:20–23; 7:37–38). This view argues that
Deut 18:15–19 refers to the establishment of the prophetic order that
finds its ultimate culmination in the Messiah. This is the view of the
majority of interpreters.[61]

---

[57] Kim, "'The Prophet like Moses,'" 246–47.

[58] Although "king" (מֶלֶךְ) in 17:15 is also singular, it may be taken as a collective and not as
a simple singular because it is not defined by the phrase "like Moses" as in Deut 18:15,18 (Kim,
"'The Prophet like Moses,'" 248).

[59] "The article of class marks out not a particular single person or thing but a class of persons, things, or qualities that are unique and determined in themselves." B. K. Waltke and
M. O'Connor, *An Introduction to Biblical Hebrew Syntax* (Winona Lake: Eisenbrauns, 1990),
13.5.1f.

[60] Kim, "'The Prophet like Moses,'" 248.

[61] Adherents of this view are C. von Orelli, *The Old Testament Prophecy of the Consummation
of God's Kingdom, Traced in Its Historical Development*, trans. J. S. Banks, (Edinburgh: T&T Clark,
1889), 132ff; P. J. Gloag, *Messianic Prophecies* (Edinburgh: T&T Clark, 1879), 137–38; Hengstenberg, *Christology of the Old Testament*, 37–40; E. J. Young, *My Servants the Prophets* (Grand
Rapids: Eerdmans, 1961), 29–37; Keil, *The Pentateuch*, 1:394–97; J. A. Thompson, *Deuteronomy:*

The essential problem with this view is that what the biblical writer intended is unclear. It is unlikely that he intended a double or progressive fulfillment. The text itself offers no evidence whatsoever that the writer saw multiple fulfillments. In fact, this sort of multiple referent interpretation would never be attempted apart from the desire to harmonize with the New Testament. It is unlikely that anyone would adopt this method by looking at the Old Testament itself, without using the New Testament as a guide.[62]

(4) The fourth interpretation is the direct messianic view, positing that "the prophet like Moses" refers exclusively to the Messiah. This interpretation was taken by some conservative, mostly older, commentators.[63] More recently, Kim has made a fresh case for the direct messianic view as follows:[64]

> (a) The singular use of *nābî'* with singular suffixes points to a specific individual. Generally, when the collective sense is intended, it is common to interchange singular and plural forms.[65] Although it is acknowledged that Deuteronomy 17 uses *melek* in a collective sense, it is maintained that no specific individual is meant, because there would only be one king at a time. Therefore, the collective use of *melek* does not require *nābî'* to be used in identical fashion.[66]

An Introduction and Commentary, ed. D. J. Wiseman, TOTC (Downers Grove, IL: InterVarsity, 1974), 213; P. C. Craigie, *The Book of Deuteronomy*, NICOT (Grand Rapids: Eerdmans, 1976), 262–64; M. G. Kline, *Treaty of the Great King: The Covenant Structure of Deuteronomy: Studies and Commentary* (Grand Rapids: Eerdmans, 1963), 101; J. S. Deere, "Deuteronomy," in *The Bible Knowledge Commentary: Old Testament*, ed. J. F. Walvoord and R. B. Zuck (Wheaton: Scripture Press, 1985), 296–97; E. S. Kalland, "Deuteronomy," EBC 3:121–23; Kaiser, *Messiah in the Old Testament*, 57–60; W. J. Beecher, *The Prophets and the Promise* (New York: Crowell, 1905), 90–92, 350–52. Beecher gives the view a slight twist, saying that the noun נָבִיא is a distributive noun as opposed to a collective. Hence, each prophet in succession was predicted and they also pointed typically to the ultimate fulfillment in the Messiah.

[62] Kim, "'The Prophet like Moses,'" 97.

[63] Adherents of this view are Delitzsch, *Messianic Prophecies in Historical Succession*, 59–65; E. H. Dewart, *Jesus the Messiah in Prophecy and Fulfillment: A Review and Refutation of the Negative Theory of Messianic Prophecy* (New York: Hunt & Eaton, 1891), 102–6; C. A. Briggs, *Messianic Prophecy: The Prediction of the Fulfillment of Redemption through the Messiah* (New York: Scribner, 1886), 110–14; D. Baron, *Rays of Messiah's Glory* (London: Wheeler & Wheeler, 1886), 181–221; D. L. Cooper, *Messiah: His Nature and Person* (Los Angeles: Biblical Research Society, 1933), 64–71; M. Reich, *The Messianic Hope of Israel*, 2nd ed. (Chicago: Moody, 1945), 35–36; W. H. Thompson, *The Great Argument of Jesus Christ in the Old Testament* (New York: Harper & Brothers, 1884), 139–66.

[64] This is a summary of the general arguments in Kim, "'The Prophet like Moses,'" 87–89.

[65] Delitzsch, *Messianic Prophecies in Historical Succession*, 61.

[66] Kim, "'The Prophet like Moses,'" 88.

(b) The prophet is compared to a single, exalted individual: Moses. Hence, the fulfillment must be a single, exalted individual.

(c) In the history of the Old Testament period, no ordinary prophet exercised the legislative, executive, priestly, or mediatorial authority that Moses did.

(d) The prophet who is like Moses had to be so special an individual that only the Messiah could fulfill the qualifications (Num 12:6–8; Deut 34:10).

(e) Other Pentateuchal messianic passages (e.g. Gen 49:10; Num 24:17–19) provide a broader context which allows for Deut 18:15–19 to be messianic.

(f) The New Testament confirms that Deut 18:15–19 is messianic (Acts 3:20–23; 7:37–38).

Having surveyed the interpretive positions, it is necessary to examine how the Old Testament itself viewed Deut 18:15–19. In so doing, it will become apparent that many years after Moses gave this prophecy to Israel, the Old Testament itself continued to look for a Moses-like eschatological prophet.

The Innertextual Considerations

There are two passages that give innertextual insight into the meaning of Deut 18:15–19: one written by Moses himself and the other by a writer at a much later date. Each of these will be discussed in turn.

Numbers 12:6–8

The first innertextual support for the messianic interpretation of Deut 18:15–19 is found in Num 12:6–8. This passage is significant because it defines what is meant by "a prophet like me [Moses]." The context of this passage lays the foundation for understanding Moses' uniqueness. In Num 11:16–30, the story is told of God establishing the seventy elders of Israel and confirming them by giving them the Spirit that Moses had (11:17) and allowing them to prophecy as Moses did (11:25).[67] In Num 12:1–5, the account of Aaron and Miriam speaking against Moses is reported. Their complaint was that God also spoke through them as prophets and not solely through Moses. God's defense of Moses is reported in Num 12:6–8, where God delineates

---

[67] Prior to Moses, Abraham was also considered a prophet (cf. Gen 20:7).

the uniqueness of Moses as a prophet. The text recounts God's words from the pillar of cloud as follows:

> Hear now my words: If there is a prophet of the Lord among you, I will make myself known to him with visions, and I will speak with him in dreams. Not so with my servant Moses; in all my house, he is faithful. Face to face[68] I speak with him even openly and not in dark sayings, And he beholds the form of the Lord; so why were you not afraid to speak against my servant Moses?[69]

The point is clear. Despite the proliferation of prophecy to the elders and to Miriam and Aaron, Moses remained unique as God's prophet and servant. This was so because God spoke directly with Moses, unlike the way He spoke with other prophets.

Numbers 12:6–8 establishes a significant innertextual foundation for interpreting Deut 18:15–19 by explaining what is meant by "a prophet like Moses." Whoever that prophet would be, he would be required to speak to God face to face.

Deuteronomy 34:10–12

The second innertextual support for the messianic interpretation of Deut 18:15–19 is found in Deut 34:10–12. This passage is significant because it establishes that many years after the death of Moses, at the close of the prophetic period, the prophet like Moses had not yet come. Thus, Israel was to continue to look for an eschatological figure who would fulfill the prophecy of the prophet like Moses.

Before examining the words of Deuteronomy 34, it is essential to examine when they were written. Deuteronomy 33–34 form an appendix to the Torah, which Moses had written. That it was written after Moses had already died is apparent from Deut 33:1. This verse introduces the poetic blessing of Moses with which he blessed Israel "before his death." Although the poem was originally written by Moses, it was obviously recorded here by someone else after Moses had died.[70] Although it has been conjectured that Joshua recorded these words,[71] the clues in the text point to a much later writer.

---

[68] The phrase פֶּה אֶל־פֶּה literally means "mouth to mouth" but is idiomatic for "face to face." See W. L. Holladay, ed., *A Concise Hebrew and Aramaic Lexicon of the Old Testament: Based upon the Lexical Work of Ludwig Koehler and Walter Baumgartner* (Grand Rapids: Eerdmans, 1971), 289.

[69] My translation.

[70] Kalland, "Deuteronomy," 219.

[71] Rashi understood the phrase "before his death" to mean "close to his death," leading to the

First, in Deut 33:1, Moses is called "the man of God," whereas before he was called "the Lord's servant." The phrase "the man of God" is not used elsewhere in the Pentateuch, but it is used to describe prophets at a later time. This leads Sailhamer to conclude that in Deut 33:1 "the words of Moses are presented as those of an ancient prophet. Moses is thus viewed as a dead prophet."[72]

Second, when recounting the death and burial of Moses in Deut 34:5–6, the text states, "And no one to this day knows where his grave is." It appears that it has been so long since Moses was buried that no one in Israel remembered the location of his grave. Moreover, the phrase "to this day" demands that there has been a significant passage of time (far more than would be appropriate if Joshua were the writer).[73]

Third, Deut 34:10 contains the clause "no prophet like Moses ever arose in Israel," which appears to assume that the end of prophecy has come. Although some versions translate the clause, "Since then no prophet has risen in Israel like Moses" (NIV, NASB), meaning that no Moses-like prophet *has yet* come, this is "not syntactically plausible."[74] Sailhamer aptly summarizes the significance of this, when he writes:

> The passage should be read in a conclusive sense, "no prophet ever came," and thus removing the possibility of a historical fulfillment sometime in Israel's past. As it stands, Deuteronomy 34:10 assumes that prophecy, or at least the office of prophecy, had already ceased and that a prophet like Moses never arose. It is worthwhile to note here that the concept of the cessation of prophecy was part and parcel with the concept of the closing of the Old Testament Canon.[75]

---

conclusion that Moses wrote this before he died ("Deuteronomy," 317). When discussing the account of Moses' death in Deut 34:5, Rashi speculates that Moses may have written "so Moses died there" before he actually died. However, he concludes that Moses wrote until Deut 34:4 and Joshua wrote from 34:5 until the end. However, the evidence points to a much later writer.

[72] Sailhamer, *Introduction to Old Testament Theology*, 244.

[73] Kim, "'The Prophet like Moses,'" 263.

[74] This is Sailhamer's conclusion (*Introduction to Old Testament Theology*, 247) based on the work of Blenkinsopp in *Prophecy and Canon*. He quotes Blenkinsopp as follows: "In all instances where this particular construction occurs in the Hebrew Bible [לֹא : : : עוֹד with the past tense] it never means 'not yet' with the implication 'it hasn't happened yet but it will later.' Following attested usage, it must on the contrary be translated 'never again,' 'never since,' or 'no longer' with no limitation of time unless expressly stated."

[75] Sailhamer goes on to state that this "does not remove the possibility of future fulfillment." Thus, at the end of the prophetic period, "the prophet which the Lord promised to send, never arose, the implication being that God would still send him in the future" (Ibid., 247–48).

On the basis of the above evidence, it is safe to say that Deuteronomy 33–34 was added to the Mosaic Torah as part of its final canonical redaction.[76]

Despite contemporary ignorance with regard to who actually wrote these chapters, they are significant because this appendix provides the keys for interpreting the Pentateuch in general and Deut 18:15–19 in particular. Reflecting a perspective offered most likely 1,000 years after the original prophecy was given, Deut 34:10–12 provides an inspired understanding of the prophecy of Deut 18:15–19.

Deuteronomy 34:10 reads, "No prophet has arisen in Israel like Moses, whom the Lord knew face to face," plainly alluding to the prophecy of Deut 18:15–19. In doing so, it seems that the writer understands the fulfillment of Deut 18:15–19 as still lying in the future and not in the past. Since the giving of the original prophecy by Moses, many prophets had arisen in Israel. However, the writer of Deut 34:10 plainly says that there has been no historical fulfillment because none of them have been like Moses. None have communicated with God "face to face." Kim clearly states the point of this discussion when she writes:

> The final paragraph of Deuteronomy 34:10ff. should be read looking at the history of Israel's prophecy retrospectively. Its final analysis after viewing all the historical prophets, including Elijah, is that the 'prophet like Moses' never came, therefore it automatically turns to the future for the fulfillment of it. He is yet to come![77]

To summarize what has been presented in this discussion of Deut 18:15–19, it was promised that the Lord would send a prophet like Moses. This has been understood in various ways, each view being noted for strengths and weaknesses. However, it was posited that the key to understanding the promise of a prophet like Moses is to see how the Old Testament itself interpreted it. Moses himself recorded one clue in Num 12:6–8, describing that which made him a unique prophet, namely, speaking to God face to face. Whoever the prophet

---

[76] Some older conservative commentators have conjectured the writer of this section to be Ezra (see A. McCaul, *The Messiahship of Jesus*, 147; D. Baron, *Rays of Messiah's Glory*, 183; M. Reich, *The Messianic Hope of Israel*, 36). This is feasible on the basis of Ezra 7:10, which literally reads, "For Ezra had set his heart to search the Law of the Lord, and to *do/make it* (עָשׂוֹת לַ) and to teach his statutes and judgments in Israel." Perhaps Ezra did play a role in the final shaping of the Pentateuch, as a scribe and writer of inspired Scripture.

[77] Kim, "The Prophet like Moses,'" 280.

like Moses would be, he would be required to speak to God in the same way—face to face. Deuteronomy 34:10–12, a passage apparently written near the close of the canon, views Israel's history of prophets retrospectively and states that the prophet like Moses never came. Israel is now to look to the future when God will send a new "Moses" who will speak to God face to face. Thus, the Old Testament itself reads the prediction of a prophet like Moses eschatologically, closing the Torah pointing Israel to the future Messiah.

Conclusion

This chapter on innerbiblical perspectives examined three passages from the Pentateuch. Each one was viewed as a messianic prophecy by later biblical writers. Although only three individual passages were examined and not every potentially messianic passage, the point was to show that later Old Testament authors did indeed consider earlier passages to be messianic. Not only does the New Testament read the Old Testament in a messianic fashion, the Old Testament reads itself messianically, long before the New Testament did. Nevertheless, not only did the writers of Scripture have messianic viewpoint, but the final redaction of the Old Testament canon bears witness to a similar outlook. Therefore, the next chapter will examine the canonical redactional evidence for the Hebrew Bible's messianic perspective.

Chapter 5

CANONICAL PERSPECTIVES ON MESSIANIC PROPHECY

The term "canon" refers to those books that have been accepted as authoritative Scripture. The books of the Hebrew canon (the Old Testament) are divided into three sections: The Law (Torah), Prophets (Nevi'im), and Writings (Ketuvim). The Hebrew Bible is called the Tanak, which is an acronym derived from the Hebrew names of these three sections of the Hebrew Bible. It is virtually without dispute that this threefold division was fixed sometime during the intertestamental period, although it is unknown who exactly was responsible for it. Nevertheless, it appears that the individual or community that shaped the Tanak in this way understood and sought to reflect the messianic message of the Hebrew Bible. The observation that the canonicler understood the Old Testament as messianic corroborates that the Hebrew Bible should indeed be read messianically. This chapter will examine the canonical evidence supporting this messianic perspective. First, it will do so by examining how the redactional shape of the Hebrew Bible sustains a messianic reading of these texts. Second, it will consider how a book's messianic message was an essential element for its inclusion in the Old Testament canon.

Shaping of the Hebrew Canon

On what basis was the Old Testament canon structured as Law, Prophets, and Writings? The conventional view, advocated by Herbert Edward Ryle,[1] was that each section was recognized as a complete whole in three different eras. He maintained that there was "a gradual development in the formation of the Canon through three successive stages."[2] First, the Torah was canonized (by the fifth century BC), then the Prophets (by the third century BC) and finally the Writings (by AD 90). Basing the canonization process purely on the historical emergence of scriptural books, Ryle concluded that there was no dis-

---

[1] H. E. Ryle, *The Canon of the Old Testament*, 2nd ed. (London: Macmillan, 1914).
[2] Ibid., 10–11.

cernible rhyme or reason for the division of books into the Prophets or the Writings.

Beckwith has challenged this view and has argued the canon of the Hebrew Bible was closed in the form of the Tanak no later than the second century BC.[3] Moreover, he has demonstrated that "a rational principle is discernible in the distribution of books between the Prophets and the Hagiographa."[4] First, he notes that the narrative books in all three sections generally cover successive historical periods: The Law covers the period from creation to the death of Moses; The Prophets covers the period from the Conquest to the Exile; The Writings covers the period from the Exile to the Return.[5]

Beckwith also identifies a second discernible principle:

> It is clear that the order of the non-narrative books in the Prophets and the Hagiographa is not chronological, and they are in fact arranged in descending order of size, with the single and trivial exception that the Song of Songs is put before Lamentations, so as to keep the three books associated with Solomon together.[6]

As seen above, the threefold structure of the Hebrew Canon is not the result of random development but rather a consequence of editorial shaping and design. However, there is further evidence of an editorial configuration, namely, that the Tanak was given its final redactional shape to give an eschatological/messianic hope. If that is so, then it would be safe to say that those who shaped the canon read it, and expected others to read it, as a messianic primer.

Sailhamer has suggested that this discernible messianic strategy in the canonical redaction of the Tanak is found in the two "canonical seams," the first seam uniting the Law and the Prophets and the second uniting the Prophets and the Writings (see Figure 5.1). He has observed that the last paragraph of the Pentateuch (Deut 34:9–12) and the first in the Prophets (Josh 1:1–9) have a pattern that is reproduced in the last paragraph of the Prophets (Mal 3:22–24) and the first in the Writings (Psalm 1).[7]

---

[3] R. T. Beckwith, "Formation of the Hebrew Bible," in *Mikra: Text, Translation, Reading and Interpretation of the Hebrew Bible in Ancient Judaism and Early Christianity*, ed. M. J. Muldur, CRINT (Minneapolis: Fortress, 1990), 39–86.

[4] Ibid., 56.

[5] Ibid., 57–58.

[6] Ibid., 58.

[7] J. H. Sailhamer, *Introduction to Old Testament Theology* (Grand Rapids: Zondervan, 1995), 239–52.

The Torah's last paragraph (Deut 34:9–12) is essentially eschato-logical and messianic. It states that at the time when prophecy ceased, the "prophet like Moses" had not come and directs Israel to look for him. Immediately after this, the opening paragraph of the Prophets (Josh 1:1–9) calls upon Joshua to exercise a new form of leadership, that of the wise scholar. He is to keep the Law and "meditate on [or "recite"] it day and night" (Josh 1:7–8). Thus, the narrative presents Joshua as the ideal wise man who models godly behavior until the eschatological prophet (the Messiah) comes.

The seam between the Prophets and the Writings is similar. The concluding paragraph of the Prophets (Mal 3:22–24) is similar to the end of the Torah. It is eschatological and messianic in its outlook, pointing to the day when Elijah will come before the Day of the Lord. When viewed canonically, it is plain that Elijah is being distinguished from the eschatological "Prophet like Moses." Elijah is to come to pre-pare the people for the arrival of the prophet like Moses (Mal 3:24). Following immediately after this section, the Writings begin with "Psalm 1, which presents the ideal of the wise man who meditates day and night on the Torah (Ps 1:2–3)."[8]

The textual and verbal links in the canonical seams are transpar-ent: Deut 34:9–12 and Mal 3:22–24 both point to the eschatological prophet, the Messiah. Joshua 1:1–9 and Psalm 1 both present the ideal wise man that prospers as he meditates on the Torah. (See Figure 5.1) It becomes obvious that the final shape of the Tanak was not the result of historical chance but the deliberate attempt to communicate the messianic message of the Hebrew Bible. In Sailhamer's words,

> The more closely we examine the final shape of the Hebrew Bible (TaNaK), the clearer it becomes that its shape and structure are not accidental. There are clear signs of intelligent life behind its formation. . . . In the later stages of the formation of the Hebrew Bible its authors were primarily concerned with making more explicit the messianic hope that was already explicit in the earliest texts.[9]

---

[8] Ibid., 249.

[9] J. H. Sailhamer, "The Messiah and the Hebrew Bible," *JETS* 44 (2001): 22. This is also the view of Horbury: "The collection of the books, therefore, and the editing of the individual books, produces a series of what can be properly called messianic prophecies, envisaging the future—sometimes evidently the immediate future." W. Horbury, *Jewish Messianism and the Cult of Christ* (London: SCM, 1998), 29.

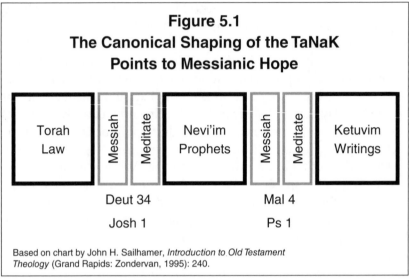

Figure 5.1
The Canonical Shaping of the TaNaK
Points to Messianic Hope

| Torah Law | Messiah | Meditate | Nevi'im Prophets | Messiah | Meditate | Ketuvim Writings |

Deut 34   Mal 4

Josh 1   Ps 1

Based on chart by John H. Sailhamer, *Introduction to Old Testament Theology* (Grand Rapids: Zondervan, 1995): 240.

Some might object to seeing intentionality in this framework, but I am reminded of a family vacation some time ago. We rented a cabin in Pennsylvania and were amazed at the perfect symmetry of the forest behind our cabin. Never before had I seen a forest in which each tree lined up to each other with the same distance in both directions, from side to side and front to back. Upon paying the bill for our stay, I commented on this phenomenon to the owner of the cabin. He replied that it was not so phenomenal–the property had previously been a Christmas tree farm. Obviously the lay of the trees was not random but intentional. This is the same conclusion that must be derived from the shaping of the Tanak. The seams of the Hebrew Bible, connecting the Law, the Prophets, and the Writings, were deliberately shaped in order to communicate an essential message of the Old Testament— that of the Messiah and his presence in the text of the Scriptures. The wise man, meditating on the Word of God, will discover the future Messiah in the words of Scripture.

The significance of the canonical redaction of the Tanak is apparent. It was designed to teach its readers to be faithful to the Torah until the Messiah comes. Hence, it is safe to say that the actual shaping of the Tanak was fashioned to present the messianic hope. In this way, the canonical redaction of the text reflects the viewpoint of the prophets, as described in chapter 4 regarding innerbiblical interpretation. Just as the prophets read the Torah messianically, so those who shaped the canon read the Tanak in the same way. This is reflected not only in the canonical redaction of the Tanak, as seen above, but also in what follows regarding the inclusion of the individual books in the Tanak.

Inclusion in the Hebrew Canon

The Discovery of Canon

Why were certain books accepted as canonical in the Old Testament while others were rejected? The traditional view is that God *determined* which books were canonical by inspiring them so that all inspired books became canonical. However, people *discovered* which books God had inspired through a variety of "earmarks," such as their authoritative message, their authorship by a prophet, their authenticity and accuracy, their dynamic power, and their reception as inspired and canonical by Israel.[10] Perhaps a simpler explanation of the discovery of canonical books is a twofold test: (1) Old Testament books were accepted as canonical if Israel had universally received them as such, and (2) if their early readers recognized the internal witness of the Holy Spirit confirming their canonical nature.[11]

There appears to be one more element that was used to discover canonicity: namely, that any canonical Old Testament book had to have a messianic hope as part of its message. The reason is that the Old Testament in its entirety is in some way messianic. That is not to say that all ancient books with a messianic hope were necessarily canonical but rather that all canonical books are indeed messianic. Sailhamer writes,

> I believe the messianic thrust of the OT was the *whole* reason the books of the Hebrew Bible were written. In other words, the Hebrew Bible was not written as the national literature of Israel. It probably also was not written to the nation of Israel as such. It was rather written in my opinion, as the expression of the deep-seated messianic hope of a small group of faithful prophets and their followers.[12]

---

[10] N. L. Geisler and W. E. Nix, *A General Introduction to the Bible* (Chicago: Moody, 1968), 130–47.

[11] J. H. Sailhamer, *How We Got the Bible* (Grand Rapids: Zondervan, 1998), 11.

[12] Sailhamer, "The Messiah and the Hebrew Bible," 23.

This is also the view of James Hamilton, who writes, "The OT is a messianic document, written from a messianic perspective, to sustain a messianic hope."[13] In rabbinic literature, there is Rabbi Johanan's famous dictum, "Every prophet prophesied only of the days of the Messiah" (*b. Ber.* 34b). The Apostle Peter also seems to advocate this view when he declared that "all the prophets who have spoken, from Samuel and those after him, have also announced these days" (Acts 3:24).

If messianic hope is the central thrust of the Hebrew Bible, then it is likely that this messianic theme was also one of the essential earmarks for recognizing the canonicity of Old Testament books. Is it possible to find a messianic theme in all the books of the Hebrew canon? That is what must be examined now.

The Messianic Theme of the Canon

The messianic "earmark" becomes even more apparent when actually looking at the sections of the Tanak and discovering that they all do reveal the Messiah. From the Law to the Prophets to the Writings, it becomes plain that the central message of each of the books is the future king who will rule the nations, namely, the Messiah.

Messiah in the Torah

Starting in the Pentateuch, the author makes messianic expectation central to the overall structure of the Torah. This becomes clear by observing that the overall structure of the Pentateuch follows a consistent pattern, namely, narrative, poem, epilogue (see Figure 5.2). So, for example, the Torah begins with an extended narrative of the primeval and patriarchal world (Genesis 1–48), followed by a poetic section containing Jacob's oracle concerning his sons (Genesis 49), and then the epilogue concerning the deaths of Jacob and Joseph (Genesis 50).[14] This structure continues throughout the Pentateuch with the poetic sections in Exodus 15, Numbers 23–24, and Deuteronomy 32–33.

It becomes evident that much like the songs in a Broadway musical, the poetic passages carry the main theme of the story. All the poems

---

[13] J. Hamilton, "The Skull Crushing Seed of the Woman: Inner-Biblical Interpretation of Genesis 3:15," *SBJT* 10 (2006): 30.

[14] J. H. Sailhamer, *The Pentateuch as Narrative* (Grand Rapids: Zondervan, 1992), 35–37.

(except the one in Exodus 15) indicate that the fulfillment of these passages will take place at "the end of days" (Gen 49:1; Num 24:14; Deut 31:29).[15] Additionally, these passages speak of a coming king, one who will ultimately receive the obedience of all people (Gen 49:8–11) and will rule over an exalted kingdom including the kingdom of Gog (Num 24:7), the end-time enemy of Israel (Ezek 38–39).[16] The structure itself points to a future messianic king.

Not only the structure but the skeleton of the Pentateuchal story follows a particular individual. This is evident in tracing the family line, or "the seed," in the Torah.[17] He is the "seed" that will descend from Eve (Gen 3:15), the future king that will descend from Abraham (Gen 17:6), the seed who will bless all nations (Gen 22:17b–19).[18] Additionally, He is the lion of the tribe of Judah, the king who will rule over all people (Gen 49:8–12), and the seed who will be a king with an exalted end-time kingdom (Num 24:7–9).[19]

Ultimately, the conclusion of the Torah (Deuteronomy 34) calls the reader to look for a prophet like Moses yet to come. The author already predicted that there would be a future "prophet like Moses" (Deut 18:15–19). Moses' unique quality as a prophet was that he spoke to God face to face (Num 12:6–8), a characteristic not found in any other prophets. Thus, none of the later prophets of Israel fulfilled the prediction of being the prophet like Moses. So, the final words of the Torah, written near the end of the canonical period, indicate that the prophet like Moses, who spoke directly to God, had not come (Deut 34:10–12). The logical conclusion is that the epilogue ends the book by directing the reader to continue looking for that prophet, the Messiah.[20] Therefore, it is plain that the Torah, taken as a whole, has as its major theme the future Messiah.

---

[15] W. Horbury, *Jewish Messianism and the Cult of Christ* (London: SCM, 1998), 27.

[16] Note also that the Masoretic Text most likely sees this passage as referring to David, who will be higher than Agag. However, all other versions take this as one who will be higher than "Gog." See chap. 3 for a discussion of this text-critical issue. See Sailhamer, "The Messiah in the Hebrew Bible," 21.

[17] T. D. Alexander, "Messianic Ideology in Genesis," in *The Lord's Anointed: Interpretation of Old Testament Messianic Texts*, ed. P. E. Satterthwaite, R. S. Hess and G. J. Wenham (Grand Rapids: Baker, 1995), 23–32.

[18] T. D. Alexander, "Further Observations on the Term 'Seed' in Genesis," *TynBul* 48 (1997): 363–367.

[19] Note the deliberate authorial linking of this passage with Gen 49:9: "He crouches; he lies down like a lion / or a lioness—who dares to rouse him?"

[20] See chap. 4 for an extended discussion on Deut 18 and the prophet like Moses. See chap. 9 for an extended discussion of Gen 3:15.

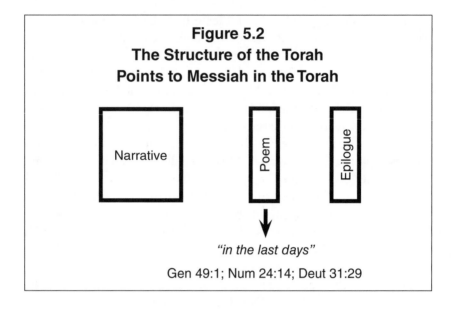

Figure 5.2
The Structure of the Torah
Points to Messiah in the Torah

Narrative   Poem   Epilogue

"in the last days"
Gen 49:1; Num 24:14; Deut 31:29

Messiah in the Prophets

The Former Prophets

The essential message of the Prophets is also the messianic hope, expanding and clarifying the message of the Torah. The former prophets, beginning with Joshua and Judges, are designed to make Israel look for a future messianic king. While the book of Joshua paints a positive picture of the initial conquest of the land, the circumstances rapidly turn negative in the book of Judges as Israel goes through a cycle of disobedience to God, discipline by God, and then deliverance by God through a chosen judge. As events spiral out of control, the author adds an appendix to the book which begins and ends with the repeated refrain, "In those days there was no king in Israel; everyone did whatever he wanted" (Judg 17:6; 21:25).

As T. Desmond Alexander explains, the role of this refrain in the narrative is to trace Israel's difficulties, at least in part, to the lack of a king. The author thereby points the reader to the anticipation of Saul and David and the establishment of kingship in Israel. The book of Judges also concludes with the horrific behavior of the tribe of Benjamin, who rape and kill a young woman from Judah. Alexander points out that "by focusing on the fate of the Benjamites and two individuals from 'Bethlehem in Judah', these chapters anticipate developments in 1 Samuel concerning the first two kings of Israel: Saul from the tribe of Benjamin and David from Bethlehem in Judah."[21] Thus, the narrative draws attention to "the tribe of Judah and the special part which it will play in establishing a monarch through whom the nations of the earth will be blessed."[22]

Although Alexander is correct in showing how the narrative uses history to point to the future Lion of Judah, there is even more to the messianic message. The book of Judges appears to have been written (or undergone final editing) not during the time of the events in the book but sometime after the fall of the Davidic dynasty and the captivity. This is evident from the time notation in Judg 18:30. There it says that the pagan priesthood begun by Moses' grandson Jonathan continued "until the time of the exile from the land." Thus, the recurring phrase, "In those days there was no king in Israel; everyone did whatever he wanted," reminds the reader that the circumstances prior to the monarchy have returned. But the solution is not to look back to David but forward, to the future restoration of kingship by the Davidic Messiah (cf. Amos 9:11–14).

The continuing narrative of 1 Samuel through 2 Kings makes the focal point the Davidic house. Saul's kingship is presented as a foil for David—Saul fails to do the will of God and his house will end. Instead, David, the man after God's own heart, the one chosen by God, is presented as the dynasty through which the Messiah will come. Central to this presentation is the Davidic covenant (2 Sam 7:12–16), wherein God's promise of seed, previously given to Abraham (Gen 22:17–18), was further expanded. This covenant is foundational for the messianic hope of the Hebrew Bible and the basis of the New Testament expectation of a future kingdom. When David wanted to build a house for God (a temple), instead God promised David that He would build a house for David (2 Sam 7:11). God affirmed that He would give David an eternal dynasty and kingdom with an eternal ruler to sit on David's throne (2 Sam 7:16). That ruler was to be one of David's sons (his seed), who would also have a father/son relationship with God (2 Sam 7:12–16).

In the course of the historical narrative of 1 Kings, it appears that this promise would be fulfilled through Solomon. In fact, since

---

[21] T. D. Alexander, *The Servant King* (Vancouver, British Columbia: Regent College, 1998), 47.
[22] Ibid., 48.

Solomon even believed that he was the potential fulfillment, he built the Temple. But the Lord warned Solomon that the promise would be fulfilled through him only if he would "walk in My statutes, observe My ordinances, and keep all My commands by walking in them" (1 Kgs 6:12). The author of 1 Kings quickly points out how miserably Solomon failed to obey God with his marriages to foreign women, who turned his heart away from God (1 Kgs 11:1–4). After Solomon failed, the promise was transferred to the next Davidic king. As a result, "beginning with the time when the oracle of Nathan fixed the hope of Israel on the dynasty of David (2 Sam 7:12–16), each king issuing from him became the actual 'Messiah' by whom God wished to fulfill His plan with regard to His people."[23] But, in fact, in the subsequent narrative, no Davidic king succeeded in obeying God completely. Instead, all of them, even the good kings, ended with failure. Hence, the book of 2 Kings ends with Israel in captivity and the Davidic covenant unfulfilled. Clearly, the author's intention was to maintain the hope and expectation that God would one day send an eternal ruler who would build the true temple of God and sit on the throne of David. Thus, the former prophets make the messianic hope the central message of the narrative from Joshua to 2 Kings.

The Latter Prophets

The latter prophets (Isaiah, Jeremiah, Ezekiel, and the Twelve [the "Minor Prophets"]) also continue to explicate the promise of Messiah previously revealed in the Torah. Although some might argue that they see the fulfillment of their words in events in their own day, in reality their focus is on the end of days and messianic fulfillment.

The book of Isaiah addresses ancient issues with a messianic perspective. While Judah would indeed be oppressed by Assyria and taken captive by Babylon, redemption would not come in those days. Rather, the hope of Israel was in the future Davidic king (Isa 9:6; 11:1–10) who would be called Immanuel (Isa 7:14). He would come as a Servant-King (Isa 42:1–9; 49:1–13; 50:4–11) who would provide a sacrificial atonement for Israel and the world (Isa 52:13–53:12). The remnant of Israel, to whom the book is addressed, was to find their comfort and hope not in Cyrus (Isa 45:1) but in the future messianic king (Isa 61:1–4).

---

[23] P.-E. Bonnard and P. Grelot, "Messiah," in *Dictionary of Biblical Theology*, ed. X. Leon-Dulfour; trans. P. J. Cahill (London: Geoffrey Chapman, 1967), 312.

The book of Jeremiah predicts that Babylon would be God's instrument of righteous wrath on His sinning people, Israel. Nevertheless, it also points to hope of restoration in the "Righteous Branch of David" who "will reign wisely as king and administer justice and righteousness in the land. In His days Judah will be saved, and Israel will dwell securely. This is what He will be named: Yahweh Our Righteousness" (Jer 23:5–6). This king would ultimately deliver Israel from a time of trouble more severe than the Babylonian exile (Jer 30:1–9) and establish a new covenant with Israel and Judah (Jer 31:31–34), just as Moses had foretold in the Torah (Deut 30:4–6).

The book of Ezekiel is a first-person account of the prophecies God gave through Ezekiel during the Babylonian exile. It reveals that hope is not to be found in the words of false prophets but instead in the far distant future, in the coming of the messianic Son of David, the true Shepherd of Israel (Ezek 34:23–24). In those days, God will restore the house of David under the Son of David, who will return the people of Israel to their land and give the people a new heart (Ezek 36:1–38). This too is the new covenant spoken of by Moses (Deut 30:4–6) and Jeremiah (Jer 31:31–34).

The Twelve Prophets also reveal that hope is to be found in a future Son of David. For example, Hosea predicts that in the last days, "The people of Israel will return and seek the LORD their God and David their king" (Hos 3:4–5). Other prophets among the Twelve promise that God "will restore the fallen booth of David" (Amos 9:11–12) and provide a king from the town of Bethlehem and the house of David to shepherd His people (Mic 5:1–4). Ultimately, the house of David and the people of Jerusalem will repent, turn to the Lord, call upon this king who had been previously pierced (Zech 12:10), and experience the opening of "a fountain" that would wash away "sin and impurity" (Zech 13:1). The Twelve concludes the Prophets with the hope of the return of Elijah to announce the Day of the Lord and the coming the Messiah (Mal 4:4–5).

Horbury summarizes the messianic perspective of the Prophets when he writes,

> There is thus a genuine thematic link between the Pentateuch and the Prophets. So Isaiah ends with a great eschatological scene of the exaltation of Jerusalem and divine judgment, which came to be associated with specifically messianic hope. Ezekiel ends with the oracles which have shaped later articulation of the eschatological events: from chapter 36 onwards the book successively mentions the outpouring of the spirit, the revival of the dry bones, the

new kingdom of David, the wars of Gog of the land of Magog, and the building of the new Jerusalem. Among the minor prophets, Hosea has an eschatological ending, Amos a Davidic ending, and Zechariah a conclusion which, for all its obscurity, is plainly and in succession messianic, royal, Davidic, Zion-centered and eschatological. The whole Book of the Twelve ends at the close of Malachi with announcement of the day of the Lord and sending of Elijah the prophet. Once again, just as in the case of the Pentateuch noted already, it is natural to read the specifically messianic prophecies, like those in Ezekiel, Amos and Zechariah, in the context of the more general prophecies of the future among which they are interspersed.[24]

So just as the Messiah is central to the message of the Torah, He is also crucial to the substantial theme of both the former and latter prophets.

Messiah in the Writings

In addition to the Law and Prophets, the Messiah also is the theme of the Writings. Beginning with the Psalms, the messianic hope is the central message. It is common for contemporary interpreters to view the Psalms as individual texts gathered with little regard for structure or theme. However, in recent years, trends have begun to shift. There is a movement to see the book of Psalms as the product of a purposeful redaction in the postexilic period with an identifiable theme.[25]

If indeed the Psalms were a postexilic redaction, as seems likely, it is most probable that the theme looks forward to the restoration of the Davidic dynasty in fulfillment of the Davidic covenant.[26] As Brevard Childs says of the royal psalms, "Indeed, at the time of the final redaction, when the institution of kingship had long since been destroyed, what earthly king would have come to mind other than God's Messiah?"[27]

---

[24] Horbury, *Jewish Messianism and the Cult of Christ*, 28–29.

[25] G. H. Wilson has effectively made the case for viewing the Psalms as having a purposeful postexilic redaction with an identifiable theme (*The Editing of the Hebrew Psalter* [Chico, CA: Scholars Press, 1985], 9–10, 182–99). However, according to Wilson, that theme looks backwards historically, focusing on the failure of the Davidic dynasty. In his view, the Psalms do not look forward to a restored Davidic dynasty under the Messiah but a return to the premonarchic days, when the Lord alone was Israel's king (pp. 214–15).

[26] D. C. Mitchell has persuasively argued for interpreting the Psalms as a coherent postexilic redaction with an eschatological/messianic theme (*The Message of the Psalter: An Eschatological Programme in the Book of Psalms*, JSOTSup 252 [Sheffield, England: Sheffield Academic Press, 1997]).

[27] B. S. Childs, *Introduction to the Old Testament as Scripture* (Philadelphia: Fortress, 1979), 516.

This postexilic messianic expectation is plainly seen, for example, in Psalm 89. The first half of the psalm celebrates the eternal Davidic covenant (vv. 1–37), the second part shifts to sorrow because postexilic conditions prevail, namely, the Davidic crown has been cast to the ground (v. 39), the walls of Jerusalem have been destroyed (v. 40), and the throne of David has been overturned (v. 44). Psalm 89 concludes with a plea for the Lord to restore the Davidic throne as promised in the Davidic covenant (vv. 49–51) because His enemies have "ridiculed every step of Your anointed [or Messiah]" (v. 51).

By recognizing the Psalms as a coherent collection of the postexilic period, the message of the entire book, not just individual songs, should be read as referring to the future king, namely, the Messiah.[28] Mitchell accurately states, "The messianic theme is central to the purpose of the collection."[29]

Other parts of the Writings also present a messianic message. In the book of Job, Job's hope of vindication is found in a "living Redeemer, and He will stand on the dust at last" (Job 19:25). Although the messianic interpretation of this passage is frequently disputed, it is hard to dismiss this as a messianic hope of redemption, particularly when read innertextually. Job desperately longs for an arbitrator or "judge" to vindicate him (9:33). He has confidence that his "advocate is in the heights" (16:19). At the end of the book, Elihu speaks of a "mediator" who is above thousands of angels (33:23) or, as Delitzsch translated it, one who "soars above the thousands and has not his equal among them."[30] The message of the book of Job is that righteous sufferers should not demand answers of the Lord but accept His sovereign decisions in all things, even suffering. Nonetheless, there is also an encouragement for them, derived from the hope of a redeemer who will mediate for righteous sufferers and vindicate them.[31]

Other wisdom literature in the Writings also has a messianic emphasis. This is evident in that the underlying source for the wisdom taught in these books, namely, the wise sage, the Messiah, is the basis

---

[28] B. K. Waltke, "A Canonical Process Approach to the Psalms," in *Tradition and Testament*, ed. J. Feinberg and P. Feinberg (Chicago: Moody, 1981), 3–18.

[29] Mitchell, "The Message of the Psalter: An Eschatological Programme in the Book of Psalms," 87.

[30] F. Delitzsch, *Biblical Commentary on the Book of Job* (Grand Rapids: Eerdmans, 1949), 230.

[31] W. C. Kaiser Jr., *The Messiah in the Old Testament* (Grand Rapids: Zondervan, 1995), 61–64.

of its message. In the book of Proverbs, there is the enigmatic woman Wisdom (Prov 1:20; 4:6; 7:4; 8:1,11–12,22–36; 9:1,11; 14:33), whom most interpreters consider merely a personification of an attribute of God. Yet, Hartmut Gese effectively argues for viewing her as a symbol of the future Messiah. Woman Wisdom, as an agent of creation (cf. Prov 3:19; 8:30), becomes the Old Testament source of the New Testament depiction of the Messiah as wisdom (Col 2:3).[32] According to Nicholas Perrin, because of the exalted description of Woman Wisdom, "more than one scholar has noticed the presence of messianic terms in the portrayal of this female figure."[33]

Building on this concept of Wisdom as Messiah, Perrin argues for a messianic reading of the book of Ecclesiastes.[34] First, he maintains that the phrase "Son of David" (Eccl 1:1), when used without Solomon's name, would be an early use of a messianic title. And even if Solomon were intended, it would be as a "prototypical Messiah." Secondly, Perrin makes a stronger argument for a messianic reading by citing the words "one Shepherd" in the epilogue (12:11). He shows definitively that the title "one Shepherd" is only used in Scripture as a messianic appellation (Ezek 34:23–24; 37:24–25).[35] The point of the epilogue would be to demonstrate the source of wisdom for the Preacher is the Shepherd (Messiah).

The relationship of the "one Shepherd" to the Preacher is similar to the call of woman Wisdom in Proverbs to her sons to "listen to me . . . For the one who finds me finds life" (Prov 8:32,35), followed by the proverbs of Solomon (Prov 10:1). In Perrin's words,

> While Solomon is the personage who gives historic and human expression to the Proverbs, it is Woman Wisdom who introduces and hence authorizes and inspires the Solomonic text. Thus, Proverbs in its final form presents an economy of authorship that, much like prophetic utterance, was at once human and divine.[36]

In an analogous way, the Preacher's words are not merely human but are given force and authority because they are given by the "one Shepherd." This Shepherd, as Perrin writes, "is the transcendent messiah.

---

[32] H. Gese, "Wisdom, Son of Man, and the Origins of Christology: The Consistent Development of Biblical Theology," *HBT* 3 (1981), 23–57.

[33] N. Perrin, "Messianism in the Narrative Frame of Ecclesiastes," *RB* 1 (2001): 58.

[34] Although Perrin holds to an intertestamental date for the authorship of Ecclesiastes, it is not essential to his interpretation of the book.

[35] Ibid., 53–54.

[36] Ibid., 59.

It is this latter assurance that substantiates the divine origin and authority of the wisdom contained within the rest of the book."[37]

The Church has long viewed the Song of Solomon as an allegorical work about the Messiah and his love for the Church, much as Judaism has viewed it as an allegory for the God of Israel's love for the people of Israel. With the contemporary rejection of allegorical interpretation, it has become far more common to view the book as a romantic song between human lovers. Nevertheless, Roland Murphy has concluded that "the eventual canonization of the work . . . can best be explained if the poetry originated as religious rather than secular literature."[38] Therefore, James Hamilton has recently averred that "the Song of Songs is in the canon because it was written from a messianic perspective in order to nourish a messianic hope."[39] Is it possible that this love song was written with the authorial intent to advance and explain the messianic hope?

One approach, proposed by Sailhamer, is to view the Song as an allegory not of Messiah's love for the Church but as Messiah's love for divine wisdom. He defends this position by citing Song 8:5b ("I awakened you under the apricot tree. / There your mother conceived you; / there she conceived and gave you birth") and proposing an intertextual reference to the prologue of the book of Proverbs and the account of the fall in Genesis 3.[40] In his view, the author of the Song intended the beloved to be understood as "wisdom" and the lover as Solomon, who represents the promised seed first mentioned in Gen 3:15.[41]

While this is plausible when read innerbiblically, an alternative view proposed by Hamilton is more likely. He posits a nonallegorical but symbolic interpretation in which King Solomon, as the son of David, "represents the ultimate expression of David's royal seed . . . the Davidic king, with all the messianic connotations that status carries."[42] Furthermore, Hamilton also sees the Song's innertextual allusions to Genesis 3, but maintains that the theme of the Song "seems to be the recovery of intimacy after alienation, and this appears to match the

---

[37] Ibid.

[38] R. E. Murphy, *The Song of Songs* (Minneapolis: Fortress, 1990), 94–95.

[39] J. M. Hamilton Jr., "The Messianic Music of the Song of Songs: A Non-Allegorical Interpretation," *WTJ* 68 (2006): 331.

[40] J. H. Sailhamer, *NIV Compact Bible Commentary* (Grand Rapids: Zondervan, 1994), 359–60.

[41] Ibid., 360.

[42] Hamilton, "The Messianic Music of the Song of Songs: A Non-Allegorical Interpretation," 337.

hope engendered by Gen 3:15 for a seed of the woman who would come as the royal Messiah to restore the gladness of Eden."[43]

After demonstrating the development of this theme of intimacy recovered throughout the Song, Hamilton concludes by pointing out that Song 7:11[Eng. 7:10] functions as a climax to the poem.[44] There it states, "I belong to my love and his *desire* is for me," using the very word for "desire" that appears in Gen 3:16 in the curse on the woman ("Your *desire* will be for your husband and he will dominate you"). The word for desire, *těšûqāh*, is used only three times in the Hebrew Bible (Gen 3:16; 4:7; Song 7:11), the first two times referring to the alienation of the fall. The author of the Song appears to be making a direct allusion to the alienation found in the curse of Gen 3:16. In Song 7:11 he seems to be saying that the messianic king will ultimately reverse the curse on the woman."[45] As Hamilton writes, "This messianic interpretation of the Song . . . explains the Song's presence in the canon and sheds light on how it exposits the Pentateuch's messianism."[46]

All the Writings contain a messianic theme.[47] Ruth ends with a Davidic genealogy, to help establish the Davidic line of the future Messiah. Lamentations, although sorrowful, has a strong element of hope, emphasizing God's ultimate restoration through the fulfillment of the Davidic covenant. Thus it ends with "LORD, restore us to Yourself, so we may return; renew our days as in former times" (Lam 5:21).

Esther is the story of God's providential preservation of Israel. It emphasizes providence in that God's name is excluded from the book. Although the Jewish people seem to have forgotten God, nevertheless He is working behind the scenes to save them. In this way, God preserves not only the people but assures the fulfillment of His promise to send the messianic redeemer to His people. Daniel presents Messiah as the hope of the Jewish people in the times of the Gentiles. In doing so, the book presents two major predictions: (1) Daniel 7 reveals "One like the Son of Man" who would be "given dominion and glory and a kingdom" (7:13–14), and (2) Daniel 9 predicts God's program for Israel and the nations, indicating precisely when Messiah would come (Dan 9:24–27).

---

[43] Ibid., 339–40.

[44] Ibid., 340–42.

[45] Ibid., 344.

[46] Ibid.

[47] Unlike our English Bibles, the Hebrew Bible ends with Ruth, Song, Ecclesiastes, Lamentations, Esther, Daniel, Ezra-Nehemia, and Chronicles.

Ezra-Nehemiah, which the ancient Jewish canon takes as one book, views the return from captivity as a promise of an even greater return. Ezra presents the return from the exile as a fulfillment of prophecy (Ezra 1:1–4), but the conclusion to Nehemiah shows how Israel had still not kept the Mosaic covenant. So, although the return from exile was part of God's kindness to Israel, it did not tell the entire story. Rather, it pointed to an eschatological day of fulfillment when Messiah would fulfill all the promises God made to His people.

The two books of Chronicles retell the history of the Davidic dynasty. But they were not written merely to glorify the past. Rather, they were composed to remind the returning exiles of the promise God had made to David (1 Chronicles 17) and cause them to look with hope and faith for a coming messianic king.[48] As Sailhamer indicates, the conclusion of the book contains the call of the Persian king Cyrus to rebuild the temple. By focusing on the temple and the messianic king who would rebuild it, the last words of the book (lit. "let him go up") "become a call for the return of the Messiah . . . thus provid[ing] a fitting bridge to the coming of the Messiah in the New Testament."[49] What has just been discussed is the messianic theme of the Writings. But this entire section has maintained that the point of the whole Tanak is to reveal Messiah, from the promise of a seed who will crush the head of the serpent (Gen 3:15) to the call for the messianic king to rebuild the holy temple (2 Chr 36:23). From the beginning to the end, from Genesis to 2 Chronicles, the entire Hebrew Bible is messianic.

Conclusion

As a child, I watched a good deal of television—probably more than was good for me. At that time, a large food company sponsored special television programs and used the commercial time to present recipes using the company's food products, particularly their cheeses. Even as a child, I was always amazed by how much cheese each of these recipes required. At the end of the program, viewers could send away for the cookbook with all the recipes from the commercials. As I grew older and began to understand advertising, I realized that it was not the tastiness of the food or the healthfulness of these meals that led to their inclusion in the cookbook. Rather, they all had one

---

[48] See Horbury, *Jewish Messianism and the Cult of Christ*, 45–46.

[49] J. H. Sailhamer, *The Books of the Bible* (Grand Rapids: Zondervan, 1998), 31.

essential requirement—they had to sell cheese. In much the same way, for books to be accepted into the Old Testament canon, they all required an essential characteristic—they had to reveal the Messiah.

The point of this chapter has been to show that messianic hope influenced the canonical redaction of the Hebrew Bible.[50] The messianic theme influenced the shaping of the Hebrew canon and became a prominent feature used to help discover which books would be included in the canon. It is not surprising, therefore, that the New Testament reads the Hebrew Bible as a messianic document.[51] So it is to this New Testament evidence we now turn.

---

[50] As Horbury has written, "The Old Testament books were so edited that they emerge collectively as a messianic document. Within the Pentateuch and the books of Joshua and Chronicles, royal and messianic themes were developed especially in the portraits of Moses, Joshua, David, Solomon and the righteous kings. Messianic hope was prominent in the prophetic books of Haggai and Zechariah. These messianic elements in the composition and interpretation of the biblical books were then reflected and developed at the end of the Persian period, not long after Alexander the Great, in the messianism of the Septuagint Pentateuch." *Jewish Messianism and the Cult of Christ,* 37.

[51] M. B. Shepherd has posited that the messianic theme of the Hebrew Bible later influenced both the rabbinic Targumim and the New Testament's understanding of the Hebrew Bible. He states, "The Targums and the NT exegete Scripture messianically. . . . These messianic readings are rooted in the text of the Hebrew Bible itself" ("Targums, New Testament, and Biblical Theology of the Messiah," *JETS* 51 [2008]: 46).

Chapter 6

NEW TESTAMENT PERSPECTIVES ON MESSIANIC PROPHECY

"Jesus' followers undertook a creative exegetical enterprise."[1] So writes Donald Juel, who maintains that the New Testament found fulfillment of messianic prophecy by eisegesis of Old Testament texts. Thus, he avers that New Testament writers were engaged in "a highly artful, even fanciful" method of interpretation.[2] He concludes that the New Testament uses midrashic methods to identify Jesus as the fulfillment of prophecy rather than accurately reflecting the real meaning of the Old Testament.[3]

This is just one of the responses that the difficulty of the use of the Old Testament in the New Testament has elicited. Throughout the centuries, commentators and theologians have sought to explain the way the New Testament used the Old.[4] It is not the purpose of this chapter to discuss the various proposals that scholars have made regarding the method that the New Testament writers used.[5] Rather, it is to demonstrate that the New Testament did not regard its own understanding of messianic hope in the Hebrew Bible to be fanciful or creative. Rather, the New Testament generally considered the Old Testament to be directly messianic, even as previous chapters of this book have argued. Therefore, this chapter will examine the New Testament perception of the messianic hope of the Hebrew Bible.

Jesus and the Messianic Hope

The identification of Jesus of Nazareth as Messiah relies on His fulfilment of messianic prophecy. For example, when the doubting John the Baptist sent his disciples from prison to ask Jesus, "Are You the One who is to come, or should we expect someone else?" (Matt 11:3), Jesus replied by quoting from Isaiah 35 and 61 to show that He

---

[1] D. Juel, *Messianic Exegesis* (Philadelphia: Fortress, 1988), 13.

[2] Ibid.

[3] Ibid., 14–19.

[4] For a historical review of the treatments of the New Testament use the Old, see E. E. Ellis, *The Old Testament in Early Christianity: Canon and Interpretation in the Light of Modern Research* (Grand Rapids: Baker, 1992), 53–74.

[5] See chap. 2 for that.

was the Messiah because He had indeed fulfilled messianic prophecy. It appears that Jesus believed in an Old Testament messianic hope and taught that to His disciples.

Jesus and the Message of the Old Testament

Plainly, Jesus considered the central message of the Old Testament to be messianic. Jesus revealed His view of Old Testament messianic prophecy in two postresurrection encounters: teaching the two disciples on the Emmaus Road (Luke 24:25–27), and teaching "the Eleven" gathered in Jerusalem (Luke 24:44–46). On those two occasions, it was Luke's intention to demonstrate that Jesus understood the Old Testament to point to the Messiah.

It is evident in Jesus' emphasis on the word "all" in both those encounters that He believed the entire Old Testament predicted the Messiah. Jesus rebuked the men on the road to Emmaus for being slow to believe in "*all* that the prophets have spoken" (*epi* pasin *hois elalēsan hoi prophētai*, Luke 24:25). He explained the Scriptures about the Messiah beginning with Moses and "*all* the Prophets" (pantōn *tōn prophētōn*, Luke 24:27). He interpreted the message about the Messiah "in *all* the Scriptures" (*en* pasais *tais graphais*, Luke 24:27). He affirmed that He had to fulfill "*everything* written about Me" (panta *ta gegrammena . . . peri emou*) in the Law, the Prophets, and the Writings (Luke 24:44). Jesus' emphasis on "all" shows that He saw the Messiah not merely in occasional isolated texts but in all the Scriptures.[6] As Ellison observed, based on this passage, "The whole Old Testament, and not merely an anthology of proof passages, was looked on as referring to Christ Jesus."[7]

In reviewing these two encounters, two concepts become evident. First, Jesus believed that the messianic prophecies were sufficiently clear that the two disciples on the Emmaus Road should have understood their meaning. He chided them, "How unwise and slow you are to believe in your hearts all that the prophets have spoken!" (Luke 24:25). The implication was that the disciples should have recognized the events of the crucifixion and the reports of the resurrection as fulfillments of Old Testament prophecies. The prophecies were not so

---

[6] I. H. Marshall, *Commentary on Luke: A Commentary on the Greek Text*, NIGTC (Grand Rapids: Eerdmans,1979), 897.

[7] H. L. Ellison. *The Centrality of the Messianic Idea in the Old Testament* (London: Tyndale, 1957), 6.

unclear that the disciples could be excused for their failure to understand. He did not say, "O poor men of faith, you could not understand what the prophets had spoken of me because they had not yet been given their full sense of meaning, their *sensus plenior*, until this very moment as I am explaining them to you!" As A. T. Robertson said, "Jesus found himself in the Old Testament, a thing that some modern scholars do not seem to be able to do."[8]

A second truth evident from these two encounters is that Jesus believed spiritual insight was necessary to understand messianic prophecy. "He opened their mind to understand the Scriptures" (Luke 24:45), demonstrating that divine enlightenment was essential to an accurate understanding of messianic prophecy.[9] In addition to diligent study of messianic texts, the disciples could not understand messianic prophecy without divine enablement.

Jesus and the Hermeneutics of the Apostles

Jesus not only interpreted the Old Testament as a messianic document but He taught the apostles his Old Testament interpretive method. Since the Messiah Himself taught the disciples how the Old Testament relates to the Messiah, Ellison states, "We can only interpret it reasonably as a claim that the Church's use of the Old Testament was in fact based on and legitimized by the teaching of its Founder."[10] Despite some who claim that apostles' use of the Old Testament was derived from their own creativity or the rabbinic midrashic method, they actually received their training in the hermeneutics of messianic prophecy from the Messiah Himself. Liefeld addresses the importance of this when he writes,

> With great clarity they show that the sufferings of Christ, as well as his glory, were predicted in the Old Testament and that all the Old Testament Scriptures are important. *They also show that the way the writers of the New Testament used the Old Testament had its origin, not in their own creativity, but in the postresurrection teachings of Jesus, of which this passage is a paradigm.*[11]

Jesus' hermeneutical perspective (that *all* the Old Testament pointed to the Messiah) is evident in Peter's preaching. In his sermon at

---

[8] A. T. Robertson. *Word Pictures in the New Testament* (Nashville: Broadman, 1930), 2:294.

[9] For an excellent discussion of the spiritual dimensions of hermeneutics, see G. Maier, *Biblical Hermeneutics,* trans. R. W. Yarbrough (Wheaton: Crossway, 1994), 53–62.

[10] Ellison, *The Centrality of the Messianic Idea in the Old Testament,* 5.

[11] Italics mine. W. Liefeld, "Luke," *EBC* 8:1053.

the portico of Solomon, recorded in Acts 3:11–26, he asserted that "all" the prophets pointed to the Messiah (Acts 3:18). Moreover, he maintained that the central message of the prophets was indeed eschatological and messianic. He stated, "All the prophets who have spoken . . . announced these days" (3:24). This reflects Jesus' earlier emphasis on the word "all" (discussed above).[12] It is apparent that Peter is only expressing what he previously learned from Jesus (Luke 24:44–46).

Jesus and the Old Testament Authors

Jesus did not believe that Old Testament authors wrote of the Messiah without understanding the meaning of their own words. Rather, they were conscious of the messianic hope included in their texts of Scripture, as is evident in John 5:45–47. There Jesus told the Jewish leaders who had rejected Him that He was not the one accusing them before the Father but that Moses was. The rationale for this statement is that if they had believed Moses, they would also believe in Jesus, "because he wrote about Me" (John 5:46). It was their failure to believe Moses' writings that caused these leaders to disbelieve Jesus' words. Leon Morris accurately assesses Jesus' meaning when he writes, "Moses' writings were prophetic. They pointed forward to Christ . . . (cf. 1:45). Therefore those who rejected the Christ did not really believe what Moses had written."[13]

The significance of John 5:45–47 with regard to messianic prophecy is that Jesus indicated that Moses knew that he was writing about the Messiah. If Moses had not known of whom he was speaking, how could he accuse those who did not believe him? Imagine how illogical that would be—Moses accusing others for failing to understand what he himself did not comprehend. Moses had to understand that he wrote of Messiah in the Torah or he would not be qualified to accuse those who did not correctly interpret the messianic hope in the Torah.

Through this brief summary, it is plain that Jesus saw Himself as the direct fulfillment of the Old Testament messianic hope. As will be

---

[12] Peter's view of the prophets' messianic focus is similar to the rabbinic saying, "All the prophets prophesied only with reference to the days of Messiah" (*Ber.* 34b).

[13] L. Morris, *The Gospel According to John*, NICNT (Grand Rapids: Eerdmans, 1971), 334.

seen, Jesus taught his view to His disciples, who in turn declared their confidence in the messianic theme of the Hebrew Bible.

The Apostles and the Messianic Hope

The apostles both believed in Jesus as Messiah and effectively proclaimed His Messiahship to ancient Jewish audiences because of their confidence in His fulfillment of messianic prophecy. This will be evident through examination of their hermeneutics and their preaching of messianic prophecy.

The Apostolic Interpretation of the Messianic Hope

Jesus' instruction that the Old Testament was inherently messianic affected the apostles—they believed that the Old Testament prophets understood that they were writing about the Messiah as well. Peter, leader of the apostles, spoke to this in two significant passages, Acts 2:29–31 and 1 Pet 1:10–12.

Acts 2:29–31

Luke wrote of Peter's first sermon, preached at Pentecost, in Acts 2:29–31. In that passage, having quoted Ps 16:8–11 as a messianic prophecy of the resurrection, Peter argued that David, writing as a prophet, had the Messiah in view and not himself. Peter asserted that David could not possibly have had himself in mind as the subject of Psalm 16 because David died and his flesh was corrupted. Moreover, David was a prophet who had confidence in God's oath (the Davidic covenant), so "Seeing this in advance, he spoke concerning the resurrection of the Messiah: He was not left in Hades, and His flesh did not experience decay" (Acts 2:31).

Significantly, Peter's perspective, that David was directly speaking of the Messiah, is in harmony with David's own understanding of his writings. In 2 Sam 23:1–7, David's last words are recorded. As discussed earlier in chapter 3, the Septuagint rendering has a distinct messianic focus. David's last words, as recorded in the Septuagint, claimed that as the man who was raised up by God, he gave prophetic oracles "concerning the Messiah of the God of Jacob, the Delightful One of the songs of Israel" (2 Sam 23:1). Furthermore, David claimed that the Spirit of the Lord spoke by him and through him (2 Sam 23:2–3), thereby recognizing his own role as a prophet. Then, David described the righteous reign of the messianic king, recognized his own failure ("for not so is my house with God"), and declared his confidence in God to bring salvation because of the everlasting Davidic covenant (2 Sam 23:3–5).

The parallels between Peter's and David's perspectives are significant. Both claimed that David's confidence was rooted in the Davidic covenant, that David's Psalms spoke directly of the Messiah, and that David could write of the Messiah because he was a prophet. It is not surprising, then, that Peter would claim that the Messiah is the subject of Psalm 16 since David, the author of that Psalm, also made that claim.

1 Peter 1:10–12

The second passage supporting the apostolic perspective that the prophets knew they were writing about the Messiah is 1 Peter 1:10–12. Although this passage is frequently cited as teaching that the prophets did not understand the messianic significance of their words,[14] this is not the meaning of these verses.

According to Kaiser, the interpretive crux is whether to translate the phrase *eis tina ē poion kairon* as "what person or time" or "what time or circumstances."[15] Kaiser makes the case that it is a tautology for emphasis, with the resulting translation "what time or circumstances."[16] Thus, the prophets searched for the time of fulfillment but not the meaning of their own words. According to this view, the prophets knew they were writing about the sufferings and glories of the Messiah, but they did not know when He would come.

On the other hand, Grudem effectively argues, based on the normal use of *tis* and *poios*, that the phrase should be translated "what person or time."[17] Although they knew that they were writing of the Messiah, the prophets searched for the identity of the Messiah (i.e., the referent) and the time of his coming.

---

[14] J. Smith, *What the Bible Teaches about the Promised Messiah* (Nashville: Thomas Nelson, 1993), 21; R. Raymer, "First Peter," in *The Bible Knowledge Commentary: New Testament*, ed. J. F. Walvoord and R. B. Zuck (Wheaton: Scripture Press, 1983), 843; E. A. Blum, "First Peter," *EBC* 12:222; P. H. Davids, *The First Epistle of Peter*, NICNT (Grand Rapids: Eerdmans, 1990), 61.

[15] W. C. Kaiser Jr., *The Uses of the Old Testament in the New* (Chicago: Moody, 1985), 19. The phrase is literally, "[researching] into what or what kind of time."

[16] Ibid., 19–20.

[17] W. Grudem, *First Peter*, TNTC (Grand Rapids: Eerdmans.1988), 74–75.

Regardless of the translation of the phrase *eis tina ē poion kairon* (either "what person or time" or "what time or circumstances"), the passage still does not support the view that the prophets failed to understand that they wrote of Messiah. Kaiser states that according to 1 Pet 1:10–12, the prophets were aware of five facts in their prophecies:

> They knew they were predicting that: (1) the Messiah would come; (2) the Messiah would suffer; (3) the Messiah would be glorified (in kingly splendor); (4) the order of events 2 and 3 was that the suffering came first, and then the glorious period followed; and (5) this message had been revealed to the prophets not only for their own day, but also for a future generation such as the church of Peter's audience (v.12).[18]

Kaiser's remarks are accurate, but his fifth point could be clearer. Peter actually stated that the prophets served the future generations with their words, not their own generation. Although the messianic predictions had relevance to the original hearers, giving comfort and hope to those who looked forward in faith, their primary relevance was to new covenant believers.[19]

The point is that, regardless of which translation is chosen, whether "what time or circumstances," or the more probable "what person or time," the prophets still knew that they were predicting the sufferings and glory of the Messiah. As Reicke says, "The prophets of the Old Testament are here looked upon as having supernatural knowledge of the eschatological events, but still being obliged to discuss the problems of their historical fulfillment."[20] Although they knew that they wrote about the Messiah, they did not know when he would come nor that Jesus of Nazareth would be the historical referent of their prophecies. According to Peter, the prophets knew the meaning of their words (they were writing about the Messiah), but it was the apostles who identified the referent as Jesus of Nazareth (see Figure 6.1).

The apostles understood Jesus to be the primary object of the prophet's predictions and did not view his messianic fulfillment in some secondary way. As a result, this affected the way the apostles used messianic hope in their preaching, proclaiming their full confidence in Jesus as the fulfillment of messianic prophecy. S. Lewis Johnson has noted the importance of this, writing,

---

[18] Kaiser, *The Uses of the Old Testament in the New*, 19–20.

[19] Grudem, *First Peter*, 71.

[20] B. Reicke, *The Epistles of James, Peter, Jude*, AB 37 (New York: Doubleday, 1964), 80.

If the apostles are reliable teachers of biblical doctrine, then they are reliable instructors in the science of hermeneutics. And what better way is there to discover their hermeneutics than to investigate their use of the Old Testament Scriptures?[21]

The Apostolic Proclamation of the Messianic Hope

In the book of Acts, the central message of the apostles to the Jewish people was that Jesus was both Lord and Messiah (Acts 2:36). According to F. F. Bruce, the apostles substantiated their claim with two arguments, one from prophecy and the other from miracles. They proclaimed that "the prophetic scriptures which foretold Messiah's coming have been fulfilled by the ministry, suffering and triumph of Jesus, and the mighty works which he performed were so many 'signs' that in Him the messianic age had arrived."[22] Both of these arguments were brought together in their proclamation of the resurrection of Jesus, which was both a mighty work of God and a direct fulfillment of messianic prophecy.[23] A survey of the apostles' use of messianic prophecy when preaching to Jewish people as recorded in the book of Acts will reveal that they viewed the Hebrew Bible as a messianic document.[24]

Peter was the first to use messianic prophecy in Jewish evangelism. At Pentecost, in his first sermon, Peter proved his central message with messianic prophecy (Acts 2:22–36). He declared that Jesus of

---

[21] S. L. Johnson, *The Old Testament in the New* (Grand Rapids: Zondervan, 1980), 23.

[22] F. F. Bruce, *The Defense of the Gospel in the New Testament* (Grand Rapids: Eerdmans, 1959) 13–14.

[23] Ibid., 14–15.

[24] The apostles found that frequently their Jewish audiences were responsive to their messianic message. This was, most probably, a result of the Jewish messianic expectation evident during Second Temple period. Luke records that there were Jewish people "looking forward to Israel's consolation" and "to the redemption of Jerusalem" (Luke 2:25,38). It was the Old Testament messianic prophecies that gave them this hope. For more on the pre-Christian use of messianic prophecy, see M. Green, *Evangelism in the Early Church* (Grand Rapids: Eerdmans, 1970), 78–111. For more on Jewish messianic expectation, see A. Edersheim, *Life and Times of Jesus the Messiah* (repr., Grand Rapids: Eerdmans, 1971), 1:78–82, 160–79; G. F. Moore, *Judaism in the First Centuries of the Christian Era* (repr., New York: Schocken, 1971), 2:323–76. For messianic expectation in the Apocrypha, Pseudepigrapha, and Qumran writings, see W. Horbury, *Jewish Messianism and the Cult of Christ* (London: SCM, 1998), 52–63. For a discussion of messianic expectation in the Targumim, see M. B. Shepherd, "Targums, New Testament, and Biblical Theology of the Messiah" *JETS* 51 (2008): 45–58; S. H. Levey, *The Messiah: An Aramaic Interpretation* (Cincinnati: Hebrew Union College–Jewish Institute of Religion, 1974). A. Laato (*A Star is Rising* [Atlanta: Scholars Press, 1997]) summarizes messianic expectation in the Qumran writings (290–316) and Tannaitic Judaism (355–93).

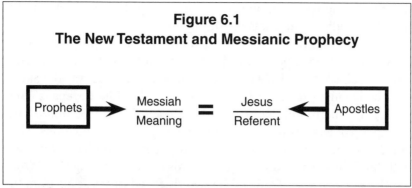

Figure 6.1
The New Testament and Messianic Prophecy

Nazareth had been raised from the dead in fulfillment of Ps 16:8–11 and that he had ascended into heaven in fulfillment of Ps 110:1.

In Peter's second sermon at Solomon's Colonnade, after the healing of the lame man (Acts 3:11–26), he argued, "But what God predicted through the mouth of all the prophets—that His Messiah would suffer—He has fulfilled in this way" (Acts 3:18). Having called on the crowd to believe in Jesus as the eschatological prophet like Moses who was foretold by Moses himself, Peter further claimed that "all the prophets who have spoken, from Samuel and those after him, have also announced these days" (Acts 3:24).

Later, when Peter made his defense before the Sanhedrin for healing the lame man, he cited messianic prophecy to explain his position (Acts 4:8–12). He charged the council with rejecting Jesus in fulfillment of Ps 118:22: "The stone despised by you builders, which has become the cornerstone" (Acts 4:11).

Stephen also made mention of messianic prophecy in his preaching. When he made his case before the Sanhedrin (Acts 7), Stephen's primary message was about Israel's long history of rebellion against God. However, Stephen's confidence in messianic prophecy became evident when he charged that the rebellious in the nation had killed the prophets "who announced beforehand the coming of the Righteous One" (Acts 7:52).

Philip also used messianic prophecy in evangelism. When the Ethiopian official (Acts 8:26–40), who apparently was a proselyte to Judaism, asked of whom the prophet spoke in Isaiah 53, Philip answered that it was Jesus (Acts 8:34–35). It is obvious that Philip considered Jesus to be the fulfillment of that prophecy. The correspondence between the description of the Servant and the events surrounding Jesus' life, death, and resurrection was so convincing that the Ethiopian believed immediately and was baptized.

Paul was another apostle who used messianic prophecy when preaching to Jewish people. In his sermon in the synagogue at Pisidian Antioch (Acts 13:16–41), he proclaimed that Jesus was the Savior God had sent to Israel in fulfillment of the Davidic covenant (Acts 13:23). Furthermore, Paul claimed that even Jesus' rejection by the leadership of Israel was a fulfillment of the prophets' predictions. They failed to recognize "the voices of the prophets that are read every Sabbath" and thus "have fulfilled their words by condemning Him" (Acts 13:27). Furthermore, Paul maintained that God raised Jesus from the dead in fulfillment of Pss 2:7 and 16:10 (Acts 13:33–37).

Paul's method in Pisidian Antioch was not unique. In fact, when he went to the synagogue in Thessalonica, he "reasoned with them from the Scriptures, explaining and showing that the Messiah had to suffer and rise from the dead, and saying: 'This is the Messiah, Jesus, whom I am proclaiming to you'" (Acts 17:1–3). Since this was Paul's custom, he followed the same procedure in Berea (Acts 17:10–15), although with greater success than in Thessalonica.

Before Agrippa and Festus, Paul maintained that in his testimony about Jesus he was "saying nothing else than what the prophets and Moses said would take place—that the Messiah must suffer, and that as the first to rise from the dead, He would proclaim light to our people and to the Gentiles" (Acts 26:22–23). This message remained the same at Rome while Paul was under house arrest. There, leaders from the Jewish community came to Paul and he "persuaded them concerning Jesus, from both the Law of Moses and the Prophets" (Acts 28:23).

Apollos also had made his reputation as an exceptional evangelist among Jewish people through his use of messianic prophecy (Acts 18:24–28). His effectiveness was rooted in his ability to convince Jews of Jesus' Messiahship by "demonstrating through the Scriptures that Jesus is the Messiah" (Acts 18:28).

In discussing the apostles' use of messianic prophecy, Dewart summarizes their method, as follows: "In all this there was an appeal . . . to the things that had been foretold by the prophets and fulfilled by the events of the life and death of Jesus of Nazareth. It is evident that Peter and Paul had strong confidence in the evidential value of fulfilled prediction.[25]

The apostles' confidence was well-founded as seen in the notable success they experienced. At Pentecost, 3,000 Jewish people believed Peter's word about Jesus as the fulfillment of prophecy (Acts 2:41). From those who heard Peter's message on messianic prophecy after the healing of the lame man, five thousand men believed (Acts 4:4). Later on, "a large group of priests became obedient to the faith" (Acts 6:7). Moreover, James was able to say to Paul, "You see, brother, how many thousands of Jews there are who have believed" (Acts 21:20).

The apostles consistently used messianic prophecy in Jewish evangelism. They did this primarily because they were convinced of its veracity through the teaching they had received from Jesus Himself (Luke 24:44–47). The apostles also found it to be an effective strategy with Jewish people because in those days Jewish people regarded the Old Testament as the basis of all religious authority.

Conclusion

I once heard about a noted evangelical Old Testament professor who had given a lecture on the Psalms. He declared that there was absolutely nothing messianic in Psalm 16. When he was asked why Peter (Acts 2:24–32) and Paul (Acts 13:34–37) had cited Ps 16:10 as a prediction of the resurrection of the Messiah, he responded by saying that he did not agree with Peter's or Paul's hermeneutics. Afterwards, several of the attendees to that lecture asked me to comment on this professor's view. I noted that it was Jesus Himself who taught Peter and Paul their interpretive method of the Hebrew Bible (Luke 24:44–46). If I were not to agree with their interpretations, perhaps that would reflect badly on my hermeneutics, not theirs.

This chapter has attempted to show that the New Testament embraced the idea that the Hebrew Bible was deeply messianic. Further,

---

[25] E. H. Dewart, *Jesus the Messiah in Prophecy and Fulfillment: A Review and Refutation of the Negative Theory of Messianic Prophecy* (New York: Hunt & Eaton, 1891), 217–18. Notably, H. J. Schoeps, who did not believe in Jesus as Messiah, recognized that the events of Jesus' life and death fit the prophetic utterances. He explained this away as either the event being inserted into the life of Jesus by the apostles as a fabrication to confirm the words of the prophets or as deliberate actions on the part of Jesus contrived to make it appear as if he were fulfilling prophecy (*The Jewish-Christian Argument: A History of Theologies in Conflict*, trans. D. E. Green [New York: Holt, Rhinehart, and Winston, 1961], 22). Either way, he recognized that the New Testament record agrees with the prophetic oracles concerning the Messiah.

that Jesus of Nazareth and his disciples believed and taught that Jesus was the fulfillment of the messianic hope of the Old Testament. Johnson rightly maintains this when he asks,

> What do the New Testament authors think of the Old Testament? Further, what adjectives would they find useful in describing it? I suggest that they hold the Old Testament to be historical revelation, strongly messianic in content, often predictive . . . in its forward look, and always inspired and inerrant in its teaching.[26]

It may be objected, as the above professor did, that the New Testament authors read the Scriptures in an atomistic and noncontextual way, using the "creative" exegetical methods of the later rabbinic midrashim. But, there could be another explanation. Perhaps the mistaken idea is the assumption that they were practicing unacceptable hermeneutics, ignoring the intended meaning of the Hebrew Bible.

More likely, Jesus and the apostles read the Hebrew Bible in a holistic way, seeing the whole Old Testament as messianic. Thus, by reading the Hebrew Bible according to the compositional strategies of the authors and the final canonical shape of the books, Jesus and His apostles accurately communicated the messianic theme of the Hebrew Bible. The following chapter will examine this proposal by investigating how the New Testament writers interpreted the Old. But the point of this chapter has been that if asked "Is the Old Testament really messianic?" Jesus and His apostles, based on the New Testament evidence, would answer with a resounding "Yes!"

---

[26] Johnson, *The Old Testament in the New*, 27.

Chapter 7

DECODING THE HEBREW BIBLE: HOW THE NEW TESTAMENT READS THE OLD

W alter C. Kaiser Jr. asked, "In their attempt to show that the Messiah and many of the events in the first century church had indeed been anticipated by the Old Testament writers, have the New Testament writers fairly cited the Old Testament quotations, according to their real truth-intention and original writer's meaning?"[1]

His question brings into sharp focus the core issue at stake in all discussions concerning the New Testament's use of the Old. Plainly, as seen in the previous chapter, the New Testament interprets the Old Testament as messianic. However, how the New Testament came to this interpretive conclusion has become a controversial subject.[2] Did the New Testament writers use the Old Testament fairly or did they read their own meanings into the texts they cited?

One common explanation is that the New Testament authors interpreted Old Testament texts according to rabbinic midrashic method. G. F. Moore defines midrashic method as

> an atomistic exegesis, which interprets sentences, clauses, phrases, and even single words, independently of the context or the historical occasion, as divine oracles; combines them with other similarly detached utterances; and makes large use of analogy of expressions, often by purely verbal association.[3]

According to this view, like the midrashim the New Testament cites the Old atomistically, arbitrarily, and so inaccurately, without any regard for the intentions of the Old Testament authors. This view is based on the idea that the New Testament authors used Old Testament texts much in the way that their Jewish contemporaries did, namely, without concern for context or authorial intent.[4] Nevertheless, frequently those who hold this view also maintain that the

---

[1] W. C. Kaiser Jr., *The Uses of the Old Testament in the New* (Chicago: Moody, 1985), x–xi.

[2] For a collection of essays on this issue, reflecting different viewpoints, see G. K. Beale, ed., *The Right Doctrine from the Wrong Texts?* (Grand Rapids: Baker, 1994).

[3] G. F. Moore, *Judaism in the First Centuries of the Christian Era* (New York: Schocken, 1975), 1:248, as cited by R. N. Longenecker, "'Who is the Prophet Talking About?' Some Reflections on the New Testament's Use of the Old," in Beale, *The Right Doctrine from the Wrong Texts?*, 381.

[4] Longenecker, "'Who Is the Prophet Talking About?' Some Reflections on the New Testament's Use of the Old," 379–84.

New Testament's interpretations can be accepted because the writers were "guided by the exalted Christ, through immediate direction of the Holy Spirit."[5] However, these interpreters would also assert that present-day interpreters should in no way mimic or use apostolic exegetical methods. Longenecker states, "I do not, however, think it my business to try to reproduce the exegetical procedures and practices of the New Testament writers, particularly when they engage in what I define as 'midrash,' 'pesher,' or 'allegorical' exegesis."[6]

Moisés Silva has objected to Longenecker's thesis, stating, "If we refuse to pattern our exegesis after that of the apostles, we are in practice denying the authoritative character of their scriptural interpretation."[7] Silva's position about the understandability of New Testament citations from the Old is mine as well.[8] The New Testament's exegesis of Old Testament texts is both discernible and reproducible. This chapter will attempt to demonstrate how the New Testament writers interpret the Hebrew Bible by examining the four Old Testament quotations in Matthew 2. The second chapter of Matthew contains four categories of Old Testament quotations that are identifiable throughout the New Testament.[9] They are not mysterious, creative, or incomprehensible but intelligible and reproducible. After examining the four classifications in Matthew 2, it will become evident that the New Testament use of the Old is accurate, comprehensible, and still usable by current interpreters of the Bible.

The narrative purpose of Matthew 2 is to show the world's reception of the Messiah, with Jewish leadership being essentially apathetic to His arrival but the Gentile Magi acting more responsive. These events foreshadow the types of reception the Messiah received in the

---

[5] Ibid., 384.

[6] R. N. Longenecker, *Biblical Exegesis in the Apostolic Period*, 2nd ed. (Grand Rapids: Eerdmans, 1999), xxxviii.

[7] M. Silva, "The New Testament Use of the Old Testament: Text Form and Authority," in *Scripture and Truth*, ed. D. A. Carson and J. D. Woodbridge (Grand Rapids: Zondervan, 1983), 164. See also S. L. Johnson Jr., *The Old Testament in the New: An Argument for Biblical Inspiration* (Grand Rapids: Zondervan, 1980), 93–94.

[8] See also G. Beale's argument that the New Testament uses legitimate hermeneutical methods to interpret the Hebrew Bible ("Did Jesus and His Followers Preach the Right Doctrine from the Wrong Texts?" *Them* 14 [1989], 89–96).

[9] Thanks to A. G. Fruchtenbaum who drew my attention to an older work: D. L. Cooper, *Messiah: His Historical Appearance* (Los Angeles: Biblical Research Society, 1958). Cooper identified four broad classifications of Old Testament quotations in the New in his examination of Matthew 2 (pp. 174–78). These became the launching pad for the basic ideas in this chapter.

rest of the gospel.[10] Nevertheless, Matthew 2 has a secondary purpose, that is, to reveal that Jesus fulfilled the messianic hope of the Hebrew Bible. Thus, Matthew's second chapter sets forth four Old Testament predictions that find their fulfilment in the life of Jesus of Nazareth.[11] The literary link of all four of these Old Testament references is that each has a geographical element: the first speaks of Bethlehem, the second of Egypt, the third of Ramah, and the last of Nazareth. Each of these Old Testament citations demonstrates a different kind of fulfillment, providing a paradigm for the four ways the New Testament uses the Old.

Direct Fulfillment: Matthew 2:5–6/Micah 5:2

The first kind of prophecy and fulfillment motif is literal prediction and direct fulfillment, as seen in Matthew's quotation of Mic 5:2.[12] After the birth narrative (Matt 1:18–25), Matthew wrote that wise men from the East arrived at the court of King Herod, asking, "Where is He who has been born King of the Jews?" (Matt 2:2). In response, Herod gathered chief priests and scribes to repeat the wise men's question to them. The Jewish scholars in turn cited Mic 5:2[Hb. 5:1]:

> And you, Bethlehem, in the land of Judah, are by no means least among the leaders of Judah: because out of you will come a leader who will shepherd My people Israel. (Matt 2:6)

The quotation appears to be a loose, paraphrastic translation of the Masoretic version of Mic 5:2[1]:[13]

> Bethlehem Ephrathah, you are small among the clans of Judah; / One will come from you to be ruler over Israel for Me. / His origin [*ûmôṣā'ōtāyw*] is from antiquity [*miqqedem*], from eternity [*mîmê 'ôlām*, lit. "from days of eternity"].

The literary strategy of Micah follows the common pattern of the prophets, alternating between prophecies of judgment and prophecies of hope. In contrast to the previous paragraph, wherein the gathering of the nations to judge Jerusalem is predicted (4:9–5:1), Micah turned

---

[10] S. D. Toussaint, *Behold the King* (Portland: Multnomah, 1980), 47.

[11] Ibid.

[12] This is the classification that Cooper labels "literal prophecy." Cooper, *Messiah: His Historical Appearance*, 174.

[13] G. L. Archer and G. C. Chirichigno, *Old Testament Quotations in the New Testament: A Complete Survey* (Chicago: Moody, 1983), 157.

to a prediction of hope and restoration in 5:2–4. There, Micah foretold the coming of a future ruler of Israel who would one day shepherd the flock of Israel. Micah also prophesied that when this king's greatness would extend to the ends of the earth, then Israel would also live securely in their land. This is clearly a messianic prediction, which conflates the two comings of the Messiah.

Micah's prophecy in 5:2 speaks of the origins of the king. It foretold that this future ruler of Israel would come forth from Bethlehem. Although this is plainly an allusion to the restoration of the Davidic house, it is also foretelling that once again a king of Israel would be born in Bethlehem. It is not only saying that Messiah would come from the Davidic line but that he would actually come from the town of Bethlehem.[14]

Additionally, Micah predicted that this king's origins would be from eternity past. The two Hebrew temporal nouns used can speak of eternity when they stand alone, although this is not always the case. Used chronologically, *qedem*, "antiquity," can refer to ancient times as in "long ago," to the earliest imaginable times as when the mountains first came to be (Deut 33:15), or to the "eternal" God and His eternal dwelling place (Deut 33:27; Hab 1:12; Pss 55:19; 68:33). The second term *'ôlām*, "eternity," usually refers to the distant or unending future (although sometimes within the context of one's lifetime). But it is also used of ancient times in the past (Ps 24:7) or of the beginning of creation (Ps 25:6; Joel 2:2) or before. According to Ps 93:2, God's "throne has been established from the beginning [lit. "from then"]; / You are from eternity." And Ps 90:2 declares, "Before the mountains were born, / before You gave birth to the earth and the world, / from eternity to eternity, You are God." When *qedem* and *'ôlām* are used together, however, as in Prov 8:22–23, they always denote eternity past (cf. Deut 33:27). In Mic 5:2, these words are placed together to emphasize the ruler's true origin, being far earlier than his arrival in Bethlehem or even antiquity. Rather, he comes from eternity past.[15]

---

[14] Even traditional Jewish sources see Bethlehem as the birthplace of Messiah. The *Targum Pseudo-Jonathan* on Gen 35:21, using the name Migdal Edar for Bethlehem, states that it is "the place from whence the Messiah shall be revealed in the last days." In the Jerusalem Talmud, *Ber.* 5a states, "The King Messiah . . . from where does he come forth? From the royal city of Bethlehem in Judah."

[15] This is possibly the source of the Talmudic idea of a preexistent Messiah. See S. Goldman, "Micah," in *The Twelve Prophets*, Soncino Books of the Bible (London: Soncino, 1957),

Kaiser accurately describes this juxtaposition of the temporal and eternal origin of Messiah as follows:

> According to his human heritage, he will descend from the family of David who lived in Bethlehem and will be born in that same town, even though he has a divine line of descent that takes him clear back to eternity. He will be both human and divine. What a mystery![16]

Thus, according to Matthew's record, when Herod asked the priests and scribes where Messiah would be born, the Jewish scholars answered correctly. They chose the correct verse (Mic 5:2) and interpreted it literally. This is a classic example of a literal prediction fulfilled directly. Micah 5:2 and its citation in Matt 2:5–6 are, in the words of Craig Blomberg, "a very straightforward scheme of prediction and fulfillment. . . . Micah prophesied that the Messiah would be born in Bethlehem, and now it has happened."[17]

The point of this book has been to posit that this kind of literal prediction and direct fulfillment are common and to be expected in the Old and New Testaments.[18] Nevertheless, this is clearly not the only way the New Testament cites the Old. In fact, the next quotation of the Old Testament in Matthew 2 demonstrates a second category of Old Testament citation, that of typical fulfillment.

Typical Fulfillment: Matthew 2:15/Hosea 11:1

The second Old Testament citation in Matthew 2 is generally understood to be "a classic example of pure typology"[19] or typical

---

175. However, while the Talmud recognizes the Messiah as preexistent, it does not see Him as eternal.

[16] W. C. Kaiser Jr., *The Messiah in the Old Testament* (Grand Rapids: Zondervan, 1994).

[17] C. L. Blomberg, "Matthew," in *Commentary on the New Testament Use of the Old Testament*, ed. G. K. Beale and D. A. Carson (Grand Rapids: Baker, 2007), 7.

[18] Direct fulfillments form the vast majority of prediction/fulfillments in Matthew. Other examples of direct fulfillments in Matthew are 1:23/Isa 7:14; 4:15–16/Isa 9:1–2; 8:17/Isa 53:4; 11:10/Mal 3:1; 12:17–21/Isa 42:1–4; 21:5/Zech 9:9; 21:42/Ps 118:22–23; 22:44/Ps 110:1; 26:31/Zech 13:7; 27:9–10/Zech 11:12–13; 27:46/Ps 22:1.

[19] Sailhamer objects to this: "When Matthew quoted Hos 11:1 as fulfilled in the life of Christ, he was not resorting to a typological interpretation. Rather, he was drawing the *sensus literalis* from the book of Hosea and it, in turn, was drawn from Hosea's exegesis of the *sensus literalis* of the Pentateuch" ("Hosea 11:1 and Matthew 2:15," *WTJ* 63 [2001]: 91). Although there is much to commend in this interpretation, particularly Sailhamer's demonstration of Hosea's dependence on Numbers 24, still it does fall short. It seems to me that Hosea was looking back to Israel's exodus from Egypt literally, not using it as a metaphor for the Messiah's future redemption as Sailhamer contends. However, Sailhamer's understanding of Hosea's dependence

fulfillment.[20] R. T. France provides a traditional definition of typology as "the recognition of a correspondence between New and Old Testaments, based on a conviction of the unchanging character of the principles of God's working."[21] This section will explore whether Matthew's citation of Hosea 11:1 as a type is valid.

After the narrative of the angel telling Joseph to flee to Egypt to save the child from Herod's soldiers, Matthew recounted that the family stayed in Egypt until Herod's death. According to Matthew, these events took place to fulfill "what was spoken by the Lord through the prophet . . . 'Out of Egypt I called My Son.'" Although Matthew's quotation is brief, and there is little to which to compare it, the rendering is distinct from the Septuagint's translation of Hos 11:1. In fact, Matthew's translation is taken from the Masoretic version and is far more literal and accurate than the Septuagint's rendering.[22] This is evident in that the Septuagint uses the word *tekna* (children) as opposed to the more literal *huios* (son) that Matthew uses.

The citation from Hos 11:1 has been found problematic through the years because Hosea was plainly speaking of Israel's departure from Egypt at the exodus and not about the Messiah. The synonymous parallelism in Hos 11:1 shows this beyond a shadow of a doubt: "When Israel was a child, I loved him, and out of Egypt I called my son." "Israel" in the first strophe is parallel to the "son" spoken of in the second strophe. Hosea undoubtedly had Exod 4:22–23 in mind, where God says "Israel is my firstborn son." Hence the same parallelism is evident in Hosea.[23]

So why does Matthew take a verse that clearly refers to Israel and then maintain that Jesus' return from Egypt is its fulfillment? According to W. S. LaSor this is a case of *sensus plenior*, meaning that while Hosea only had Israel in mind, God had the fuller messianic sense in His mind.[24] As Carson points out,

---

on Numbers does indeed, as will be seen, make Matthew's typical interpretation not farfetched but entirely defensible.

[20] Ibid. Cooper categorizes this example in Matt 2:15 as a "literal prophecy with typical import" (*Messiah: His Historical Appearance*, 175).

[21] R. T. France, *The Gospel according to Matthew*, TNTC (Grand Rapids: Eerdmans, 1985), 40. Cf. idem, *Jesus and the Old Testament: His Application of Old Testament Passages to Himself and His Mission* (London: Tyndale, 1971), 38–43.

[22] Archer and Chirichigno, *Old Testament Quotations in the New Testament: A Complete Survey*, 147.

[23] Cooper, *Messiah: His Historical Appearance*, 175.

[24] W. L. LaSor, "Prophecy, Inspiration, and *Sensus Plenior*," *TynBul* 29 (1978): 49–60.

So blunt an appeal to what God has absolutely hidden seems a strange background for Matthew's insisting that Jesus' exodus from Egypt in any sense
fulfills the Hosea passage. This observation is not trivial; Matthew is reasoning with Jews who could say, "You are not playing fair with the text!"[25]

Blomberg states that the Old Testament author need not have intended the future Messiah when he wrote but rather that "for believing Jews, merely to discern striking parallels between God's actions in
history, especially in decisive moments of revelation and redemption,
could convince them of divinely intended 'coincidence.'"[26] While an
improvement on LaSor's *sensus plenior*, is it really a sufficient explanation for Matthew's typological interpretation? Carson's objection appears to be just as valid a response to Blomberg as it was to LaSor—it
does not appear to be fair to the Old Testament text. Although this
is indeed an example of typical fulfillment, there should be and is a
more plausible explanation for Matthew's usage of Hos 11:1 as a type
than merely noting striking parallels.

The basis of Matthew's use of Israel as a type of the Messiah is
from Numbers 23 and 24, which presents Israel as a general type of
the Messiah. Moreover, that type specifically identifies coming out
of Egypt as a point of correspondence between Israel and the future
Messiah.[27] This becomes apparent by examining the second and third
Balaam oracles (Num 23:22–24; 24:7–9).

The second Balaam oracle (Num 23:22–24) describes God's care
for the nation of Israel. Singular pronominal suffixes are used of Israel
in 23:21, treating the people of Israel as a collective singular. But in
23:22, there is a deliberate shift to a plural pronoun to clarify that
the whole people of Israel is in view. Thus, Num 23:22a (*ʾēl môṣîʾām
mimmiṣrāyim*) literally reads, "God brings [hiphil participle] *them* out
of Egypt." The phrase *hen ʿām* in Num 23:24 (lit., "Behold, a people") makes it plain that Balaam's second oracle is about the whole
people of Israel. In summary, the oracle states that God brings Israel
out of Egypt (23:22a), that He is for Israel like the horns of a wild ox
(23:22b), and that Israel will be as powerful as a lion (23:24).

---

[25] D. A. Carson, "Matthew," *EBC* 8:92.

[26] Blomberg, "Matthew," in Beale and Carson, *Commentary on the New Testament Use of the
Old Testament*, 8.

[27] Note also the vine imagery applied to Israel in the Old Testament (Ps 80:8 ["You uprooted
a vine from Egypt"]; Isa 5:1–7; 27:2–6; Jer 2:21; 12:10; Ezek 15:1–8; 19:10–14; Hos 10:1), which
Jesus applied to Himself in John 15:1.

The third Balaam oracle (Num 24:5–9) begins by describing the fruitfulness of Israel (24:5–6). Then, in Num 24:7, it predicts a future "seed" or descendant of Jacob (literally, "And his [Jacob's] seed is in the many waters"). Furthermore, this "seed" will also be a king with an exalted kingdom (24:7). In the Masoretic Text, the king is said to be higher than Agag, but other ancient versions read "He shall be higher than Gog," the end-time enemy of Israel.[28] The combination of his exalted kingdom and his superiority to Gog, no doubt, was the foundation for the ancient Targum's correct interpretation of the third Balaam oracle as a reference to the future Messiah.

What is especially significant is that the third oracle, juxtaposed to the second, deliberately uses similar descriptions of its subject (24:8–9). However, just as deliberately, there is a difference, namely, a shift to the singular pronoun. While in the second oracle God brings "them [Israel]" out of Egypt, in the third, (lit.) "God brings him [the future king] out of Egypt" (*'ēl môṣî'ô mimmiṣrāyim*).[29] Further, the third oracle, in a fashion similar to the second, states that God is for him (the king) like the horns of a wild ox and that the king will be as powerful as a lion.[30]

The author of the Pentateuch is using a significant compositional strategy in placing these two oracles next to each other. Figure 7.1 shows the deliberate repetition of phrases. The oracles are intentionally similar (same phrases) and intentionally different (singular versus plural pronouns). The writer's strategy was intended to establish a pattern or a type: what God will do for Israel, He will also do for the future king of Israel. Sailhamer makes this point when he writes,

> The writer's purpose appears to be to view the reign of the future king in terms taken from God's great acts of salvation in the past. The future is going to be like the past. What God did for Israel in the past is seen as a type of what he will do for them in the future when he sends his promised king.[31]

By placing the two oracles side by side, the author of the Pentateuch deliberately establishes one of the foundational types found in

---

[28] This variant reading is more preferable; see my more thorough discussion of this text in chap. 3.

[29] See Sailhamer, "Hosea 11:1 and Matthew 2:15," 94–95.

[30] "He crouches, he lies down like a lion or a lioness—who dares to rouse him?"(24:9). This is an almost literal repetition of the messianic prophecy in Gen 49:11. The use of an innertextual reference gives further confirmation that Num 24:7–9 is referring to the messianic king.

[31] J. H. Sailhamer, *The Pentateuch as Narrative* (Grand Rapids: Zondervan, 1992), 408.

Figure 7.1
The Typology of the Balaam Oracles

Israel's past experience prefigures the King's future experience.

Israel	**King**
Num 23:18–24	*Num 24:7–9*
• God brings **them** out of Egypt	• God brings **Him** out of Egypt
• God is for **them** like the horns of an Ox	• God is for **Him** like the horns of an Ox
• **Israel** is like a lion	• The **King** is like a lion

---

the Bible—Israel as a type of the future King-Messiah. Beyond this general typology, these two Balaam oracles provide a specific similarity between the people of Israel and the future king of Israel—God will bring them both out of Egypt.

Understanding this typology lays the foundation for Matthew's typical use of Hos 11:1. While others have noted that perhaps Matthew was making a subtle allusion to Num 24:8,[32] and some have even suggested that Matthew may have been citing Num 24:8 directly,[33] they both miss the point. Matthew understood that the Pentateuch had established Israel as a type of the future King Messiah. Furthermore, he understood that the Torah had established a specific parallel between Israel and the future king, namely, that God would bring them both out of Egypt. Hence, based on this established typology, Matthew saw it as perfectly sound, when narrating God's deliverance of Messiah from Egypt, to cite Hos 11:1, which speaks of God bringing Israel out of Egypt.

The question remains, "Why not just cite Num 24:7?" The answer is that Matthew was not just describing the journey from Egypt—he wanted to emphasize the Messiah's relationship to His Father as Son. The Hosea passage states that "Out of Egypt I called my Son." This was so important to Matthew that he rejected the Septuagint

---

[32] See R. H. Gundry, *Matthew: A Commentary on His Literary and Theological Art* (Grand Rapids: Eerdmans, 1982), 34.

[33] According to W. D. Davies and D. C. Allison, "For those familiar with the LXX, Matthew's quotation would have seemed closer to Num 24.8 than to Hos 11.1. This explains the scribal note in the margin of ‬ℵ [Codex Sinaiticus], which ascribes the text to Numbers" (*A Critical and Exegetical Commentary on the Gospel according to Saint Matthew,* ICC [Edinburgh: T&T Clark, 1988], 1:262n8).

translation of Hos 11:1 ("Out of Egypt I called my children") and made his own, more accurate translation of the Hebrew text, using the word "Son."[34]

The purpose of this discussion has been to demonstrate that Matthew did not indiscriminately flip through his Hebrew Bible and pull a verse out of context to "fulfill" a nonexistent prediction of the Messiah. Nor did he arbitrarily and without biblical justification create a far-fetched typical interpretation. Matthew's case of typical fulfillment exemplifies deep knowledge of the Scriptures, using a valid type well established in the Torah.[35]

Although the point of this book has been to show that the Old Testament has a clear messianic hope, a secondary purpose is to show that the New Testament uses the Old in a reasonable way. Matthew's typical citation of Hos 11:1 makes perfect sense in light of the type established by Moses in the Pentateuch. However, what is Matthew's meaning in the next Old Testament quotation? That, too, will be seen as a logical and fair use of the Old Testament.

Applicational Fulfillment: Matthew 2:16–18/Jeremiah 31:15

The third Old Testament citation in Matthew 2 is an example of applicational fulfillment.[36] In this section, Matthew recorded Herod's response to being outwitted by the Magi. In relating the events of the Slaughter of the Innocents, when every male child under age two in Bethlehem was slaughtered,[37] Matthew states, "then what was spoken by Jeremiah the prophet was fulfilled" and cites Jer 31:15:

[34] Gundry, *Matthew: A Commentary on His Literary and Theological Art*, 33. Also Davies and Allison, *A Critical and Exegetical Commentary on the Gospel according to Saint Matthew*, 1:262–64.

[35] Typology is less common than what some expect, but it is still present in the New Testament. One example is in Acts 13:47, where Paul quotes Isa 49:6. The Isaiah passage refers directly to the Messiah, who establishes a pattern or type for His followers. In this fashion, they are appointed as lights for the Gentiles. Another example is the typology of Melchizedek found in Hebrews 7. The basis of this type is the linkage between the Messiah and Melchizedek in Psalm 110:4.

[36] This is what D. L. Cooper calls "literal prophecy plus an application." *Messiah: His Historical Appearance*, 175. Also see my chap. 2, n. 84.

[37] The historicity of this account is frequently denied. Yet it is entirely in keeping with what is known of Herod's character and actions. Moreover, since Bethlehem was so small, the deaths, though grievous in that community, would have numbered in the dozens, not the thousands. Therefore, it is no surprise that there is no extrabiblical record of this event. See R. T. France, *The Gospel of Matthew*, NICNT (Grand Rapids: Eerdmans, 2007), 84–85.

A voice was heard in Ramah,
a lament with bitter weeping—
Rachel weeping for her children,
refusing to be comforted for her children
because they are no more.

Matthew's quotation appears to be closer to the Masoretic Text than the Septuagint but does show some dependency on the LXX.[38] The context of the quote from Jeremiah is essentially an eschatological declaration of hope. The chapter revolves around an expectation of the end-time deliverance of Israel. Yet tucked into the middle of Jeremiah 31 is the reason that Judah needed to be reminded of her future deliverance—the death and exile of Jewish youth at the hands of the Babylonians.

Jeremiah 31:15 speaks of Ramah as the place of weeping because it was there the Babylonians gathered the captive young men of Judah before sending them into exile (Jer 40:1–2). There Rachel was said to weep for her children. Obviously, the matriarch Rachel had been long dead when Jeremiah wrote. So Jeremiah did not use her name literally (i.e., weeping from her grave) but rather symbolically, representing all of Jewish mothers.[39] Thus, Jeremiah states that Jewish mothers were weeping for their sons who had died in the war with Babylon and for the young men who were being taken to a distant land as captives. Jeremiah was referring to the deep pain of Jewish mothers at the loss of their young men to Nebuchadnezzar and the Babylonians. So the question is, Since Jer 31:15 refers to the Babylonian exile, how could Matthew cite the Slaughter of the Innocents as fulfilling this text?

According to France, "This is one of Matthew's most elusive OT quotations, and few claim with any confidence to have fathomed just what he intended." France goes on to speak of Matthew's "creativity" in formula quotations.[40] Some might consider Matthew's quotation of Jer 31:15 to be midrashic interpretation?[41] Longenecker maintains that the New Testament frequently quotes the Old without concern

---

[38] Archer and Chirichigno, *Old Testament Quotations in the New Testament: A Complete Survey*, 136–37.

[39] *Bereshit Rabbah* 71:2, commenting on Gen 29:31, identifies the matriarch Rachel as the principal or chief mother of Israel and cites Jer 31:15 in support of this idea.

[40] France, *The Gospel of Matthew*, 88.

[41] "*Midrash* derives from a Hebrew word meaning 'to seek' and refers to interpretive exposition." K. Snodgrass, "The Use of the Old Testament in the New," in Beale, *The Right Doctrine from the Wrong Texts?* (Grand Rapids: Baker, 1994), 42

for its literary context, even as ancient rabbis did in their midrashic interpretations.

Therefore, according to this midrashic view, Matthew's quotation is merely an atomistic quotation offered without any regard for Jeremiah's intention, the literary context, or the original meaning of the verse. Matthew could quote Jeremiah in this way because he was operating under the inspiration of the Holy Spirit, but modern interpreters must never reproduce this sort of atomistic exegesis.[42]

One problem with citing midrashic background as the explanation of the New Testament's exegesis of the Old is that this is historically anachronistic. It is based on rabbinic exegesis of a later time but substantially misunderstands how pre–AD 70 Jewish interpreters used biblical texts. David Instone-Brewer has examined all the instances of pre–AD 70 protorabbinic exegesis. He concludes that unlike later rabbinic methods, Jewish exegesis in the prerabbinic period before the destruction of the Temple was concerned with using Scripture in context. He writes, "Every single scribal exegesis examined could be quoted as an example to show that Scripture was interpreted according to its context."[43] Moreover, at that time, protorabbinic exegetes would have posited that "Scripture does not have a secondary meaning" and they would have indeed been concerned with discovering "the primary or plain sense of the text."[44] Klyne Snodgrass summarizes this distinction when he writes, "In the earlier rabbinic material, midrashic interpretation is fairly straightforward, but later rabbinic practices often focused more on individual words and even letters. The result is a 'creative' exegesis in which the original concern of the text is often lost."[45] So if the New Testament writers were truly using a Jewish hermeneutic from the first century, their citations should have been concerned with context and the true meaning of the text.

A second flaw in taking New Testament citations of the Old as creative exegesis in the form of midrash is that it misunderstands the true purpose of midrash. The point of midrash is not to pull texts out of context. Rather, a more correct understanding of midrash is that it was to show the continuing relevance of Scripture to contemporary

---

[42] Ibid., 384–85.
[43] D. Instone-Brewer, *Techniques and Assumptions in Jewish Exegesis before 70 CE* (Tübingen: J. C. B. Mohr, 1992), 167.
[44] Ibid., 169.
[45] Snodgrass, "The Old Testament in the New," 42.

life. Even Longenecker recognizes that the purpose of midrash was "to contemporize the revelation of God given earlier for the people of God living later in a different situation."[46] The focus of midrash was on the application of ancient texts in later circumstances.[47] This should not be surprising since the midrashim are homiletic in nature and application is the priority of preaching.

Applicational fulfillment, the third category of Old Testament citation, did indeed use Scripture midrashically in conformity with early protorabbinic methods. This was not an arbitrary (or even creative) form of interpretation that showed no regard for context or original meaning. So, in Matt 2:16–18, Matthew was citing an Old Testament text, deriving a principle found in that text, and showing its relevance to his own day and time. Matthew was *applying* Scripture, not twisting it.

A question might be, why did the New Testament authors not specify what principle they were applying? The answer is that they expected the principle to be so obvious to their readers that it did not require further explication. Moving from exegesis to biblical principle to contemporary application is so intuitive that the writers expected their readers to discern the bridging principle even as they read it.

Contemporary readers of Scripture apply God's Word in much the same way, moving from an exegetical idea to contemporary relevance without explaining the process but still doing so accurately. For example, a number of years ago, my family faced a serious medical problem. To encourage me, many of my friends would assure me that all would be fine because "we had the best doctors and the best hospital." I would always respond with Ps 20:7: "Some trust in chariots and some in horses, but we trust in the Name of the Lord our God" (NIV). I never explained that this text actually was not about how to face a medical emergency but what Israel's attitude should have been when going to war. Nor did I say the principle of this text is that we are not to trust in human might but in God's protective care. And I did not state that although we may have excellent medical care, the application for me was that we were to trust God in dealing with serious illness, not physicians or hospitals. I did not explain all this because

---

[46] Longenecker, "'Who Is the Prophet Talking About?' Some Reflections on the New Testament's Use of the Old," 381.

[47] Snodgrass, "The Old Testament in the New," 42.

it was intuitive—I expected my hearers to comprehend what I was saying without explication, and they did.

The reason for Matthew's citation of Jer 31:15 was to show that Scripture had a continuing relevance. As David L. Cooper wrote, "Matthew simply applies the language of this prophecy to a similar situation of his day."[48] Just as Rachel represented Jewish mothers who wept at the death and exile of their sons, so Jewish mothers once again mourned when wicked Herod murdered their children. And Rachel has continued to lament and has refused to be consoled for her children as they have been murdered by Crusaders, Nazis, and terrorists. Sadly, this is a Scripture that has had continuing relevance for centuries.

To summarize, the third category of New Testament citation of the Old is applicational fulfillment. It uses the text in a way that protorabbinic writers did before AD 70, seeking to apply ancient biblical texts to their contemporary situation. Applicational fulfillment recognizes that ancient texts have continuing relevance. By quoting these texts, the writers understood a principle in a biblical passage and then applied it to their contemporary situation.[49] Thus, Matthew recognized that Jeremiah wrote of the suffering of Rachel, the personification of Jewish mothers, at the exile. He, in turn, applied the principle that the Jewish mothers of Bethlehem still wept because of the suffering of their children at the hands of wicked Herod.

Summary Fulfillment: Matthew 2:19–23

The fourth prophecy and fulfillment motif in Matthew 2 is summary fulfillment.[50] The Matthew narrative relates the events for the Messiah's family after the death of Herod. The Lord appeared to Joseph in a dream and told him it was safe to return Mary and the toddler Jesus to the land of Israel. However, when Joseph found Archelaus ruling over Judea, he was afraid to return there[51] and instead went to his hometown of Nazareth.[52] According to Matthew, this was "to

---

[48] Cooper, *Messiah: His Historical Appearance*, 177.

[49] Some other examples of applicational fulfillment in Matthew are 4:6/Ps 91:11–12; 13:14–15/Isa 6:9–10; 13:35/Ps 78:2; 15:8–9/Isa 29:13.

[50] This is what Cooper calls "literal prophecy plus a summation." *Messiah: His Historical Appearance*, 175. See my chap. 2, n. 84.

[51] The text implies but leaves unstated what is known from Josephus—that Herod Archelaus was brutal in his treatment of his subjects, including the murder of 3,000 Judeans celebrating Passover upon the ascension to the throne (*Antiquities* 17.342).

[52] Although Matthew fails to mention that this was Joseph's home town.

fulfill what was spoken through the prophets, that He will be called a Nazarene" (2:23).[53]

Of course, the long recognized difficulty with Matthew's fulfillment formula here is that in no place does the Hebrew Bible predict that "He shall be called a Nazarene." As a result, a number of possible explanations have been proposed.

The most popular is to take Matthew's citation as a play on words derived from the Hebrew word *neṣer* used of the "branch" in Isa 11:1. There it speaks of Messiah, the Branch, who will spring forth from the obscurity of Jesse's household.[54] The difficulty with this view is that the word play is entirely absent in Greek, the language of Matthew's gospel and makes no sense of the fulfillment.

A second option has been to view Jesus as a "Nazarite."[55] Some even cite the phrase "The boy will be a Nazarite" (Judg 13:7) in support of this interpretation. However, the word Nazarite (*nāzîr*) has an entirely different root and spelling from Nazareth (*nṣrt*) in Hebrew and is in no way related to being a Nazarene. Moreover, the verse in Judges is a prediction of the birth of Samson, not the Messiah. Above all, Jesus was not a Nazarite, nor does an upbringing in Nazareth connect Him to the Hebrew word for Nazarite.

The best interpretation is to view this as a summary fulfillment, meaning that the phrase "He shall be called a Nazarene" summarizes a teaching from the prophets about the Messiah.[56] This is supported from within the text because here alone Matthew states that this fulfills the words of the "prophets" (plural), referring to many prophecies,

---

[53] Against almost all other translations, the HCSB translates this correctly, taking the Greek word ὅτι not as introducing a direct quotation but rather an indirect statement. As R. T. France explains (*The Gospel of Matthew*, 91), "The quotation-formula [in 2:23] differs from all Matthew's other formulae in two respects: instead of a single prophet (named or anonymous) he speaks here of 'the prophets,' and the participle *legontos* ('who said') which leads into all the other quotations is missing; in its place is *hoti* ('that'), which sometimes functions as the equivalent of our quotation marks, but can also indicate not so much a direct quotation as a paraphrase or summary of what was said. These two distinctive features together suggest strongly that what Matthew is here providing is not a quotation of a specific passage but rather a theme of prophecy (as in 26:56, where again plural 'prophets' are mentioned and no particular passage is cited)."

[54] According to France, this is the view "mentioned in most commentaries." *The Gospel of Matthew*, 92n10.

[55] Multiple authors have adopted this interpretation, including McNeile, Schaeder, Schweizer, Sanders, Zuckschwerdt, Soares, Prabhu, Brown, and Allan. See Davies and Allison for citations (*Matthew*, 1:276).

[56] This view is ably supported by both France, *The Gospel of Matthew*, 94–95, and Carson, "Matthew," 8:97.

not just an individual one. Moreover, the conjunction *hoti* which indicates an indirect statement shows that Matthew was not referring
to a specific quotation but a general idea—a paraphrase of Matt 2:23
would be that Jesus grew up in Nazareth "to fulfill the general teaching of the prophets that the Messiah would be a Nazarene."

Matthew is not unique in using this sort of citation to summarize a
biblical lesson. For example there is an Old Testament example of just
such a citation. Ezra 9:10–12 states,

> Now, our God, what can we say in light of this? For we have abandoned the
> commands You gave through Your servants the prophets, saying: "The land
> you are entering to possess is an impure land. The surrounding peoples have
> filled it from end to end with their uncleanness by their impurity and detest-
> able practices. So do not give your daughters to their sons in marriage or take
> their daughters for your sons. Never seek their peace or prosperity, so that
> you will be strong, eat the good things of the land, and leave it as an inheri-
> tance to your sons forever."

Ezra's quotation cannot be found anywhere in the Hebrew Bible. Rather, he was summarizing the teachings found in Deut 11:8–9, Isa 1:19
and Ezek 37:25.[57]

But what theme is Matthew summarizing by calling Jesus a Nazarene? He is using "Nazarene" as a term of derision and is summarizing
the Old Testament teaching that the Messiah was to be despised. That
"Nazarene" was itself a disparaging term in the first century is evident
from Nathanael's reaction to hearing of a Messiah from Nazareth, ob-
jecting "Can anything good come out of Nazareth?" (see also John
7:41–42,52). Moreover, in the only other place Matthew uses "Nazarene," it is used in a derogatory way (Matt 26:71).[58] Thus, according to Matthew, the prophets taught that Messiah would be despised.
Moreover, Matthew maintained that the negative reaction to Messiah's
coming from the poor, despised village of Nazareth would epitomize
the derisive attitude of Israel to her King.

Although Judaism tended to emphasize the glorious Messiah, the
Hebrew Bible repeatedly presents the Messiah as a despised figure. For
example, see the psalms of the rejected and suffering Messiah (Pss 22
and 69). Zechariah speaks of Israel esteeming her future messianic king

---

[57] Davies and Allison (*The Gospel of Matthew*, 1:275) suggest that there is a rabbinic example
of a summary quotation in *b. Ketub.* 111a, but I cannot identify it in my reading of that text.

[58] France adds that the phrase "He shall be called" is referring specifically to "derogatory
name calling." *The Gospel of Matthew*, 94.

with the value of a dead slave (Zech 11:4–14 referring to Exod 21:32). Isaiah predicts most clearly that the Messiah would be "One who is despised" and "abhorred by people" (49:7), that He would suffer "scorn and spitting" (50:6), that He would arise from obscurity "like a root out of dry ground" (53:2), and that He would be "despised and rejected by men" (53:3). Thus, Matthew, using summary fulfillment, encapsulates all that the prophets wrote of the Messiah being despised and scorned with the terse phrase "He shall be called a Nazarene."[59]

Conclusion

S. L. Johnson, Jr. has asked,

> Can we reproduce the exegesis of the New Testament? Unhesitatingly, the reply is yes, although we are not allowed to claim for our results the infallibility of the Lord and His apostles. They are reliable teachers of biblical doctrine and they are reliable teachers of hermeneutics and exegesis. We not only *can* reproduce their exegetical methodology, we *must* if we are to be taught their understanding of Holy Scripture. Their principles, probably taught them by the Lord in His post-resurrection ministry, are not abstruse and difficult. They are simple, plain, and logical. The things they find in the Old Testament are really there.[60]

Johnson has answered his question correctly. The point of this chapter has been to show that the New Testament writers did not interpret the Hebrew Bible in a creative, atomistic, or noncontextual way. Rather, their hermeneutics were contextual and reflective of the intent of the Old Testament passages. Although New Testament authors commonly cited direct fulfillments of Old Testament messianic prophecies, they also noted typical, applicational, and summary fulfillments (see chap. 2, n. 84). Too often it is present-day interpreters that fail to see the true meaning of Old Testament texts by limiting themselves to their historical rather than their literary sense. Therefore, it is contemporary readers that need to adjust their lenses to see the Hebrew Bible as the New Testament authors did, as a messianic book written with a messianic intention.

---

[59] Some might object that summary fulfillment is unique to Matt 2:23 so it should not even be considered a category of prophetic fulfillment. This is not the case. Although rare, it is also found in Matt 26:56, Acts 3:18–24, and Rom 1:2.

[60] Johnson, *The Old Testament in the New: An Argument for Biblical Inspiration*, 93–94. Italics his.

Chapter 8

RASHI'S INFLUENCE ON THE INTERPRETATION OF MESSIANIC PROPHECY

If messianic hope is so evident using a literary reading of the Hebrew Bible, why is it that so many contemporary exegetes fail to recognize it? Assuming the good will and strong exegetical ability of biblical scholars, particularly among those from the world of evangelical biblical studies, it is surprising that so many prefer a historical reading of Old Testament texts rather than an eschatological, messianic interpretation. Luke records that the Messiah Jesus saw Himself in the text of the Hebrew Bible (Luke 24:25–27,44–46). Therefore, it is especially unexpected that so many who accept the authority of the New Testament and the deity of Jesus view Old Testament texts as having their fulfillments in historical figures rather than the future Messiah. Old Testament scholar Louis Goldberg noted this trend of interpretation and lamented that contemporary evangelical scholarship had begun to deny "any messianic message in key passages, i.e., Psalm 22, Isaiah 7:14, as well as others."[1] Moreover, he bemoans that such approaches find all fulfillments "at the time of writing" rather than being considered predictions of the Messiah.[2] As such, Goldberg is shocked that these evangelical Old Testament scholars agree more readily with Jewish anti-Christian polemicists than with the Messiah Jesus' own explanation of the Old Testament.[3]

Other evangelical scholars, in an attempt to remain faithful to the words of Jesus and to the historical interpretation of the Old Testament, have adopted alternative interpretations: *sensus plenior* (dual fulfillment), typical fulfillment, and midrashic fulfillment. These methods enable them to maintain a historical interpretation, with a fulfillment in an event or person at the time of writing and a future fulfillment by Jesus, and still claim fidelity to the words of Jesus. Why does contemporary evangelical scholarship focus so exclusively on historical

---

[1] L. Goldberg, "Another Voice by an Anti-Missionary and a Seeming Evangelical Concurrence" (paper presented at the Lausanne Consultation for Jewish Evangelism, March 1998), 30–31.

[2] Ibid., 31.

[3] Ibid., 32. Goldberg raises the problem but offers no explanation for this trend.

fulfillment and find messianic fulfillment perhaps only in secondary meanings, if at all, rather than direct prediction and fulfillment?

Perhaps one answer to this question can be found in the work and influence of the great Jewish biblical commentator, Rabbi Shlomo Yitzkhaki (1040–1105), most commonly known by his acronym, Rashi. His interpretive methods, along with the approaches of the medieval Jewish commentators whom he influenced, ultimately found their way into Christian commentaries. Is it possible that Rashi's more historical approach ultimately affected the way Christians interpret messianic prophecy? That is the question that will be examined in this chapter.

Rashi's Life

Rashi was born in Troyes, France, east of Paris, near the German border.[4] Little is known of his childhood, resulting in a stream of legends about his early life. His studies began in Worms and continued in Mainz. Thereafter, he returned to Troyes and established a rabbinical academy. Although only 21 years old, he was appointed the rabbinical judge of the community. His school was so highly regarded that Jewish students gathered there from all over Europe to study under this master of Scripture and Talmud. Although serving as a rabbi, teacher, and a judge, Rashi earned his living as a vintner.

Rashi's two greatest accomplishments were his commentaries on the Talmud and on the Hebrew Bible. His Talmud commentary, completed by his grandson, Samuel ben Meir, became the standard of interpretation of this esoteric work of Jewish law. As a result, Rashi's commentary is always published alongside the actual text of the Talmud. In similar fashion, his biblical commentary seems more like an annotated Bible than a commentary. Eschewing lengthy philosophical or theological comments, Rashi focused on elucidating the meaning of the biblical text. Merely by clarifying the meaning of a word or explaining the context or syntax of a text, Rashi brought clarity to the reader. Much like modern study Bibles, Rashi's commentary became the indispensable guide for Jewish people seeking meaning from the Scriptures.

---

[4] The summary of Rashi's life in this section is derived from the entry "Rashi" in G. Wigoder, *Dictionary of Jewish Biography* (New York: Simon and Schuster, 1991), 409–10.

During Rashi's lifetime, there were drastic changes for Jewish people. For the first part of his life, Jews in France enjoyed autonomy in all religious affairs. The Jews of Troyes enjoyed good relations with the crown and with their Christian neighbors. Granted much economic freedom, the Jews of Troyes worked as merchants and traders, serving both the Jewish and Christian communities. Jews also worked in skilled labor, engaging in metalworking, gold- and silversmithing, glasswork, coinstamping, and winemaking—even providing wine for the churches' use in the Mass. As a general rule, the Gentile populace got along well with their Jewish neighbors.[5]

This changed radically in 1096 with the onslaught of the First Crusade. Although Troyes, France, itself was spared from the violence that many European Jewish communities experienced, the not-too-distant Rhine Valley Jewish communities were destroyed by the attacks of the Crusaders. Seeking to kill infidels in the Holy Land, the Crusaders also slaughtered the Jewish people in their path.[6] Although Rashi produced the bulk of his works during the earlier time of stability, the parts of his commentaries written during and after the First Crusade were certainly influenced by those terrible times.[7]

Another significant aspect of Rashi's life and times was that he was born into a polemical era. Even before the Crusades had brought so much suffering to European Jews, public religious disputations between Christians and Jews had become quite common. The focus of these disputations was always the Bible and the question most commonly addressed was, Is Jesus of Nazareth the promised Messiah of the Old Testament? Christian disputants frequently offered allegorical defenses of their interpretations, while Jewish polemicists often presented more literal and historical interpretations to defend their understanding of the biblical text.[8] These disputations, along with the First Crusade, certainly affected Rashi's understanding of messianic texts. Plainly, the conditions of Rashi's life and times caused him to develop a biblical hermeneutic that would greatly influence both Jews and Christians.

---

[5] E. Shereshevsky, *Rashi: The Man and His World* (Northvale, NJ: Aronson, 1996), 60–61; H. Hailperin, *Rashi and the Christian Scholars* (Pittsburgh: University of Pittsburgh Press, 1963), 15–28.

[6] R. Chazan, *In the Year 1096* (Philadelphia: Jewish Publication Society, 1996).

[7] Ibid., 108.

[8] Shereshevsky, *Rashi: The Man and His World*, 61–62.

Rashi's Methods

Classical Jewish interpretation of the Bible has been characterized by four methods, summarized by the acronym PaRDeS, spelled with the four Hebrew consonants פ, ר, ד, ס (*P, R, D, S*). They stand for *Peshat* (meaning "simple" and referring to the plain meaning of the text), *Remez* (meaning "hint" and referring to an allusion to another teaching in a secondary biblical text), *Derash* (meaning "search" and referring to the homiletical interpretation of the text in terms of relevance and application), and *Sod* (meaning "secret" and referring to mystical interpretation). Thus, the four basic Jewish interpretive methods were plain, allusion, homiletical, and mystical.[9] According to the Talmud, peshat is the most foundational, expressed by the dictum, "A verse cannot depart from its plain meaning (peshat)."[10]

Early rabbinic literature emphasized derash (homiletical), while medieval mystics favored sod (mystical). Medieval Jewish philosophers made use of remez (allusion), but the preferred method of medieval rabbinical interpreters of Scripture was peshat (simple). Rashi was the interpreter who more than any other influenced later medieval Jewish interpreters to emphasize this method.

The first interpreter to accentuate peshat was Saadia Gaon (880–942). He did so in response to a group within Judaism known as the Karaites (literally, Scripturalists). The Karaite movement rejected rabbinic tradition and law and instead focused on the Scriptures alone as the source of conduct for Jewish people. Saadia's purpose was to defend rabbinic tradition; therefore, he did it using the Scriptures, the Karaite source of authority. His emphasis on the peshat interpretation resulted from the grave threat of the Karaites against traditional Judaism. Thus, in the words of Erwin I. J. Rosenthal, Saadia's "close atten-

---

[9] *Encyclopædia Britannica Online*, s.v. "Peshat," http://www.britannica.com/ EBchecked/ topic/453371/peshat (accessed Nov. 20, 2009). See also C. Pearl, *Rashi* (New York: Grove Press, 1988), 25–26. Pearl gives a clear illustration of the use of all four methods in the interpretation of Gen 18:5. According to the peshat, Abraham gave refreshment to his three visitors. According to the remez, the verse teaches that although a guest may be invited to lead grace after meals, the master of the house must offer the blessing over the bread at the start of a meal as seen in the phrase "I will fetch a morsel of bread." According to the derash, it is observed that Abraham only promised a morsel, yet he actually provided a feast. Hence, the homiletical lesson is that "good people try to do more than they promise." Finally, according to the sod, Abraham's promise of bread mystically refers to the teaching of the Torah, the true staff of life. Hence, Abraham offered spiritual refreshment.

[10] *b. Sabb.* 63a.

tion to, and concentration on, the plain meaning of Scripture" was a result of his using "the weapons of his opponents."[11]

Saadia also used the plain meaning of the Bible in response to the rationalist philosophers of Islam. In his attempt to explain humanity's sources of knowledge, Saadia included the Bible as divine revelation. As a result, he "clearly defined when and where a departure from the literal meaning was justified, or required."[12]

Nevertheless, it was not Saadia who revolutionized Jewish interpretation, but Rashi, born some 100 years after the death of Saadia.[13] The circumstances of Rashi's times led him to make the most substantive use and to adjust ever so slightly the meaning of peshat. Rashi lived in an era of religious disputations between Christians and Jews, which included both public debates and written pamphlets designed to convince Jewish people of the messiahship of Jesus based on messianic prophecy. Therefore, Rashi initiated the attempt to rebut Christian interpretation of messianic passages through the use of peshat.[14] Thus, Rashi's commentaries reflect his desire to counter Christianity. Rosenthal states, "Many a comment on a passage in the Pentateuch, in Isaiah, Jeremiah, Ezekiel or the Psalms is concluded with the statement that his interpretation is according to the plain sense and serves as 'an answer to the Christians.'"[15]

But Rashi's use of peshat took on an additional nuance. In order to refute Christian claims, Rashi made a significant shift in the meaning of peshat: he equated the simple meaning of the text with the historical interpretation. This means that Rashi would often rebut the Christian claim that a given verse was messianic and referred to Jesus by countering that it referred "to a biblical historical person or event."[16] Hence, Rashi no longer understood the peshat as the *plain* sense of the text but the *historical* sense. Moreover, Rashi frequently argued for the historical sense of a passage even if this meant that "he had to depart from traditional exposition."[17]

---

[11] E. I. J. Rosenthal, "The Study of the Bible in Medieval Judaism," in *The Cambridge History of the Bible*, ed. G. H. Lampe (Cambridge: Cambridge University Press, 1969), 2:257.

[12] Ibid.

[13] As Rosenthal says, "By far the greatest and most enduring impact was made by Rashi . . . who commented on almost the entire Hebrew Bible." Ibid., 261.

[14] Ibid., 264.

[15] Ibid., 262.

[16] Ibid., 263.

[17] Ibid., 262.

Rashi's changes were important because most previous Jewish interpreters had accepted the traditional messianic interpretations found in the midrash collections as reflecting the peshat of those biblical passages. In fact, the line between peshat and derash had indeed become blurred.[18] Therefore, Rashi, in rejecting traditional interpretations, was not necessarily, as is sometimes maintained, departing from an allegorical messianic interpretation and instead adopting a literal one. Rather, he was departing from the literary and messianic interpretation to a historical understanding.

Besides defending Judaism from Christian attempts at conversion of the Jewish people, Rashi had a secondary purpose in his methods, namely to give courage to Jewish people, who were seriously suffering during the Crusades. Rashi sought to bring encouragement by citing some traditional messianic passages and interpreting them as the future hope of the Jewish people.[19] Thus, some of Rashi's interpretations are quite messianic while others are historical. The deciding factor was whether a particular messianic passage could be understood to refer to the first coming of Jesus or to Jesus' deity. If this was an issue, then Rashi would commonly interpret those texts as referring to a historical figure. However, if the passage fit the traditional Jewish conception of the Messiah or referred to what Christians perceived as the Second Coming, Rashi would maintain the messianic interpretation.

Rashi was unique as an interpreter. He became beloved and revered for his unique ability to combine traditional derash with innovative peshat. Moreover, he wrote for the common person, making the Bible accessible to the entire Jewish community. Beyond making the Scriptures understandable, Rashi included an occasional application or homily, showing a pastoral concern for his readers.[20] But as will be evident, Rashi's greatest impact would be to transform both Jewish and Christian interpretation of the Bible, particularly in the realm of messianic prophecy.

---

[18] Rosenthal (ibid., 260–61) demonstrates that in many cases the Midrash was understood to present the *peshat* meaning of a biblical text.

[19] E. I. J. Rosenthal, "Medieval Jewish Exegesis: Its Character and Significance," *JSS* 9 (1964): 265.

[20] Rosenthal, "The Study of the Bible in Medieval Judaism," 262.

Rashi's Influence on Jewish Interpretation

Rashi's innovative approach to the Bible exercised a profound influence in the world of Jewish biblical scholarship. Those who followed Rashi's view of peshat as referring to the historical sense include his grandson, Samuel ben Meir (also known as Rashbam, 1085–1174), Joseph Bekhor Shor (twelfth century), David Kimchi (also known as Radak, 1160–1235), Abraham ibn Ezra (1089–1164), and Don Isaac Abravanel (1437–1509). Building upon Rashi's work, these scholars also used the historical sense to combat Christological interpretation and even emphasized this approach more than Rashi. As Rosenthal writes, "The medieval commentators link the *peshat* with the 'answer' (or rejoinder) to the Christians and thus establish a clear connection between the literal method and anti-Christian polemic."[21] Moreover, they linked the literal with the historical interpretation.[22]

For example, Rashbam, writing so that the Jewish people might remain loyal to Judaism,[23] also used peshat far more extensively than even his grandfather Rashi and considered his own emphasis to be superior to his esteemed teacher.[24] Rashbam maintained that he had debated with Rashi and that his grandfather had admitted that "if he had the opportunity he would compose different commentaries according to the new *peshat* interpretations coming to light every day."[25]

Joseph Bekhor Shor, also adopted peshat as historical sense and did so with even more gusto than Rashbam. Bekhor Shor held to a rationalistic interpretation of Scripture, emphasizing the historical referent even more than both Rashi and Rashbam.[26] He criticized the Christian understanding of virtually every messianic passage in the Hebrew Bible and even disputed the specific interpretations of Jerome. Generally, he found the referent for these passages in the history of Israel rather than in an eschatological Messiah.[27]

The polemical nature of David Kimchi's commentaries is evident in his repetitive use of phrases such as "If somebody were to object, you

---

[21] E. I. J. Rosenthal, "Anti-Christian Polemic in Medieval Bible Commentaries," *JJS* 11 (1960): 119.

[22] Ibid., 116–17.

[23] Rosenthal, "The Study of the Bible in Medieval Judaism," 266.

[24] E. L. Greenstein, "Medieval Bible Commentaries," in *Back to the Sources*, ed. B. W. Holtz (New York: Simon and Schuster, 1984), 243.

[25] Rashbam, cited by E. L. Greenstein, "Medieval Bible Commentaries," 243.

[26] Greenstein, "Medieval Bible Commentaries," 246.

[27] Rosenthal, "The Study of the Bible in Medieval Judaism," 265–66.

must answer . . ." or "The Christians interpret this psalm [as refer-ring] to Jesus but you must answer them. . . ."[28] And when interpret-ing the Psalms, Kimchi repeatedly insists that they must refer not to the Messiah but to the historical figure of David.[29]

Abraham ibn Ezra was a Spanish scholar who insisted on using pe-shat to interpret the Torah. In his commentary on the Torah, ibn Ezra argues that Christian commentators find "riddles and allegories," a method that yields vanity and hot air. Rather he maintains that the Torah must be understood according to the peshat.[30]

Don Isaac Abravanel also insisted that the peshat of the Hebrew Bible be used to combat Christian interpretation of the messianic pas-sages. He compiled a special book on messianic passages to refute the Christian claim that Jesus was the Messiah. As with the other medi-eval Jewish commentators, he linked the peshat to historical rather than literary interpretation.[31]

This examination of Rashi's influence on medieval Jewish interpre-tation reveals that just as he sought to refute a Christological inter-pretation of the Hebrew Bible by appealing to the peshat, so did the Jewish commentators who followed him. Additionally, they appropri-ated Rashi's reformulation of peshat as containing the historical mean-ing rather than the literary. These biblical interpreters even surpassed Rashi in abandoning previously maintained midrashic interpretation of the Hebrew Scriptures. Nevertheless, Rashi's influence was not limited to Jewish interpreters. Most importantly, his ideas and influence also found their way into the Christian interpretation of the Hebrew Bible.

Rashi's Influence on Christian Interpretation

It was not only Jewish interpreters that adopted Rashi's method of interpretation. First, Roman Catholic, and then Protestant interpret-ers also found his method useful for understanding Scripture. Rashi's influence on Catholicism is first seen among the Victorines, beginning with Hugo of St. Victor (d. 1141) and then his disciple, Andrew of St. Victor (d. 1175).[32] Rashi was so influential with Andrew that he even

---

[28] Rosenthal, "Anti-Christian Polemic in Medieval Bible Commentaries," 120.

[29] Rosenthal, "The Study of the Bible in Medieval Judaism," 271.

[30] Rosenthal, "Anti-Christian Polemic in Medieval Bible Commentaries," 118–19.

[31] Rosenthal, "The Study of the Bible in Medieval Judaism," 273.

[32] Hugo's and Andrew's reliance on Rashi has been ably documented by H. Hailperin, *Rashi and the Christian Scholars* (Pittsburgh: University of Pittsburgh Press, 1963), 105–11.

adopted his nonmessianic interpretations of classical messianic passages frequently used by Christians as prooftexts for the messiahship
of Jesus. For example, when faced with Rashi's historical interpretation of Isa 7:14 as referring to a young woman in the days of Isaiah,
Andrew could not respond. For Andrew, the "literal interpretation"
was Rashi's historical sense.[33]

In the same vein, Andrew followed Rashi's lead in his interpretation
of the fourth Servant Song, the famous fifty-third chapter of Isaiah.
Rather than interpreting it as referring to the messianic Suffering Servant (i.e., Jesus), Andrew, dependent on Rashi, explained the servant
historically as referring to collective Israel, suffering at the time of
the Babylonian captivity.[34] So historical and non-Christological are
Andrew's interpretations that upon review Beryl Smalley exclaims,
"Reading Andrew, one sometimes has to rub one's eyes! It is extraordinary to think that this was written at St. Victor, by a pupil of Hugo,
that he was begged to continue his work, begged to resume his ab-
bacy, and finally buried 'with great honor.' The twelfth century is full
of surprises."[35]

Certainly the most significant Catholic interpreter to rely on Rashi
was Nicholas de Lyra (1270–1349). One of the most prolific Catholic
commentators, he is known for his *Postilla litteralis super totam Bib-
liam* (i.e., *Literal Notes over the Whole Bible*). The purpose of the work
is explained by Nicholas: "In like manner, I intend, for making clear
the literal sense, to introduce not only the statements of the Catholic
doctors, but also of the Hebrews, especially of Rabbi Salomon, who
among the Hebrew doctors has spoken most reasonably."[36] So extensively did Nicholas rely on Rashi that he became known as "Rashi's
Ape."[37] Christian Hebraist Johannes Reuchlin even sarcastically commented that if Rashi's words would be cut from Nicholas's notes, few
pages would remain.[38]

Although Nicholas was heavily influenced by Rashi's literal method,
when it came to messianic passages, he did object to Rashi's treating
the peshat as referring to a historical personage rather than a messianic

---

[33] B. Smalley, *The Study of the Bible in the Middle Ages* (Oxford: Blackwell, 1952), 163.

[34] Ibid., 164–65.

[35] Ibid., 165–66.

[36] As cited by E. H. Merrill, "Rashi, Nicholas de Lyra, and Christian Exegesis," *WTJ* 38 (1976): 71.

[37] Ibid.

[38] Erwin I. J. Rosenthal, "Rashi and the English Bible," *BJRL* 24 (1940): 139.

figure. Using a literal hermeneutic, Nicholas set out to demonstrate that Jesus was the Messiah through the literal interpretation of messianic prophecy. For example, in demonstrating the messianic interpretation of Psalm 2, he wrote, "Proof, however, is not valid from the mystic sense, but from the literal only . . . one ought to say that the Psalm is understood of Christ *ad litteram* [literally]." Additionally, he wrote, "But no proofs are evidence except out of the literal sense, as was said above. And thus it is evident according to the learned men, converted from Judaism, that that psalm is understood as referring to Christ *ad litteram*."[39]

Following Jewish interpretations earlier than Rashi's, Nicholas sought to demonstrate that the literal sense of various traditional messianic passages proved that they were indeed messianic prophecies. Some key passages that he discussed were Gen 49:10, Num 24:17–19, Psalm 72, Zech 9:9–10, Isa 7:14, 52:13–53:12, and Psalms 2, 45, 110, always making the case for a messianic interpretation.[40] Afterwards, others used Nicholas's commentaries and therefore inadvertently adopted Rashi's views. For example, a well-known jingle about Martin Luther was *Si Lyra non lyrasset, Lutherus non saltasset* ("Had Nicholas not played the lyre, Luther would not have danced"),[41] indicating even Luther's dependence on Nicholas and unconsciously on Rashi.

With the Reformation, scholars became concerned with using the Old Testament in its original language and therefore began to study Hebrew. These Christian Hebraists learned Hebrew and Old Testament from rabbis. Along with the Bible and Hebrew language, they also studied Rashi and the other medieval interpreters.[42] According to Rosenthal, medieval Jewish exegesis "made an important contribution to Christianity by helping to establish that *Hebraica veritas* at which the Reformation aimed in its struggle for the authority of the Word of God."[43]

Yet, the purpose of medieval Jewish exegesis was polemical. Peshat was used as a tool to advance an antimessianic, historical interpretation of messianic texts. Thus, the literal sense of the Scriptures became identified with the historical sense. Hence, when the

---

[39] Hailperin, *Rashi and the Christian Scholars*, 178.
[40] Ibid., 156–84.
[41] A. S. Wood, "Nicholas of Lyra," *EvQ* 33 (1961): 196.
[42] Rosenthal, "The Study of the Bible in Medieval Judaism," 264.
[43] Ibid., 279.

Reformers borrowed literal interpretation from Rashi and other medieval Jewish exegetes, they were not as critical as Nicholas and in effect they embraced antimessianic interpretations designed to combat Christianity.[44]

The adoption of historical interpretation caused a quandary for Protestant Christianity. If the Hebrew Bible found its fulfillment in historical referents, then how did it predict the coming of the Messiah? The issue was, In what sense was the Old Testament messianic if the peshat did not seem to indicate a messianic interpretation?

One way of resolving this dilemma was offered by Peter Cunaeus (1586–1638), who advanced the idea of a Christian *kabbalah*. This was distinct from Jewish mystical kabbalistic teaching. According to Cunaeus, there was a true kabbalah, passed down orally alongside the Scriptures from the Old Testament times and through the New Testament. This kabbalah provided the deeper meanings of Old Testament texts not readily apparent in the peshat interpretations.[45] In effect, it set up a twofold approach to messianic prophecy: First, there was the literal or historical meaning discerned in the peshat, referring to a historical character or event. But there also was the secondary, mysterious messianic meaning, discovered by Christian kabbalah, referring to Christ. This dual approach is evident today in the *sensus plenior* or typical approaches to messianic prophecy. According to these methods, the literal meaning of an Old Testament text finds its fulfillment in an Old Testament character or event. However, the messianic meaning is also present in a secondary fulfillment or a type. This dual interpretive method has led to a minimizing of messianic hope in that it denies that the messianic interpretation is the true peshat of the Old Testament.

Rashi's Effect

The central effect of Rashi and other medieval Jewish interpreters on post-Reformation Christian interpretation was a less messianic understanding of the Old Testament. Rashi and the other medieval Jewish interpreters, arguing from a historical understanding of peshat, advanced a nonmessianic understanding of a number of key messianic

---

[44] J. Sailhamer, *Introduction to Old Testament Theology* (Grand Rapids: Zondervan, 1995), 140–41.

[45] Ibid., 142.

texts. Afterwards, Christian interpreters adopted their views as the true peshat of those passages as well, leading to a demessianized understanding of the Old Testament, as is evident even in contemporary Christian interpretation of the Hebrew Bible. The following are just a few examples of this trend.

Genesis 3:15

Prior to Rashi, Christians understood Gen 3:15, which speaks of a seed of the woman who will crush the head of the serpent, to be the first messianic prophecy of the Old Testament. The midrash had recognized the messianic nature of this text: "Eve had respect to that seed which is coming from another place. And who is this? This is the King Messiah."[46] Moreover, David Kimchi even recognized it as messianic when he wrote, "Messiah, the Son of David, who shall wound Satan, who is the head, the King and Prince of the house of the wicked."[47]

Rashi, however, interpreted Gen 3:15 naturalistically to refer to conflict between snakes and humanity, stating, "You will not stand upright and you will bite him on the heel, and even from there you will kill him."[48] A few centuries later, reformer John Calvin followed Rashi's naturalistic approach, saying, "I interpret this simply to mean that there should always be the hostile strife between the human race and serpents, which is now apparent."[49] Not surprisingly, it is common for evangelical scholars today to understand Gen 3:15 as a conflict between snakes and humanity just as Rashi and Calvin did. For example, John Walton adapts this historical interpretation to mean that there will be perpetual strife between humans and evil. He writes, "The verse is depicting a continual, unresolved conflict between humans and the representatives of evil." Walton continues, "It is therefore haphazard to adopt a messianic interpretation of the text. If we are going to take this text at face value, even on a canonical scale, we must conclude that 3:15 describes only the ongoing struggle between

---

[46] *Gen. Rab.* 23:5

[47] D. Kimchi, cited by D. L. Cooper, *Messiah: His Nature and Person* (Los Angeles: Biblical Research Society, 1933), 28.

[48] Rashi on Gen 3:15, in *Complete Tanach with Rashi*, CD ROM, ed. and trans. A. J. Rosenberg (Brooklyn, NY: Judaica Press, 2007). Subsequent citations of Rashi derive from this same source.

[49] Calvin, *Commentary on the First Book of Moses Called Genesis*, trans. J. King (Grand Rapids: Baker, 2005), 1:167.

evil (represented by the serpent and all representatives of evil that succeed it) and humanity generation through generation."[50]

Psalm 2

Psalm 2 is another example of Rashi's influence on messianic interpretation. The Midrash on Psalms quotes 2:8 ("Ask of Me, and I will give thee the heathen for thine inheritance, and the ends of the earth for thy possession") and then interprets it messianically: "God, speaking to the Messiah, says: If thou dost ask for dominion over the nations, already they are thine inheritance; if for the ends of the earth, already they are thy possession."[51] Plainly, ancient rabbis understood the anointed king of Psalm 2 to be a reference to the Messiah.

As opposed to this interpretation, Rashi understood the text as having a historical referent, writing, "Our Sages [*Ber.* 7b] expounded the passage as referring to the King Messiah, but according to its apparent meaning [the *peshat*], it is proper to interpret it as referring to David himself."[52] Today, it is fairly common for evangelical scholarship to see the Psalms as essentially historical and to follow Rashi's view that Psalm 2 addresses David or the Davidic king. For example, Gerald Wilson states that Psalm 2 is "in its original setting and intent" nothing more than "a psalm regarding the powers and blessing of the human Davidic kings."[53]

Isaiah 9:6

In another case, the Midrash understood Isa 9:6 [Hb. 9:5] to refer to the Messiah. It states, "I have yet to raise up the Messiah, of whom it is written, 'For a child is born to us.'"[54] Although the Midrash does not address the meaning of the Messiah's supernatural throne titles, it does identify the Messiah as the child spoken of in the verse. Nevertheless, Rashi, in an attempt to avoid the apparent deity of the child, understands the titles as follows: "The Holy One, blessed be He, Who

---

[50] J. H. Walton, *Genesis: The NIV Application Commentary* (Grand Rapids: Zondervan, 2001), 226, 235–36. See further my discussion of Gen 3:15 in chap. 9.

[51] *Midr. Tehillim* 2:10, in *The Midrash on Psalms*, trans. W. G. Braude (New Haven: Yale University Press, 1987), 1:41–42.

[52] Rashi on Ps 2:1.

[53] G. H. Wilson, *Psalms*, NIVAC (Grand Rapids: Zondervan, 2002), 108. C. C. Broyles takes a similar view, identifying Psalm 2 as part of the "liturgy at the enthronement of the Davidic king in preexilic times." *Psalms*, NIBC (Peabody, MA: Hendrickson, 2002), 44.

[54] *Deut. Rab.* 1:20.

gives wondrous counsel, is a mighty God and an everlasting Father, called Hezekiah's name, 'the prince of peace.'"[55] To accomplish this interpretation, Rashi must take God as the subject of the third person singular verb "he called," although it is more likely that it is an indefinite personal subject ("one calls").[56] As a result of Rashi's identification of God as the subject of the verb, the divine titles do not describe the Messiah but God Himself, thereby avoiding the Christian idea of a divine Messiah. Additionally, Rashi breaks with the midrashic idea that the verse speaks of the Messiah and rather identifies the child with Hezekiah.

Today, evangelical scholarship has adopted variations of Rashi's historical interpretation. For example, John D. W. Watts writes of John Goldingay, "Goldingay has now resurrected a view held by many Jewish scholars of the medieval period, such as Rashi, that the first three pairs of names refer to God. It is he who names the prince of peace."[57] Watts also denies the messianic nature of Isa 9:6, writing, "The verses do not function as messianic predictions in this context."[58] Goldingay, in his commentary on Isaiah, adapts Rashi's view, taking all four couplets as descriptions of God (i.e., a theophoric name) rather than a description of the child. He writes, "It would be quite natural for this fourfold name in v. 6, too, to be a statement about God—and not a statement about this son." He concludes that the titles should be translated as one long, theophoric name of God: "A wonderful counselor is the Mighty God; the Everlasting Father is a Prince of Peace."[59]

Isaiah 42:1–9

Isaiah 42:1–9 is yet another example of shifting interpretation because of Rashi's influence. This passage, the first of the famous Servant Songs, was recognized as messianic in the ancient *Targum Jonathan*, paraphrasing it as "Behold, my servant, the Messiah, whom

---

[55] Rashi on Isa 9:5.

[56] GKC, 460. That is, the construction is an impersonal passive.

[57] J. D. W. Watts, *Isaiah 1–33*, 2nd ed., WBC (Nashville: Nelson, 2002), 176.

[58] Ibid., 174.

[59] J. Goldingay, *Isaiah*, NIBC (Peabody, MA: Hendrickson, 2001), 71, 73. P. D. Wegner, writing before Goldingay, took a virtually identical view, also identifying the four couplets as a long theophoric name: "a wonderful planner [is] the mighty God; the Father of eternity [is] a prince of peace [or well-being]." "A Re-examination of Isaiah IX 1–6," *VT* 42 (1992): 111–12.

I bring, my chosen one, in whom one delights."[60] The Midrash also understood this text to be speaking of the Messiah. In the Midrash on Psalm 2, it notes the relationship between the people of Israel who are called God's son (Exod 4:22) and the future Messiah, also called God's Son in Psalm 2. Then it lists a number of passages, including Isa 42:1 (also Isa 52:13; Ps 110:1, Dan 7:13–14), and says, "All these goodly promises are in the decree of the King, the King of kings, who will fulfill them for the lord Messiah."[61]

Rashi, however, rejects the messianic interpretation of Isa 42:1 and instead identifies collective Israel as the historical referent. He writes, "Behold My servant Jacob is not like you . . . Israel is called 'My chosen one' (Ps. 135:4) 'For the Eternal chose Jacob for Himself.' Scripture states also (infra 45:4): 'For the sake of My servant Jacob and Israel My chosen one.'" Once again Rashi takes the peshat to be the historical meaning rather than the literary sense. Modern critical scholarship has followed Rashi's historical approach to messianic texts, but so have some contemporary evangelical scholars. For example, Goldingay follows Rashi, stating, "The implication is that 42:1–9 describes Jacob-Israel's role. Jacob-Israel is Yahweh's servant, and this is Yahweh's servant's role."[62] Watts also takes a historical sense for the passage but differs in interpretation by identifying the servant as Cyrus the Great rather than collective Israel. Either way, these historical interpretations follow Rashi's rejection of the messianic interpretation.[63]

Zechariah 6:9–15

Another example of Rashi's influence in changing messianic interpretation is seen in Zech 6:9–15. This passage relates a role-play wherein Joshua the high priest is crowned as a representative of the Messiah, who will unite the offices of priest and king and be named "Branch."

> Take silver and gold, make crowns and place them on the head of Joshua son of Jehozadak, the high priest. You are to tell him: This is what the LORD of Hosts says: Here is a man whose name is Branch; He will branch out from His

---

[60] *Targum Jonathan* 42:1, in *The Chaldee Paraphrase on the Prophet Isaiah*, trans. C. W. H. Pauli (London: London Society's House, 1872), 142.

[61] *Midr. Tehillim* 2:9, in *The Midrash on Psalms*, 1:40–41.

[62] Goldingay, *Isaiah*, 239.

[63] J. D. W. Watts, *Isaiah 34–66*, WBC (Nashville: Nelson, 1987), 119.

place and build the LORD's temple. Yes, He will build the LORD's temple; He will be clothed in splendor and will sit on His throne and rule. There will also be a priest on His throne, and there will be peaceful counsel between the two of them. (Zech 6:11–13)

The word for "crown" in Hebrew is plural and has been alternatively translated as a glorious crown, reflecting the grandeur of it, or as a combined crown, reflecting both royalty and priesthood. In either case, Joshua is viewed as symbolic, enacting a role-play of the future Messiah.[64]

This is the view of the Midrash as well. It asks, "What is the name of the Messiah?" Then, after giving various names from differing Old Testament texts, it says, "His name is 'Branch' as it is stated, 'Behold, a man whose name is Branch, and who shall branch forth from his place, and build the Temple of the Lord' (Zech. 6:12)."[65]

Rashi rejects the messianic interpretation and opts for a historical one, writing concerning the Branch, "He is Zerubbabel, mentioned above (3:8): 'Behold, I bring My servant, the Shoot,' since his greatness burgeoned little by little. Some interpret this as referring to the King Messiah, but the entire context deals with the [time of the] Second Temple."[66] Remarkably, Rashi is arguing that his view reflects the peshat, the simple meaning of the text, although Zerubbabel is nowhere to be found in this text. Thus, according to Rashi, the Branch refers to Zerubbabel, who will build the Second Temple, rather than the Messiah, who, in uniting the priestly and royal offices, will build the eschatological Temple.

Rashi's historical interpretation has become common among those with a high view of Scripture. Rather than identify the Branch as the Messiah, Eugene H. Merrill writes that it is "certain that Zerubbabel in view in the present oracle."[67] Merrill explains the plural "crowns" as one for Joshua and one for Zerubbabel, despite Zerubbabel not even being mentioned in this passage.[68]

To summarize the point of this section, Rashi and other medieval Jewish interpreters, in seeking a polemical tool to combat Christian

---

[64] For a more detailed explanation, see W. C. Kaiser Jr., *The Messiah in the Old Testament* (Grand Rapids: Zondervan, 1995), 213–15.

[65] *Lam. Rab.* 1:16 §51.

[66] Rashi on Zech 6:12.

[67] E. H. Merrill, *An Exegetical Commentary: Haggai, Zechariah, Malachi* (Chicago: Moody Press, 1994), 197.

[68] Ibid., 198.

interpretation of the Old Testament, adjusted the meaning of peshat, changing it from the literal (or literary) sense to the historical sense. They then used the peshat, even if it contradicted the messianic interpretation of earlier rabbinic sages, to combat the messianic interpretation of the Old Testament and the identification of Jesus as the Messiah. With the Reformation, when Christian interpretation of the Bible moved from an allegorical approach to a literal one, even unconsciously Christian interpreters began equating the literal meaning of the Hebrew Bible with the historical sense. As a result, much of contemporary, Christian interpretation uses anti-Christian Jewish polemic to interpret messianic passages of the Hebrew Scriptures.

Conclusion

The point of this discussion of the importance of Rashi and medieval Jewish interpreters has been to show that their anti-Christian polemic has subtly crept into Christian interpretation of the Old Testament. This is a result of Rashi's shift in the use of peshat from the literal/literary meaning to the historical sense. It would be far better to link the peshat of these biblical texts not to the historical sense but to their literary meaning. This will yield a more accurate comprehension of the actual intent of the Old Testament authors and point to the essential messianic meaning of these texts. As Sailhamer states,

> By paying careful attention to the compositional strategies of the biblical books themselves, we believe in them can be found many essential clues to the historical meaning intended by the authors—clues that point beyond their immediate historical referent to a future messianic age. . . . Those clues, we also suggest, point to an essentially messianic and eschatological focus of the biblical texts.[69]

---

[69] Sailhamer, *Introduction to Old Testament Theology*, 154

Chapter 9

AN EXAMPLE FROM THE LAW: INTERPRETING GENESIS 3:15 AS A MESSIANIC PROPHECY

Concerning Gen 3:15, Gerald Sigal, in his polemic against Christianity, rails that "there is absolutely no proof to assume that this verse is messianic," finding a reference to Jesus here to be "exegetically untenable."[1] So I was not surprised when a young Jewish follower of Jesus encountered Sigal's interpretation and asked me to explain the evidence for taking Gen 3:15 as a messianic text. However, I was caught unawares some years later when that same Jewish follower of Jesus went to an evangelical Bible college and reported to me that more than a few of the Bible and theology professors there taught the very same view of Gen 3:15 as Sigal. These professors, all with a high view of Scripture, explained that the serpent in Genesis 3 was a mere snake and did not represent Satan. Moreover, they insisted that the curse on the serpent was only referring to the perpetual hostility that would ensue between snakes and humanity and that the messianic interpretation was founded on allegory and eisegesis. Once again, I was called upon to bolster the faith of this young follower of Jesus.

It seems that the classic understanding of Gen 3:15 as the protoevangelium, or the "first gospel," has eroded dramatically, even among those who hold to inspiration and inerrancy. Is the messianic interpretation really exegetically untenable? Did the author of this text intend it to be read only of the perpetual hatred between snakes and people? The trend in Old Testament interpretation is to answer these questions affirmatively.

The first eight chapters of this book have made the argument that despite contemporary evangelical biblical scholarship's tendency to interpret the Hebrew Bible with a historical sense, the Old Testament should be read as a messianic text, designed by its authors to promote a messianic hope. It seems imperative to test this thesis by examining

---

[1] G. Sigal, *The Jew and the Christian Missionary: A Jewish Response to Missionary Christianity* (New York: KTAV, 1981), 3. As would be expected, Sigal follows Rashi's medieval interpretation of this verse.

texts from within the Hebrew Bible. In this chapter and the two that follow, I will examine one passage per chapter from each of the three main sections of the Hebrew Bible: the Law, the Prophets, and the Writings. Each passage has long been understood as a messianic text. However, because of the trend of contemporary interpretation, each one is now commonly understood as historically fulfilled. I will attempt to show why the particular passage under examination should still be interpreted as a messianic text. The first passage to be considered, Gen 3:15, is from the Pentateuch (the Law or Torah). Here the beginning of the messianic message of the Old Testament is found.

The Context of Genesis 3:14–15

After the creation narrative (Genesis 1–2), the author of the Pentateuch explains the beginning of sin in God's new creation (3:1–19). Opening with the serpent's temptation of Eve (3:1–5), the story then tells of the first couple's sin (3:6–7). Falling prey to the three main areas of temptation—the lust of the flesh ("the woman saw that the tree was good for food"), the lust of the eyes ("delightful to look at"), and the pride of lifestyle ("it was desirable for obtaining wisdom"; cf. 1 John 2:16)—both Eve and Adam eat of the fruit of the tree of the knowledge of good and evil, and sin enters the world.

Next the author relates the consequences of Adam and Eve's sin (3:8–19). First, Adam and Eve seek to flee from God's presence (3:8–10). Then they confess their sin to Him, albeit by blaming others (3:11–13). Adam confesses first, blaming the woman for giving him the fruit (3:11–12); afterwards, Eve confesses, blaming the serpent for deceiving her (3:13); finally, the serpent does not confess as he has no one else to blame. Having heard the confessions, God responds by delivering His curse in reverse order from the previous confessions. First, the Lord addresses the serpent (3:14–15), proclaiming the judgment that will be the focus of this chapter. Then, speaking to the woman, God pronounces the curse of marital discord that she will endure (3:16).[2] Finally, God declares judgment on the man, altering the man's primary focus from his original task of worshiping and obeying (Gen 2:15) to laboring by the sweat of his brow (3:17–19).[3]

---

[2] For an explanation of the curse of discord, see R. C. Ortlund Jr., "Male-Female Equality and Male Headship: Genesis 1–3" in *Recovering Biblical Manhood and Womanhood: A Response to Evangelical Feminism*, ed. J. Piper and W. Grudem (Wheaton, IL: Crossway, 1991), 108–9.

[3] It is commonly understood that Adam was put into the Garden of Eden "to work it and

The curse on the serpent is the focus of this chapter. In Gen 3:14–15 the serpent is first told that he is more cursed than the rest of the animal kingdom. Further, the serpent will be required to crawl on its belly and eat dust. Moreover, the curse also speaks of enmity between the serpent and the woman and between the serpent's seed and the woman's seed, and of crushing blows from the woman's seed upon the serpent and from the serpent upon the woman's seed. Through the years, the meaning of this curse has become the subject of considerable interpretive disagreement.

The Interpretations of Genesis 3:14–15

The Naturalistic View

Interpreters have adopted four basic explanations of the curse on the serpent. The first of these is a *naturalistic* view, seeing the serpent simply as an animal and the woman's seed as collective humanity. In this view, championed by Claus Westermann, the curse is merely an etiology, like one of Rudyard Kipling's *Just So Stories*. It identifies why snakes slither and also why snakes and humanity seem to be in perpetual conflict.[4] Westermann gives two main arguments to

keep it" (ESV). However, it is more likely that the phrase should be translated "to worship and obey" (see U. Cassuto, *A Commentary on the Book of Genesis*, trans. I. Abrahams [Jerusalem: Magnes, 1989], 1:122–23) indicating God's purpose for humanity's placement in the garden was to worship Him. As a result of the curse, man must spend his time working hard, with the sweat of his brow, rather than devoting all his time to worship and obedience (3:17–19). See also J. Sailhamer, "Genesis," *EBC* 1:45.

[4] C. Westermann, *Genesis*, trans. J. J. Scullion, CC (Minneapolis, MN: Fortress, 1994), 258–59. Similar to Westermann, *The NET Bible*, a translation with translation notes done by evangelical scholars, adopted the naturalistic interpretation in its beta text ("they will attack your head, but you will attack their heels"; *The NET Bible*, 1st beta ed. [Richardson, TX: Biblical Studies Press, 2001]), though the current version reads "her offspring will attack your head, and you will attack her offspring's heel" (copyright 2005–2009, http://bible.org/netbible/ [accessed July 12, 2010]). Also, the translation notes categorize the messianic interpretation as "allegorical" and state that "the etiological nature of v. 15 is apparent. . . . Ancient Israelites, who often encountered snakes in their daily activities . . . would find the statement quite meaningful as an explanation for the hostility between snakes and humans." Additionally, an evangelical Old Testament scholar that seems to agree with Westermann is R. B. Chisholm Jr. In two book reviews, Chisholm takes writers to task for espousing a messianic interpretation. He finds it "disappointing" that B. K. Waltke and C. J. Fredericks offer "the traditional interpretation of 3:15 without interacting with approaches that challenge this interpretation as being pure allegory that is unsubstantiated linguistically or contextually." Review of *Genesis: A Commentary*, by B. K. Waltke with C. J. Fredericks, *BSac* 161 (2004): 118. Chisholm also chides C. J. Collins for interpreting Gen 3:15 "as a so-called protoevangelium," maintaining that Collins goes "against the trend of modern scholarship" in defending "the traditional (in the reviewer's

support the naturalistic interpretation. First, he maintains the word *zera'* (seed) must be understood collectively. Hence, the seed of the woman is speaking of a line of the woman's descendants and therefore cannot refer to an individual, messianic descendant. Secondly, according to Westermann, the passage is a pronouncement of judgment and so, according to form criticism, it would not contain a promise of victory and hope in the midst of judgment.[5]

In response to the lexical argument that the word "seed" is limited to a collective sense, this is simply incorrect. The word can also be used with an individual meaning as well. For example, the word "seed" is used of an individual in the very next chapter (4:25) when Eve identified Seth as the particular seed (translated "child") given in place of Abel.[6]

With respect to the form-critical argument about the unlikelihood of a message of hope in the midst of a judgment pronouncement, this fails to consider the context of Genesis. That the God of mercy should offer hope in the midst of judgment is not surprising. In fact, in the early chapters of Genesis, He does this regularly. For example, after judging Cain for murdering his brother, God mercifully "placed a mark on Cain so that whoever found him would not kill him" (Gen 4:15), thereby offering hope in the midst of judgment. Also, when God judged the earth for its ever-escalating sin (Genesis 6–8), He chose to show mercy to the family of Noah, saving them (Gen 6:18) and granting hope in the midst of judgment. Additionally, when God judged Babel and scattered humanity over the earth (Gen 11:1–10), He also chose to call Abram out of Ur of Chaldees and bring him to the promised land (Gen 12:1–9), thereby offering hope in the midst of judgment. Likewise, when God judged the iniquity of Sodom with destruction, He sent angels to rescue Lot and his family (Gen 19:1–29) "because [of] the Lord's compassion for him" (Gen 19:16). In light of the broader context of the book of Genesis, it is to be expected that even in the midst of judgment for the fall of Adam and Eve, God would offer hope of mercy and deliverance.

---

opinion, quasi-allegorical) view." Review of *Genesis 1–4: A Linguistic, Literary, and Theological Commentary* by C. J. Collins, *BSac*, 165 (2008): 372.

[5] Westermann, *Genesis*, 260.

[6] Other examples of the individual usages in Genesis are 15:3; 16:10; 21:13; 22:18; 24:60; 38:8–9.

The Symbolic View

A second interpretation, similar to the naturalistic explanation, is the *symbolic* view. Defended ably by John H. Walton, this view rejects the messianic interpretation as foreign to "the author's intention" and "the audience's understanding."[7] Rather, he maintains that the passage is to be read, at least partially, symbolically. In his words, "The verse is depicting a continual, unresolved conflict between humans and the representatives of evil."[8] This view can be characterized as symbolic because "it would have been evident to the Israelite audience that the serpent represented something evil—if the role of Satan was unknown to them."[9] Thus, according to Walton, the verse is predicting a perpetual struggle, albeit without any hope of victory for humanity (the woman's seed) over the forces of evil (the symbolic seed of the serpent).[10]

Walton supports the symbolic view by maintaining the collective sense of the word "seed," arguing that a particular individual redeemer is not in view in the verse. Second, he maintains that the verb translated "strike" should be read comparably, as equal blows. Thus, both the woman's seed and the serpent's seed "strike" each other, showing that there is no sense of victory of the woman's seed. Moreover, the snake described would have been understood as a poisonously deadly one.[11] Therefore, Walton concludes, "Given the repetition of the verb and the potentially mortal nature of both attacks, it becomes difficult to understand the verse as suggesting an eventual outcome to the struggle."[12]

In response, all that was said previously of the collective sense of "seed" applies to this view as well. As shown above, the word can bear an individual meaning. Moreover, that both the serpent and the woman's seed strike each other with equal death blows does not in any way refute the messianic view.[13] An acceptable messianic view would hold that both blows are deadly—indicating that the Messiah will indeed die and through His death have victory over the serpent.

---

[7] J. H. Walton, *Genesis*, NIVAC (Grand Rapids: Zondervan, 2001), 234.

[8] Ibid., 226.

[9] Ibid., 233.

[10] Ibid., 226.

[11] Ibid.

[12] Ibid.

[13] The traditional messianic view does indeed take the serpent's blow to the heel of the woman's seed as a nonmortal strike, while the seed of the woman's crushing blow to the head is seen as a mortal attack. This is frequently viewed as a sign of the victory of the woman's seed. See W. C. Kaiser Jr., *The Messiah in the Old Testament* (Grand Rapids: Zondervan, 1995), 41.

The *Sensus Plenior* View

The third approach to these verses sees them through the lens of *sensus plenior* or fuller meaning. This interpretation adopts the naturalistic interpretation described above. For example, Gordon Wenham writes, "On the face of it, the saying looks like a mere etiology. It is an explanation of why men try to kill snakes, and why snakes try to bite men." Additionally, Wenham maintains that the author of Genesis only wanted to describe "lifelong mutual hostility between mankind and the serpent race."[14]

Beyond the author's intent, Wenham suggests that there may be a possibility of a secondary, messianic understanding added to these verses based on later revelation—"a *sensus plenior*" as he calls it. Nevertheless, he also warns that "it would be perhaps wrong to suggest that this was the narrator's own understanding."[15]

Of course, all the objections to the naturalistic interpretation raised above apply to this view as well. Additionally, the whole idea of *sensus plenior* is highly questionable. The only meaning in a given text is that which the author intended. To say the Holy Spirit meant something other than what the human author understood contradicts the very idea of biblical inspiration. In fact, the doctrine of inspiration serves to confirm the truth of the human author's words—the Holy Spirit does not contradict their words with alternative or additional meanings.[16]

The Messianic View

The essential *messianic* view is that Gen 3:15 ultimately predicts the coming of a future individual (a "seed") who will have victory over the serpent through His own death.[17] Various suggestions for the messianic significance have been offered through the centuries.[18]

---

[14] G. J. Wenham, *Genesis 1–15*, WBC (Waco, TX: Word Books, 1987), 80.

[15] Ibid., 81. This is also the view of V. P. Hamilton, who writes, "I am most comfortable with LaSor's use of the verse as an illustration of *sensus plenior.*" *The Book of Genesis: Chapters 1–17*, NICOT (Grand Rapids: Eerdmans, 1990), 200.

[16] For an able defense of the single meaning of Scripture, see W. C. Kaiser Jr., "The Single Intent of Scripture," in *Evangelical Roots*, ed. K. Kantzer (Nashville: Thomas Nelson, 1978), 123–41.

[17] The two most recent and responsible presentations of the messianic interpretation are by T. D. Alexander, "Messianic Ideology in Genesis," in *The Lord's Anointed*, ed. P. E. Satterthwaite, R. Hess, and G. Wenham (Grand Rapids: Baker, 1995), 19–32; and J. Hamilton, "The Skull Crushing Seed of the Woman: Inner-Biblical Interpretation of Genesis 3:15," *SBJT* 10 (2006): 30–54.

[18] A messianic interpretation was offered by the LXX, ancient Jewish Targumim (*Pseudo-

Some have proposed that in Gen 3:15 there is an alleged prediction of the virgin birth because of the use of the phrase "her seed."[19] Others have maintained that these verses teach that the seed of the woman would only experience a crippling blow while at the same time administering a deadly blow to the serpent. Both of these approaches read more into the text than is warranted and, as a result, have led many to doubt the messianic interpretation.

A more likely explanation is that the author of the Torah offered a hint of a coming redeemer in Gen 3:15 and then used the rest of the Pentateuch to identify Him as the future Messiah. Later Old Testament writers also recognized the seed as the future deliverer and referred to Gen 3:15 as a messianic text. It is this innerbiblical approach that I will take to defend the messianic interpretation of Gen 3:15.

The Innerbiblical Exposition of Genesis 3:14–15

The messianic view as espoused here posits that Gen 3:15 teaches that the seed of the woman, although being struck, will also strike the serpent and his seed and thereby win victory for humanity. This text is just the beginning of the story. As John Sailhamer says, "More is at stake in this brief passage than the reader is at first aware. A program is set forth. A plot is established that will take the author far beyond this or that snake and his 'seed.'"[20]

Preliminary Considerations

Before examining the innerbiblical evidence supporting a messianic interpretation of Gen 3:14–15, some preliminary considerations must be established as a foundation for reading it messianically. First, *the messianic interpretation fits the broader context of Genesis.* As shown above, salvation in the midst of judgment is a common theme in the early chapters of Genesis. Just as God provided hope in the midst of punishment for Cain after murdering Abel by giving him a mark to protect him (Gen 4:15), so the Lord spared Noah and his family when He judged the world (Gen 6:18). Additionally, the judgment

---

Jonathan, *Neofiti, Onqelos*) and the church fathers Justin and Irenaeus. For a more detailed recounting of this history of interpretation, see Alexander, "Messianic Ideology in Genesis," 27–29.

[19] This is unlikely since Ishmael and his descendants are called Hagar's seed (Gen 16:10) and no one would contend that Ishmael was virgin born.

[20] J. H. Sailhamer, *The Pentateuch as Narrative* (Grand Rapids: Zondervan, 1992), 107.

of the city of Babel (Gen 11:1–10) was followed by the call of Abram (Gen 12:1–9), once again offering hope despite judgment. So it is to be expected that in the Bible's first pronouncement of judgment, God would offer the hope of salvation in the midst of judgment.

A second foundational element is that *the serpent must be identified as something other than just a mere snake.* It appears to be, in the words of C. John Collins, "the mouthpiece of a Dark Power, whom later texts would call Satan."[21] A number of factors lead to this observation. For example, snakes cannot talk, even in Genesis. The genre of this text is not ancient myth with talking animals or a fairy tale like *The Chronicles of Narnia.* Rather, it is a realistic biblical narrative that expects its readers to accept the facts of the story.

There is additional evidence that this text is describing more than a mere serpent but an animal that is animated by an evil force. A snake, as part of the creation, is not inherently evil but part of what the text calls "very good" (Gen 1:31). Furthermore, a mere serpent from the good creation, apart from an evil force animating it, would have no reason to challenge God's words or tempt humanity. Additionally, it is not the serpent's seed that will be crushed by the woman's seed after a long conflict but the serpent itself, indicating a longevity not normal for mere snakes.[22]

Significantly, later biblical writers identified Satan with the serpent of Genesis (Rom 16:20; Rev 12:9). Sailhamer writes, "Such a reading of this passage does not lie outside the narrative implications of the verse. . . . It is unlikely that at such a pivotal point in the narrative the author would intend no more than a mere reference to snakes and their offspring and the fear of them and their offspring and the fear of them among humankind."[23] Although in Gen 3:14 the Lord addresses the actual serpent, in the following verse (3:15), He appears to address the

---

[21] C. J. Collins, *Genesis 1–4: A Linguistic, Literary, and Theological Commentary* (Phillipsburg, NJ: P&R, 2006), 156.

[22] Critical scholar J. Skinner recognizes this: "The serpent, therefore, belongs to the category of 'beasts of the field,' and is a creature of Yahwe. And an effort seems to be made to maintain this view throughout the narrative (v. 14). At the same time, it is a being possessing supernatural knowledge, with the power of speech, and animated by hostility towards God." Skinner concludes that "behind the sober description of the serpent as a mere creature of Yahwe, there was an earlier form of the legend in which he figured as a god or a demon." While admitting the textual issue at hand, Skinner offers an unwarranted, critical, antisupernatural, and mythological explanation. See J. Skinner, *A Critical and Exegetical Commentary on Genesis,* ICC (Edinburgh: T&T Clark, 1994), 71–72.

[23] Sailhamer, *The Pentateuch as Narrative,* 107.

dark power animating it. I believe this is similar to the way the king of Tyre is addressed in Ezek 28:1–10 followed by an oracle against Lucifer, the anointed cherub, as the power behind the throne (cf. Ezek 28:11–19), yet with no textual indication of a change of addressee.

The point is that when the original readers considered Genesis 3, they would have recognized that its author wrote of more than a mere serpent. As such, they would have expected not a long conflict between snakes and humanity, but a battle between a terrible dark force and a divinely powered deliverer.

Yet a third preliminary consideration is that *ancient Jewish interpreters also explained Gen 3:15 messianically.* For example, the problem of identifying the serpent was resolved in Jewish theology "by the doctrine that the serpent of Eden was the mouthpiece of the devil."[24] As a result, ancient Jewish interpreters also viewed the woman's seed as the messianic victor over the serpent. This messianic reading of Gen 3:15 is evident in the Septuagint[25] and the rabbinic literature of the Targumim *Pseudo-Jonathan, Neofiti, Onqelos*[26] and the midrash *Genesis Rabbah* 23:5.[27] Not surprisingly, many scholars recognize that ancient Jewish sources read Gen 3:15 (and other passages) messianically but dismiss their interpretations as far-fetched. Is it not also possible that these ancient Jewish interpreters were sensitive to the nuances of the text, read them carefully, and understood their meaning? It is just as likely that the LXX, the Targumim, and the midrashim read Gen 3:15 messianically because that was the true meaning embedded in the text. Does a careful examination of the text support that thesis? To this we now turn.

Intextual Considerations[28]

Genesis 3:14

God's pronouncement of judgment (3:14) is directed to the serpent proper—meaning the actual animal and not the dark force behind

---

[24] Skinner, *A Critical* and *Exegetical Commentary on Genesis*, 73. Skinner cites Wis 2:24; 1 *En.* 69:6; 2 *En.* 31:3ff; *Pss. Sol.* 4:9; and *Gen. Rab.* 29.

[25] See R. A. Martin, "The Earliest Messianic Interpretation of Genesis 3:15," *JBL* 84 (1965): 425–27.

[26] M. B. Shepherd, "Targums, New Testament, and Biblical Theology of the Messiah," *JETS* 51 (2008): 52–53.

[27] "Eve had respect to that seed which is coming from another place. And who is this? This is Messiah the King."

[28] "Intextual" refers to examination of the details within the text itself."

it. Since a serpent from the animal kingdom is an amoral being, it is surprising that the animal itself would be cursed. The purpose of cursing the animal is for it to become a perpetual reminder of the devastating destruction caused by the role of the serpent in the sin of Adam and Eve.

Nevertheless, this curse should not be understood as changing the actual physical condition of all snakes but more likely declaring the meaning of their normal characteristics. Thus, when God proclaimed that the serpent would crawl on its belly, it does not mean that serpents previously had legs. Rather, crawling would now forever be understood as a sign of defeat.[29] When the Lord declared that the serpent would "eat dust," it was only a figurative statement since serpents do not really subsist on a diet of dust. Rather, since they crawl on the dust of the earth, serpents are said to "eat dust" as a sign of perpetual humiliation.[30] Moreover, the serpent was cursed more[31] than the whole of the animal kingdom. This indicates that although the whole creation was cursed (Rom 8:20–21), including all the animals, the serpent was even more cursed. That serpents are more cursed is echoed in Isa 65:25 ("'The wolf and the lamb will feed together, and the lion will eat straw like the ox, but the serpent's food will be dust! They will not do what is evil or destroy on My entire holy mountain,' says the LORD").[32] There it is promised that the effects of the curse on the animal world will be reversed in the future messianic kingdom— the wolf and the lion will no longer be predatory beasts, but "the serpent's food will be dust." Unlike the rest of creation, when the effects of the fall are reversed, the curse on the serpent will remain forever. In this way, the serpent will remain an eternal outward symbol of the spiritual defeat of the dark force behind the fall.

---

[29] This is the case with other biblical signs as well. For example, rainbows existed before God declared that it would be the sign of His covenant with Noah (Gen 9:12–17), as did circumcision before the Lord declared that it was the sign of His covenant with Abraham (Gen 17:9–14).

[30] See Pss 72:9; Isa 49:23; Mic 7:17 for this figure of speech.

[31] The particle מִן is used in a comparative sense in Gen 3:14.

[32] As G. V. Smith points out, "If this refers back to the curse on the snake in Gen 3:14 [which he apparently agrees that it does], it appears that the curse on the snake is not lifted. The snake will not be allowed to eat normal food but will suffer the humiliation of eating dirt just like some of God's other enemies did" (Isaiah 40–66, NAC [Nashville: B&H, 2009], 724). Nevertheless, in the coming messianic age the "serpent" will no longer be allowed to do any harm (cf. Isa 11:6–9).

Genesis 3:15

Several intextual observations can be made with regard to Gen 3:15. First, the Lord's curse turns its direction from the serpent to the evil power that animated it. Some might object that this is unlikely since there is no explicit shift indicated in the text. However, since this was an unusual animal, able to speak and desirous of tempting as indicated above, it was surely animated by that dark force later revealed as Satan. As E. J. Young puts it, "Almost imperceptibly, the language passes from the actual serpent to address the evil one who has used the serpent. In v. 14 the serpent had been in the foreground, and in the present verse the tempter himself appears."[33]

A second intextual consideration has to do with the word "hostility." The Lord declared that there would be "hostility" between the cursed one and the woman. The Hebrew word *ʾêbâ* as used in the Hebrew Bible always refers to enmity between moral agents (persons, not animals).[34] This would indicate that the enmity would be between the woman and Satan as the force animating the serpent.[35]

Yet a third observation has to do with the word "seed." The text states that the judicial hostility would not be limited to the woman and the tempter but would extend to their seed as well. The word *zeraʿ* (seed) is always a singular form in the Hebrew Bible, even when used collectively as referring to groups. Nevertheless, the word can also refer to an individual.[36] The best English translation would be "offspring," a word that has the same flexibility as the Hebrew, referring either an individual or a group.

Moreover, there is an ambiguity to the term "seed" in that it can oscillate from the collective to the individual usage. Walter Kaiser writes that the word "is deliberately flexible enough to denote either one person who epitomizes the whole group . . . or the many persons in that whole line of natural and/or spiritual descendants."[37] The flexibility of meaning is seen in the meaning of the "holy seed" of Isa 6:13.[38] The same ambiguity of meaning is seen in the seed of David in

---

[33] E. J. Young, *Genesis 3: A Devotional and Expository Study* (Edinburgh: Banner of Truth, 1983), 102.

[34] See Num 35:21–22; Ezek 25:15; 35:5.

[35] Kaiser, *The Messiah in the Old Testament*, 41.

[36] As mentioned previously, זֶרַע is used a number of times in Genesis with an individual sense (4:25; 15:3; 16:10; 21:13; 22:18; 24:60; 38:8–9).

[37] W. C. Kaiser, "זֶרַע," *TWOT* 1:253.

[38] For a thorough discussion of the flexibility of the term as it oscillates from a collective

2 Sam 7:12. There it refers collectively to all David's descendants and "is applied 'individually' to each of the sons of David who assume his throne."[39]

This very same kind of oscillation is at work in Gen 3:15. After promising the hostility that will exist between the woman and the tempter, it also predicts that the hostility will exist between the seed of the tempter and the seed of the woman. In this phrase, "seed" is used in a general sense, referring to the collective offspring of both the woman (meaning humanity) and the tempter (meaning his followers). The enmity begun between the tempter and the woman will continue in their descendants and followers.

Immediately afterwards, however, the verse shifts the meaning of seed from a collective group to a particular individual descendent of the woman. The evidence for this is that a singular pronoun and a singular verb are used to refer to the seed. Jack Collins has demonstrated that when a biblical author has a collective sense for "seed" in mind, he uses plural pronouns and verbal forms to describe it. However, when he has an individual in mind, he uses singular verb forms and pronouns to describe the "seed."[40]

In Gen 3:15, the biblical author uses singular pronouns and verb forms in reference to the seed, so he plainly has a specific offspring in view. Thus, when the text says "*He* will strike your head," it means that a particular, future individual, descended from the woman, will strike the head of the tempter. Moreover, the blow given by this individual is not on a descendant of the tempter but on the tempter directly, which points to its supernatural longevity mentioned above.

A final observation pertains to the word *šûp* ("strike"). Although some have argued that the two usages of the verbs are not identical, this is unlikely.[41] Kaiser correctly recognizes that the word is used

---

to an individual sense, see Hamilton, "The Skull Crushing Seed of the Woman: Inner-Biblical Interpretation of Genesis 3:15," 32–33.

[39] W. Wifall, "Gen 3:15–A Protoevangelium?" *CBQ* 36 (1974): 363.

[40] J. Collins, "A Syntactical Note on Genesis 3:15: Is the Woman's Seed Singular or Plural?" *TynBul* 48 (1997): 141–48. J. Walton dismisses the validity of this syntactical rule, arguing that Gen 22:18 and 24:60 violate it. In so doing, he rejects Collins's careful work without support and dismisses Alexander's thoughtful examination of Gen 22:18 and 24:60 ("Further Observations on the Term 'Seed' in Genesis" *TynBul* 48 [1997]: 363–67) as mere "special pleading." Walton's dissent from the detailed studies by Collins and Alexander requires more than dismissive rejection without substantiation.

[41] Cassuto, *A Commentary on the Book of Genesis*, 161; D. Kidner, *Genesis: An Introduction and Commentary*, TOTC (Downers Grove, IL: Inter-Varsity, 1967), 70–71.

twice in Gen 3:15: once to describe the action of the woman's seed against the head of the tempter, and once to describe the action of the tempter against the heel of the woman's seed. A rare word, *šûp* has its only other plain usage in Job 9:17.[42] There the parallelism indicates that the word means to "batter" or "strike." Thus, in Gen 3:15 it indicates that both the woman's seed and the tempter will strike violent blows on each other.[43]

Kaiser maintains that the two blows are different despite the same word being used to describe them. The distinction, he says, is that "crushing the head and crushing or bruising the heel is the difference between a mortal blow to the skull and a slight injury to the victor."[44] This seems mistaken. Since in the context the tempter has taken the form of a serpent (*nāḥāš*), it is likely that the tempter's blow would be equated with a serpent's bite. And in the case of this animal, the Hebrew generally uses it to speak of a venomous and lethal snake.[45] Most likely, therefore, the text is speaking of two comparable death blows: the future redeemer will strike the head of the tempter and thereby kill it, and at the same time the tempter will strike the heel of the redeemer and kill him.

Although some have objected that this somehow renders the messianic view invalid,[46] that would be far from true. Rather, it indicates that the woman's seed will indeed have victory, but the victory will be achieved through suffering his own death. This appears to be how the writer of Hebrews understood this verse. In an apparent midrash on Gen 3:15 he writes, "so that through his [Jesus'] death He might destroy the one holding the power of death—that is, the Devil—and free those who were held in slavery all their lives by the fear of death" (Heb 2:14–15).

Desmond Alexander states, "Viewed solely within the context of ch. 3, it is virtually impossible to sustain a messianic interpretation of 3:15. Considered, however, in the light of Genesis as a whole, a messianic reading of this verse is not only possible but highly probable."[47] This may indeed be an overstatement since there are intextual clues supporting a messianic reading. Nevertheless, Alexander is correct in

---

[42] "He *batters* me with a whirlwind and multiplies my wounds without cause." A possible use in Ps 139:11 is disputed.

[43] Kaiser, *The Messiah in the Old Testament*, 41.

[44] Ibid.

[45] For example, see Num 21:6–9. See also R. Alden, "Nahash," *TWOT* 571–72.

[46] Walton, *Genesis*, 226.

[47] Alexander, "Messianic Ideology in Genesis," 32.

noting that the rest of Genesis, and I would say the rest of the Pentateuch and the whole Hebrew Bible, make the messianic interpretation
virtually certain. Thus, we proceed to the innertextual and intertextual considerations on Gen 3:15.[48]

Innertextual Considerations

Innertextual references to Gen 3:15 should not be limited to the
book of Genesis. From the time of the writing of the Pentateuch, it
was considered one book rather than five.[49] Thus, the entire Torah
should be examined for innertextual references to this text.

Immediately, in fact, in the very next chapters of Genesis, the trail
of the two seeds becomes evident. First, Cain, representing the wicked seed, slays Abel (Gen 4:1–16). The text then presents the wicked
line of Cain (Gen 4:17–24), followed by the establishment of the righteous line of Seth (4:25). The righteous line is traced in the genealogy
of Seth to Noah (Gen 5:1–32). The author continues to be concerned
with following the godly "seed," tracing the genealogy of the special
line from Shem (Noah's descendent) to Abram (11:10–31), leading to
the call of Abram (Gen 12:1–3). Genesis continues to be concerned
with tracing the promised line, showing God's choice of Isaac (not
Ishmael), Jacob (not Esau), and the twelve sons of Jacob.[50]

God renews His covenant promises to Abraham and his "offspring"
(literally "seed"), assuring him that "kings will come from you" (Gen
17:6–7). The same promise is also made to Sarah (Gen 17:16)[51] and
Jacob (35:11).[52] Ultimately, in a messianic prediction, the promise is
narrowed to Judah, whose descendent will be the royal Messiah, to
whom all peoples will offer obedience (Gen 49:9–10). This is significant because it shows that the future descendent predicted in Gen
3:15 will come from a royal dynasty.[53]

---

[48] "Innertextual" considerations refers to the way the same author in the same book makes
allusions or cites the text under consideration. "Intertextual" considerations refers to the way
the other books of the Bible allude to or cite the text under consideration.

[49] Sailhamer, *The Pentateuch as Narrative*, 1–2.

[50] At the same time, Genesis also traces the wicked line. Alexander writes, "By his murderous
actions Lamech mirrors his ancestor Cain (4:19–24) . . . the activities of the Canaanites living
in Sodom (19:4–8) resemble those of their ancestor Ham, the father of Canaan (9:21–22; "Messianic Ideology in Genesis," 24n11).

[51] "kings of peoples will come from her."

[52] "kings will descend from you."

[53] Alexander, "Messianic Ideology in Genesis," 26–27.

Not only will that future descendent rule all people; Abraham is also promised that his seed will bless the nations (Gen 22:17–18). It might be thought that the use of "seed" in Gen 22:17–18 requires a collective sense because it promises that Abraham's seed would be "as numerous as the stars of the sky and the sand on the seashore." But Alexander has shown that this is yet again one of the cases where the word "seed" oscillates from the corporate to the individual.[54] Beginning with the collective sense, the word "seed" indeed refers to the numerous descendants Abraham would have. However, a new thought begins in the middle of v. 17,[55] promising Abraham that "your offspring will possess the gates of his[56] enemies." Following the same Hebrew syntax as found in Gen 3:15, the author uses the third person singular pronoun and verb, indicating that this use of seed has a particular individual in view.[57] Thus Abraham is promised numerous descendants and also a particular descendant who will bless all nations of the earth.[58]

A further innertextual reference to Gen 3:15 is found in Num 24:5–9.[59] There in an eschatological text (cf. "in the last days" Num 24:14) Jacob is promised that "water will flow from his buckets" and that "his seed will be in the many waters."[60] The next phrase, using a synonymous parallelism, describes Jacob's seed as "His king" who "will be higher than Gog" and whose "kingdom will be exalted."[61] Just as Genesis develops that the woman's seed would spring from a royal dynasty, so this oracle identifies the seed as the end-time messianic king who will defeat the enemies of Israel and rule over an exalted

---

[54] Alexander, "Further Observations on the Term 'Seed' in Genesis," 363–67.

[55] Alexander points out that this sentence does not have a "*vav*-consecutive," indicating a new thought. "A striking feature of the final clause is the way in which it does not begin with a *vav*-consecutive; rather it is introduced by the imperfect of the verb יִרַשׁ preceded by a non-converting *w*. This syntactical arrangement leaves open the possibility that the זֶרַע referred to in the final clause differs from that mentioned in the first part of the verse. Whereas the first זֶרַע obviously refers to a very large number of descendants, the second would, following Collins' approach, denote a single individual who is victorious over his enemies." Ibid., 365.

[56] The HCSB, NASB, NIV, NKJV, and NET Bible all translate the third person singular pronoun here as "their." The KJV and ESV translate the singular pronoun accurately as "his."

[57] A similar promise is made to Rebekah (Gen 24:60) using the same Hebrew syntax. She is promised that her "seed" will (lit.) "possess the gate of his enemies," showing that she will have a particular descendent with unique royal authority.

[58] This appears to be the way Paul read Gen 22:18 in Gal 3:16. See C. J. Collins, "Galatians 3:16: What Kind of Exegete Was Paul?" *TynBul* 54 (2003): 75–86.

[59] See previous discussions of this passage chaps. 3 and 7.

[60] This is my own literal translation.

[61] The MT has it as "higher than Agag," but the LXX, Samaritan Pentateuch, and other versions more correctly have it as "Gog," the end-time enemy of Israel.

kingdom. Moreover, Num 24:9, in a virtual quotation of Gen 49:9, identifies the seed as the lion of the tribe of Judah (cf. Gen 49:9–10).

In the very next oracle in Num 24:17–19, the promise of the future messianic king ("A star will come from Jacob, and a scepter will arise from Israel")[62] makes a thematic allusion to Gen 3:15. In Num 24:17 there is a prediction that the messianic king "will smash the forehead of Moab," an enemy of Israel. Although Num 24:17 uses different words than Gen 3:15 for both the blow struck and the head that is crushed,[63] the thematic literary allusion is plain. The expectation is that when the messianic king arrives, he will crush the heads of Israel's enemies, reminding the readers of the promise that Eve's offspring would crush the head of the enemy.

It seems that Genesis in particular, as well as Numbers, make innertextual references to the promise of the woman's seed. In so doing, it clarifies that when Gen 3:15 speaks of a future seed that will crush the head of the tempter, it has a particular, royal individual in view and not a mere collection of human beings. But it is not only the Pentateuch that refers to the promise in Gen 3:15—the rest of the Hebrew Scriptures do as well.

Intertextual Considerations

The rest of the Hebrew canon makes extensive direct and thematic allusions to Gen 3:15, firmly identifying the woman's seed as a royal and messianic figure.[64] Perhaps the most significant way that later biblical writers develop the "seed" theme is in the Davidic covenant. David is promised a "seed" who will have an eternal house, kingdom, and throne (2 Sam 7:12–16),[65] reminding readers of the promise of the royal seed described in Genesis (3:15; 17:16; 35:11; 49:9–10).

Psalm 89:10 [Hb. 89:11] alludes to Gen 3:15 by stating that the Lord "crushed" Rahab, who is the ancient sea-dragon and a demonic

---

[62] See the previous discussion of this passage in chap. 4.

[63] In Gen 3:15 the word for "strike" is שׁוּף and the word for "head" is רֹאשׁ; Num 24:17 uses מָחַץ for "smash," and the word for "forehead" is פֵּאָה.

[64] For the most extensive discussion of the intertextual evidence for this thesis, see Hamilton, "The Skull Crushing Seed of the Woman: Inner-Biblical Interpretation of Genesis 3:15," 34–43. There he shows how the entire Hebrew Bible makes reference to themes of "broken heads," "broken enemies," those who are "trampled underfoot" and who "lick the dust," as well as "stricken serpents."

[65] See also Ps 89:4,29,36 [Hb. 89:5,30,37].

figure.[66] Further, Davidic kings are said to crush their enemies beneath their feet (Ps 89:23; 2 Sam 22:37–43). In a specific allusion to Gen 3:14–15, Ps 72:9 states that the messianic king will have his enemies bow before him and "lick the dust." In a transparent allusion to Gen 3:15, Mic 7:17 predicts that in the eschatological future the enemy nations will submit to the Lord and "lick the dust like a snake." Speaking of that same future time in an innertextual reference to Gen 3:15, Ps 8:6 proclaims that the messianic king will have "everything under his feet." The same image of ultimate defeat of the nations is found in Ps 110:1, where the messianic king is promised that God will make His enemies a footstool for His feet.[67] The intertextual references to Gen 3:14–15 support the ideas found throughout Genesis that the seed of the woman would come from the family of Abraham and the royal tribe of Judah. Ultimately, they confirm that Messiah will bring victory over the tempter, the ancient serpent, that is, the Devil.

Conclusion

In view of the preliminary considerations and careful observations of the intextual evidence in Gen 3:14–15 as well as the innertextual and intertextual references, it seems appropriate to understand Gen 3:15 as the first specific messianic prophecy of the Bible. Alexander is correct when he writes, "While many modern writers have been particularly dismissive of the traditional messianic understanding of 3:15, it is they, and not their predecessors, who have failed to grasp the true significance of this passage within its wider context."[68]

Furthermore, what this text reveals about the Messiah is significant. While not predicting the virgin birth of Messiah, it does promise that Messiah will descend from humanity and that He will destroy the evil force that tempted Eve, humanity's ancient enemy later revealed as Satan. Moreover, in defeating this enemy, the Messiah himself will be struck, bringing victory over the enemy of our souls through His own death.

---

[66] See W. Bacher and J. Z. Lauterbach, "Rahab," *JE* . See also Ps 87:4; Job 9:13; 26:12; Isa 30:7, 51:9.

[67] Wifall ("Gen 3:15–A Protoevangelium," 363–65) has noted these references and has maintained that Genesis was composed afterwards as a pre-history to them. While not accepting his critical perspective, his recognition of the linkage supports the messianic interpretation.

[68] Alexander, "Messianic Ideology in Genesis," 32

Chapter 10

AN EXAMPLE FROM THE PROPHETS: INTERPRETING ISAIAH 7:14 AS A MESSIANIC PROPHECY

The Virgin Birth in Question

In his book *Velvet Elvis*,[1] Rob Bell asked,

> What if tomorrow someone digs up definitive proof that Jesus had a real, earthly, biological father named Larry, and archaeologists find Larry's tomb and do DNA samples and prove beyond a shadow of a doubt that the virgin birth was really just a bit of mythologizing the Gospel writers threw in to appeal to the followers of the Mithra and Dionysian religious cults that were hugely popular at the time of Jesus, whose gods had virgin births? But what if as you study the origin of the word *virgin*, you discover that the word *virgin* in the gospel of Matthew actually comes from the book of Isaiah, and then you find out that in the Hebrew language at that time, the word *virgin* could mean several things. And what if you discover that in the first century being "born of a virgin" also referred to a child whose mother became pregnant the first time she had intercourse?[2]

After raising these questions, Bell wonders if belief in the virgin birth is even necessary, although he goes on to affirm the historic Christian faith, including the virgin birth.[3] Nevertheless, Bell's conjecture regarding "Larry, the human father of Jesus" is troublesome because many evangelicals have accepted some of the presuppositions presented here.

For centuries, Christians understood Isaiah 7 to be a prediction of the virgin birth. Now it is not uncommon for evangelicals to assert that the Hebrew word Isaiah used does not mean "virgin" at all, but rather "young woman." Moreover, the passage is not viewed as a prediction of Messiah's birth but rather of a child born in Isaiah's day. Bell's popular-style book reflects the trend in contemporary evangelical Old Testament scholarship that denies that Isaiah was predicting the virgin birth of the Messiah. For example, John Walton understands Isaiah predicting the natural birth of a child to a young woman in the

---

[1] R. Bell, *Velvet Elvis* (Grand Rapids: Zondervan, 2005).

[2] Ibid., 26–27.

[3] Ibid., 27.

court of King Ahaz.[4] He writes, "Exegesis gives us no clue that Isaiah had been aware that he was speaking of the Messiah. The child's name merely expressed the hope that accompanied God's deliverance."[5] It must be recognized that Walton and other evangelical scholars who agree with his view take this position not to deny a biblical essential but rather to affirm biblical scholarship and sound exegesis. But is their approach to interpreting Isaiah 7 as accurate and safe as they suppose?

For now, the evangelical commitment to faith in Jesus and His virgin birth is secure. But will not the questioning of the predictive value of Isaiah 7 or, as Bell does, the questioning of even whether belief in the virgin birth of Jesus is essential for evangelical faith lead to a slippery slope culminating in a spiritual disaster? It seems that if we are to maintain faith in the virgin birth over the long term, it will be necessary to address the seemingly troublesome Isaiah 7 passage. Is it possible to view Isaiah's prophecy as a direct messianic prediction while still practicing sound exegesis? In this chapter, that is precisely what I propose to do.

The Virgin Birth in Prophecy

In my experience, Isa 7:14 is the most controversial of messianic prophecies. Disputes revolve around a variety of issues, chiefly, the meaning of the word *'almāh*, the relationship of Isaiah's "sign" to the context, the way the original readers of the prophecy would have understood it, and Matthew's citation of this verse in support of the virgin birth.

As a result, interpreters have divided into three primary views of the passage and even among these views, expositors present their own unique perspectives. The first view held by many traditional Christian interpreters is to see the prophecy as a *direct prediction* of the virgin birth of the Messiah. Taking different approaches as to how the prophecy relates to the original context, they each conclude that the word *'almāh* means "virgin" and refers to the mother of Jesus.

A second position, frequently held by critics and Jewish interpreters, is that of a purely *historical interpretation*. It takes Isaiah's promise to be that a young woman in the eighth century BC would have sexual

---

[4] J. H. Walton, "Isa 7:14: What's in a Name?" *JETS* 30 (1987): 289–306.
[5] Ibid., 300.

relations and then give birth to a child that would serve as a sort of hourglass for Judah—before that child reached a certain age, the two kings threatening Judah would be removed.

Third, a common approach taken by contemporary Christian scholars is to view the prophecy as having some sort of *dual* or *multiple fulfillment*. Isaiah is understood to refer to the natural birth of a child in his own day as a sign to Judah. Nevertheless, they contend that this does not exhaust the meaning. Rather by double fulfillment, *sensus plenior*, type, a later rereading, progressive fulfillment, or even by the use of first-century Jewish hermeneutics, the prophecy also refers to the virgin birth of Jesus.

I believe that by placing the prophecy in context, through a careful reading of the text of Isaiah 7 and relating it to innerbiblical interpretations of the passage, a view that supports a direct prediction of the virgin birth makes the most sense. That would explain Matthew's reason for citing Isa 7:14 as a prediction of the virgin birth.

The Context of the Prophecy

The historical setting of the prophecy was a threat against Judah around the year 734 BC. At that time, Rezin, king of Syria (Aram) and Pekah, king of the northern kingdom of Israel, formed an anti-Assyrian alliance. They in turn wanted Ahaz, king of Judah, to join their alliance. When he refused, they decided to make war against Ahaz to force the issue (7:1). The northern alliance against Ahaz caused great fear in the royal family of David (7:2) because the goal was not just to conquer Judah but also to "set up the son of Tabeel as king" in the place of Ahaz (7:6). Their plan would place a more pliable king on the throne and also put an end to the Davidic house. This threat provides a significant detail in understanding the passage. While some have contended that there would be no reason to foretell the coming of the Messiah, the danger to the house of David explains the messianic concerns of the passage. It was the Davidic covenant (2 Sam 7:12–16; 1 Chr 17:11–14) that led to the expectation of a future Messiah who would be a descendant of David. Therefore, if Ahaz and the entire royal house were to be destroyed, it would bring an end to the messianic hope. A long-term prophecy of the birth of Messiah would assure the Davidic house and the readers of the scroll of Isaiah that the messianic hope was indeed secure.

With this threat looming, the Lord sends Isaiah to give assurance to Ahaz, telling him to meet Ahaz "at the end of the conduit of the upper pool, by the road to the Fuller's Field" and specifically to bring his son, Shear-Jashub (7:3). Frequently, commentators overlook this command to bring the boy as if it were an unnecessary detail. Nevertheless, it seems strange to include this precise requirement if it had no significance. As we will see, this seemingly minor detail will play a significant role in understanding the passage.

At the conduit of the upper pool, Isaiah gave Ahaz his God-directed message: "It will not happen; it will not occur" (7:7). The Lord, through Isaiah, promised that the attack would not succeed and that the alliance would be broken. In fact, Isaiah predicted that within 65 years, the northern kingdom of Israel would no longer be recognized as a people (7:8, "Ephraim will be too shattered to be a people"). This prediction came true in three phases. First, Tiglath-pileser, king of Assyria, conquered Israel in 732 BC and sent many captives back to Assyria (2 Kgs 15:29). Second, Assyria destroyed the northern Kingdom in 721 BC, deporting much of the Israelite population to Assyria and settling the land of Israel with other peoples (2 Kgs 17:24). It was completely fulfilled in 669 BC when Ashurbanipal enacted the final population transfers between Israel and Assyria (Ezra 4:2,10). Thus in 669 BC, 65 years from the date of the events described in Isaiah's prophecy, the northern kingdom was indeed "too shattered to be a people" (7:8) and the land was inhabited by Samaritans, a people of mixed ethnicity (Ezra 4:2).[6]

To confirm the promise that the attack on Judah would not succeed, the Lord offered a sign to Ahaz of his own choosing.[7] The king was told that the sign could come "from the depths of Sheol to the heights of heaven" (7:12). This is an obvious merism,[8] calling Ahaz to ask God for a sign that would be stupendous enough to elicit faith.

---

[6] J. J. Davis and J. C. Whitcomb, *A History of Israel* (Grand Rapids: Baker, 1980), 429–34.

[7] J. Walton has speculated that Isa 7:10 ("Then the Lord spoke again to Ahaz . . .") begins a new setting for the prophecy at a later time and that Isaiah and his son Shear-Jashub were no longer present at the conduit of the upper pool. He also cites a number of sources both supporting and rejecting this conjecture ("Isa 7:14: What's in a Name?" 289). J. Oswalt correctly affirms that 7:10 is a continuation of Isaiah's meeting at the upper pool. He writes that the word "*again* may merely indicate a second part of a single conversation, vv. 3–9 being the promise and vv. 10,11 the challenge (cf. Gen. 18:29; etc.). There being no evidence of a change in time or location, it seems best to see the paragraph as a direct continuation of vv. 1–9" (*The Book of Isaiah: Chapters 1–39*, NICOT [Grand Rapids: Eerdmans, 1986], 204).

[8] A merism is a figure of speech in which "the totality or whole is substituted by two con-

Although the Hebrew word for "sign" (*'ôt*) does not necessarily require a miracle, it does include the supernatural within its range of meaning (cf. Exod 4:8–9,17,28,30; 7:3; 10:1–2; Num 14:11,22; Deut 4:34; 6:22; 7:19, etc.). In light of the nature of the offer, it appears that Ahaz was to ask for a miraculous sign.

Nevertheless, Ahaz, with false piety, refuses to test God. The disingenuous nature of his response is plain in that this is a king who had so little regard for the Lord that he practiced idolatry, even offering his own son as a child sacrifice to Molech (2 Kgs 16:3; 2 Chr 28:3). While he might claim biblical justification (Deut 6:16) for his refusal to ask or to test the Lord (7:12), this seems ridiculous because the Lord Himself has just called upon him to do so. So, when Ahaz was under his greatest threat, he refused the Lord's comfort and rejected the offer of a sign. In response, Isaiah declared that nonetheless, the Lord would give a sign—one that would become a source of controversy for generations.

The Contents of the Prophecy

The most significant difficulty in interpreting the prophecy is that on a cursory reading it appears that the sign would be fulfilled within just a couple of years of Isaiah's meeting with the king and not more than 700 years later with the birth of Jesus. The reason for this difficulty is the failure to read the prophecy carefully and pick up the clues the author has left. A close reading of the text will disclose not just one prophecy here but two—a long term prediction addressed to the house of David (7:13–15) and a short-term prediction addressed to Ahaz (7:16–25).

The Long-Term Prophecy to the House of David: The Birth of Messiah (Isaiah 7:13–15)

Since the northern alliance was threatening to replace Ahaz with the son of Tabeel, the entire house of David was being endangered. Were Syria and Israel to succeed, the messianic promise of a future son of David who would have an eternal house, kingdom, and throne (2 Sam 7:16) would be demolished. This provides the need for a long-term sign of hope that despite the menace to the house of David, the

---

trasting or opposite parts." See R. B. Zuck, *Basic Bible Interpretation* (Wheaton, IL: Victor Books, 1991), 151.

Messiah would be born, with the sign of His coming being His virgin birth. The details of this prophecy are as follows:

"*"Listen, house of David!"* Isaiah's declaration of the Lord's sign shifted the direction of the prophecy away from Ahaz to the whole house of David (7:13). This is evident not only from the vocative "house of David" but also from the change of singular pronouns and verbs of command (7:4,5,11) to plural. When addressing Ahaz alone, the *singular* was used. However, in 7:13–14, Isaiah used the second person *plural*. This is not an obvious change in the English Bible, but in v. 13 the imperative verb "listen" is plural, the expression "Is it not enough for *you*" is plural, and "Will *you* also try" is plural. Then in v. 14 "you" is plural.[9] The reason for the shift is that God was clearly fed up with this wicked and sanctimonious king, so he addressed the royal house he represented. Moreover, it was not only Ahaz that was being threatened but the entire house of David.[10]

"*Therefore the Lord Himself will give you a sign.*" Although Ahaz, as the head of the house of David, had tried God's patience, Isaiah promised that the Lord Himself would still grant a sign—but one that would now be of God's own choosing. As mentioned above, the Hebrew word for "sign" can refer to the miraculous or the non-miraculous. However, in light of the previous offer of a sign "from the depths of Sheol to the heights of heaven," it would appear that the sign to follow would be of a miraculous nature. Moreover, this is how Isaiah used the same word in the parallel situation with Hezekiah (Isa 38:1–8). There as a "sign" that Hezekiah's life would be extended, the shadow on the stairway would miraculously retreat ten steps (38:7–8).[11]

"*[Behold] the virgin will conceive [lit. the virgin (is) pregnant], have a son, and name him Immanuel.*" The Lord called special attention to

---

[9] English cries out with the need for a second person plural. Hence, the southern colloquialism "Y'all" or the Brooklynese "Youse."

[10] An implication is that the sign offered in vv. 13–15 was no longer intended to encourage Ahaz to have faith since he was now under judgment. Note the prophet's change from "*your* God" in v. 11 to "*my* God" in v. 13. See J. A. Motyer, *The Prophecy of Isaiah: An Introduction and Commentary* (Downers Grove, IL: InterVarsity, 1993), 84.

[11] See the discussion of the word "sign" or אוֹת in D. L. Cooper. *Messiah: His Nature and Person* (Los Angeles: Biblical Research Society, 1933), 36–37. R. L. Reymond maintains that since "the referent of the word 'sign' in v. 11 clearly is of that order [this] lends strong credence to the presumption that, when God declared in v. 14 that He Himself would give a 'sign' since Ahaz had refused to ask for one, the words that then followed upon His declaration that He would give a 'sign' also entailed the miraculous" (*Jesus, Divine Messiah: The Old Testament Witness* [Ross-Shire, Scotland: Christian Focus, 1990], 24).

the ensuing sign by beginning with the word *hinnê*, traditionally rendered "behold!" (e.g., KJV, NASB, RSV, ESV), and often now "look!" (e.g., NRSV, JPS, NET, NLT[2]). When used in similar constructions in the Hebrew Bible (Gen 16:11; 17:19; Judg 13:5–7), the word *hinnê* serves to call attention to a birth of special importance.[12] The sign that the Lord promised the house of David is that of a pregnant *'almāh* who would bear a son. The use of the article (frequently untranslated in modern English versions) with the word *'almāh* indicates that the Lord has a specific woman in mind. It is not some generic woman in the court of Ahaz but one whom the prophet sees in particular.

Controversy has surrounded the word *'almāh* since the second century when Aquila substituted "young woman" (Gk. *neanis*) in his Greek translation of the Hebrew Bible for the LXX translation of "virgin" (*parthenos*). Was Isaiah speaking of a virgin or merely a young woman?[13] Various arguments have been put forward to make the case for translating the word as virgin.

Etymologically, *'almāh* is derived from a word which means "to be sexually strong, sexually mature, sexually ripe or ready."[14] This would seem to emphasize the age of the woman (pubescent) rather than indicating whether she was sexually active. Cyrus Gordon has argued that ancient (pre-Mosaic) Ugaritic, which is cognate to Hebrew, used the word parallel to *'almāh* of a virgin goddess. Since the Ugaritic annunciation formula used a very similar construction to Isa 7:14, Gordon concluded that *'almāh* should rightly be translated "virgin."[15] Furthermore, many have maintained that the Septuagint translation

---

[12] E. J. Young not only cites these verses but also shows that the Ras Shamra literature does the same (*Studies in Isaiah* [Grand Rapids: Eerdmans, 1954], 159–60). The word הִנֵּה is a deictic particle whose function is generally to call attention to what follows. It occurs first in Gen 1:29 calling attention to His announcement of His abundant provision of food for Adam and Eve and thus serving as an important part of the context for the temptation narrative in chap. 3.

[13] Walton (*NIDOTTE*) has made the case for translating *'almāh* as "young woman." His strongest argument is that when used as an abstract noun in Isa 54:4, *'ālûmîm* ("youth") is used with "a metaphorical attribution of this term to Israel, she is also described as having a husband (v. 5) and of being barren (v. 1). In parallel phrases the 'shame' of her [*'ālûmîm*] is paired with the shame of her widowhood." He maintains that this "would suggest a close connection with childbearing," thus concluding that the word does not indicate virginity. However, a closer look at Isa 54:4 will demonstrate that while Israel is indeed being spoken of figuratively as a woman, the promise the Lord is making is that "you will forget the shame of your *virginity* [*'ālûmîm*], and the reproach of your widowhood you will remember no more." The contrast is between Israel's youth (before she married, hence a virgin) and when she was a widow (again with no husband, after she married). Isaiah's usage of the abstract noun *'ālûmîm* would seem to indicate virginity.

[14] BDB, 761.

[15] C. H. Gordon, "Almah in Isaiah 7:14," *JBR* 21 (1953): 106.

of ʿalmāh with the Greek word parthenos ("virgin") is evidence that in the pre-Christian era, the word was understood as referring to virginity.[16]

The best way to determine the meaning of ʿalmāh is by examining its usage throughout the Hebrew Bible. If there were a place in Scripture where it clearly refers to a non-virgin, it would widen the range of meaning to make it possible that it might refer to a non-virgin in Isa 7:14. However, in every situation the word is used either of a virgin or in an indeterminate, neutral sense.

Genesis 24:43. Here Rebekah, the soon-to-be wife of Isaac, is called an ʿalmāh. This chapter of Genesis describes Rebekah as a "girl" (naʿărāh, 24:14), a virgin (bětûlāh, 24:16), and a maiden (ʿalmāh, 24:43). These three synonyms are used to describe a virginal young woman.[17]

Exodus 2:8. In this passage, Miriam, the sister of Moses, is called an ʿalmāh. As a young girl, still in the home of her parents, it is legitimate to infer that the word includes the idea that she was a virgin.

Psalm 46:1. In this verse, the superscription uses the word as a musical direction. So it is indeterminate, not supporting or contradicting the meaning virgin.

Psalm 68:25. This verse refers to a musical worship procession in which ʿălāmôt (plural of ʿalmāh) play the timbrels. Perhaps this verse is indeterminate, not speaking to the virginity of the maidens. But possibly it hints at virginity because it calls to mind Jephthah's daughter who lamented her being offered as a sacrifice to the Lord (Judg 11:34–40). While some commentators believe that Jephthah's daughter was an actual human sacrifice, others maintain that she was given by Jephthah to lifelong service in the tabernacle. Thus, she was never

---

[16] For example, see E. E. Hindson, *Isaiah's Immanuel* (Phillipsburg, NJ: P&R, 1978), 67–68. G. Delling (παρθένος, *TDNT* 5:826–37) maintained that the word παρθένος did not yet mean "virgin" when the LXX was translated. While this is questionable, the Isaiah translator clearly understood עַלְמָה as a virgin and so rendered the feminine singular adjective הָרָה ("pregnant") as a feminine singular verb ("will conceive"; ἐν γαστρὶ ἕξει). Surprisingly, most interpreters miss what has long been seen as an attempt by the translator to come to terms with the "difficulty" of a "pregnant virgin" in Isa 7:14.

[17] In response to the proposal that if Isaiah had wanted to stress the girl's virginity, he would have used the word בְּתוּלָה, see G. J. Wenham, "*Bĕtûlâ*: A Girl of Marriageable Age," *VT* 22 (1972): 325–48, who points out that virginity was not a *necessary* element of the semantic content of בְּתוּלָה any more than it is with the English word "girl." He also argues, "It is not until the Christian era that there is clear evidence that *bĕtûlâ* had become a technical term for 'virgin'." Motyer concludes that עַלְמָה suited the task of expressing virginity better than בְּתוּלָה (*The Prophecy of Isaiah*, 84).

to marry and went with her friends to mourn her virginity. If this is the case, then perhaps it indicates that serving in the temple was restricted to virgins. Therefore, the damsels in the Temple worship procession, spoken of in Ps 68:25, would be virgins.

1 Chronicles 15:20. Once again, the word is used as a musical direction. So it is neutral, not supporting or contradicting the meaning "virgin."

Song of Songs 1:3. This verse refers to the love of the *ʿălāmôt* for Solomon. These are not married women but maidens who wanted husbands but have not yet been married. Therefore, the word would imply the concept of virginity.

Song of Songs 6:8. This description of the king's harem includes three categories: sixty queens, eighty concubines, and *ʿălāmôt* without number. The queens are those whom the king has married, the concubines are those with whom he has had sexual relations, and the *ʿălāmôt* are the virgins who will one day be elevated to either concubine or queenly status. If these *ʿălāmôt* were not virgins, they would be in the concubine category. Hence the use of the word here is of virgins.

Proverbs 30:19. This verse is the most controversial of the usages since it describes "the way of a man with an *ʿalmāh*." The entire proverb is found in 30:18–20 and refers to four wonderful and incomprehensible things: an eagle in the sky, a serpent on a rock, a ship in the sea, and a man with an *ʿalmāh*. Some have maintained that what unites these four is in each one something disappears. A soaring eagle is easily lost from sight. A serpent quickly slithers off the rock, disappearing from sight. A ship can be lost in a fraction of time. And a virgin can lose her virginity to young man very quickly. If this were the true interpretation of the proverb, the word *ʿalmāh* would indeed be virgin. But since there is no moral evil in the first three examples, it seems unlikely that the fourth would call extramarital sex "wonderful." Moreover, the contrast with the adulterous woman in 30:20 would imply that the *ʿalmāh* in the previous verse was not engaged in illicit sex. Probably the best way to understand this proverb is as referring to the mysterious and wonderful qualities of youthful attraction.[18] Thus, it once again would refer to a virgin.

---

[18] This is the view of Hindson, *Isaiah's Immanuel,* 38–39 and also D. Hubbard, who describes it as "the positive picture of romance" (*Proverbs* [Waco, TX: Word, 1989], 465–66). W. McKane, while denying that *ʿalmāh* means "virgin," interprets the proverb as referring to the "irresistible

In every usage of the Hebrew Bible, the word ʿalmāh either refers to a virgin or has a neutral sense.[19] Based on this study, it appears that Isaiah chose his words based on precision. While the Hebrew bĕtûlāh could refer to a virgin of any age, ʿalmāh would refer to a virgin that has just arrived at puberty. She is a maiden in the truest and purest sense. So, there does not seem to be cause to abandon the traditional interpretation of ʿalmāh as a "virgin" except for an antisupernatural or antimessianic bias.[20]

This virgin, according to the translation, will be with child. However, the Hebrew in the verse is even more emphatic. It uses the feminine singular adjective hārāh ("pregnant"), so the clause is more accurately rendered "Behold, the virgin is pregnant" or "Behold the pregnant virgin." Were it not for the context calling for a sign as deep as Sheol or high as heaven, such a translation would seem impossible. However, the prophet by means of a vision sees a specific pregnant virgin before him who would be the sign of hope for the house of David.[21] This indeed would meet the qualification of being "from the depths of Sheol to the heights of heaven."

"And she will call his name Immanuel." The virgin mother of the child will recognize His special nature. Therefore, she will give Him the title "Immanuel," which means "God with us."[22] The message to Judah was that God would be with them in a special way through this child. The title hints at the divine nature of the boy. Even clearer is Isa 8:8, which describes the Assyrian conquest of Judah, saying that the Assyrians will sweep over Judah, "and its spreading streams will fill your entire land, Immanuel!" If the child Immanuel were not divine, Isaiah would not identify the land as belonging to Him.[23] Moreover,

---

and inexplicable attraction which draws together the man and the woman" (*Proverbs: A New Approach* [Philadelphia: Westminster, 1970], 658).

[19] For a more thorough discussion of the meaning of ʿalmāh, see R. Niessen, "The Virginity of the עלמה in Isaiah 7:14," *BSac* 546 (1980): 133–50.

[20] The antimessianic bias is readily apparent in the great Jewish biblical commentator Rashi, who interprets ʿalmāh as "virgin" in Song 1:3 and 6:8 but argues for "young woman" in Isa 7:14. This same bias motivated Aquila in his second century Greek translation of the Hebrew Bible, changing the LXX *parthenos* to *neanis* (young girl).

[21] This vision explains why Isaiah speaks of a future event in the present tense.

[22] Some have objected to Matthew's use of this passage in the birth narrative (Matt 1:23) because Mary did not name the child "Immanuel." However, "Immanuel" is not the given name of the Messiah. Rather, it was to be seen as a symbolic, descriptive throne title. Similarly, David's son was given the name Solomon, but his descriptive royal title was "Jedidiah" or "Beloved of the Lord" (2 Sam 12:24–25).

[23] See Motyer, *The Prophecy of Isaiah*, 86.

in the next great vision of the coming Davidic king (Isa 9:6), the child receives other divine throne titles including "Mighty God" and "Eternal Father." Isaiah was not merely promising a future Davidic king who would secure the line of David. He was not only promising that He would have a supernatural birth. Ultimately, the prophet has revealed that the Messiah would be God in the flesh, Immanuel.[24]

"By the time he learns to reject what is bad and choose what is good, he will be eating butter [or curds] and honey." The Lord continues his description of the virgin-born Davidic Messiah, giving a clue to the situation into which He would be born (7:15). Many mistake the butter and honey He would eat as the food of royalty, ignoring the context in Isaiah 7 itself. Later in the chapter Isaiah writes of the coming Assyrian oppression, when Assyria would shave the land (7:20). At that time, fields will not be cultivated and will become pastures for oxen and sheep (7:23–25). The effect of this will be an overabundance of dairy (or butter/curds) because of the pasturing of livestock, and an excess of honey because bees will be able to pollinate the wild flowers. Therefore, because of "the abundant milk they give," a man "will eat butter, for every survivor in the land will eat butter and honey" (7:21–22). So, in this passage, butter and honey do not represent the food of royalty but rather the food of oppression. The point then of the description of the coming virgin-born, Davidic king eating butter and honey is to accentuate that he would be born during a time of political oppression. In other words, the prophecy of Messiah concludes with a hint that He will be born and grow up ("learn[ing] to reject what is bad and choose what is good") at a time when Judah is oppressed by a foreign power.[25]

With this, Isaiah has completed his first prophetic message. With the northern confederation of Syria and Israel threatening to replace Ahaz with a substitute king, the entire house of David was imperiled and with it, the messianic hope. Isaiah has come with a message of hope—the future Son of David would indeed be born someday. The supernatural sign that will reveal His identity is that He will be born of a young virgin and have a miraculous divine nature. Moreover, He

---

[24] Reymond, *Jesus, Divine Messiah: The Old Testament Witness*, 31–34.

[25] "The 'butter and honey' serve as figures for an oppressed land: natural rather than cultivated products; cf. vv. 22–23 . . . Fulfillment: the moral growth of Jesus, learning to distinguish between good and evil (cf. Luke 2:40,52), yet in a land that was afflicted—as it worked out historically, by the Romans—and no longer ruled by the dynasty of David" (J. B. Payne, *The Encyclopedia of Biblical Prophecy* [Grand Rapids: Baker, 1973], 293).

will grow up during a time of oppression over the Jewish people and their land. With the assurance that the house of David and the messianic hope are both secure, the prophet turns his attention to the immediate threat and gives a near prophecy to wicked King Ahaz.

The Short-Term Prophecy to Ahaz: The Sign of Shear-Jashub (Isaiah 7:16–17)

While many have considered v. 16 to be a continuation of the prophecy in 7:13–15, the grammar of the passage suggests otherwise. The opening phrase in Hebrew can reflect an adversative nuance, allowing for a disjunction between the child described in 7:13–15 and the one described in verse 16. There is a different child in view in this verse.[26]

The Identity of the Child. So who is the child in 7:16? In light of Isaiah being directed to bring his own son to the confrontation with the king at the conduit of the upper pool (cf. 7:3), it makes most sense to identify the lad as Shear-Jashub. Otherwise there would be no purpose for God directing Isaiah to bring the boy. Thus having promised the virgin birth of the Messiah (7:13–15), the prophet then points to the very small boy that he has brought along and says, "But before *this* lad (using the article with a demonstrative force) knows enough to refuse evil and choose good, the land whose two kings you dread will be forsaken."[27] In this way, Shear-Jashub functioned as a sign to the king.

---

[26] The two Hebrew words, כִּי בְּטֶרֶם, are only used twice in the Hebrew Bible, and the other use, in Isa 8:4, may indeed be causal. However, the causal nuance does not make sense here. NIV and NLT (first edition) recognize the contrast with the translation "but before."Calvin and more recently R. Vasholz ("Isaiah and Ahaz: A Brief History of Crisis in Isaiah 7 and 8," *Presb* 13 [1987]: 82–83) recognized the adversative phrase כִּי בְּטֶרֶם as signaling a new and different boy under discussion. Oswalt argues to the contrary: "It is not necessary to separate v. 16 from v. 15; in fact, the opening *ki* of v. 16 can be taken as causal, indicating why the child will eat curds and honey: Judah will be delivered from her neighbors' threat" (*The Book of Isaiah: Chapters 1–39*, 213). However, the causal nuance makes no sense if the curds and honey represent the food of oppression, as it plainly does in the next paragraph. How would Judah's deliverance explain why the child would eat curds and honey, the food of oppression?

[27] Calvin and Vasholz, "Isaiah and Ahaz," 83, maintain that 7:16 begins a second prophecy but that it is not a particular boy but a generic child, leading to the idea, "but before a boy grows old enough to refuse evil and choose good." To come to this view they must claim a generic use of the article, which is not supported by the context. Cooper (*Messiah: His Nature and Person*, 150–51) and A. Fruchtenbaum (*Messianic Christology* [Tustin, CA: Ariel Press, 1998], 37) have recognized that the boy is Shear-Jashub, but they mistakenly and without syntactical warrant begin his description in 7:15, seeing only 7:13–14 as referring to the Messiah. To my knowledge, only W. Kelly, *An Exposition of the Book of Isaiah* (London: Paternoster, 1897), 144–45; and H. Bultema, *Commentary on Isaiah*, trans. D. Bultema, (Grand Rapids: Kregel, 1981), 108, have

Appropriately, Isaiah could tell Judah in the very next chapter, "Here I am with the children the LORD has given me to be signs and wonders in Israel from the LORD of Hosts who dwells on Mount Zion" (8:18).

The Identity of the Addressee. To whom does Isaiah make this prediction? What is not evident in the English text is plain in the Hebrew. The prophet returned to using the second-person singular pronoun in 7:16 ("the land of the two kings *you* [sg.] dread"). In 7:10–11 he used the singular to address King Ahaz. Then, when addressing the house of David with the prophecy of Messiah, he shifted to the plural. But in 7:16, he addressed King Ahaz, using the singular pronoun once again and giving him a near prophecy: before Shear-Jashub would be able to discern good from evil, the northern confederacy attacking Judah would fail. Within two years, Tiglath-Pileser defeated both Israel and Syria, just as the prophet had predicted.

Having completed his long-term prophecy, Isaiah gave a short-term prophecy. In doing so, he followed a frequent pattern in his book. He consistently did this so his readership could have confidence in the distant prediction by observing the fulfillment of the near one.[28]

The Confirmation of the Prophecy

The messianic interpretation of Isaiah 7:13–15 does not only stand strongly through a careful reading of the text itself, but it is also confirmed by innerbiblical allusions to the prophecy. While some have argued that only Matt 1:23 reads Isa 7:14 as a messianic prophecy, that is really not the case. To begin with, Isaiah himself substantiates the messianic reading with two passages that follow. Isaiah's contemporary Micah does the same.

Isaiah 9:6–7

After giving hope to the house of David that the promise of the Davidic covenant was secure, as would be seen in the birth of Immanuel (7:13–15), Isaiah proceeded to identify when the Son of David would come. He described the time of judgment to fall on Judah (Isaiah 8) when Judah would be "dejected and hungry" and would "see only distress, darkness, and the gloom of affliction" (8:21–22). At that time

---

written that 7:16 begins a second, distinct near prophecy *and* identified the lad as Shear-Jashub. Kelley states that others hold this view, but he does not cite anyone.

[28] Vasholz, "Isaiah and Ahaz: A Brief History of Crisis in Isaiah 7 and 8," 82.

it will be said that "the people walking in darkness have seen a great light; a light has dawned on those living in the land of darkness" (9:2). This light was the Son of David described in Isa 7:13–15.[29] He was the child who would be born and given four glorious, twofold titles: "Wonderful Counselor, Mighty God, Eternal Father, Prince of Peace" (9:6). He would sit "on the throne of David and over his kingdom, to establish and sustain it with justice and righteousness from now on and forever" (9:7). Just as this future king would be called Immanuel, indicating His deity, so also would the other throne titles reflect His divine nature.[30] The point of Isa 9:1–7 was to alert the house of David that the virgin-born King for whom they were to look would only come after a long period of darkness. Nevertheless, He would indeed come, possessing a divine nature, to establish a righteous and eternal kingdom.

Isaiah 11:1–10

Although Isaiah 9 clarifies that the Son of David would come after a time of darkness, Isaiah 11 elucidates even further that Immanuel, the virgin-born Child, on whom the hopes of the entire Davidic house rests, will come in the distant future. Only after the mighty tree of David was cut down "with terrifying power" (10:33) and the Davidic dynasty had become a mere stump would a shoot "grow from the stump of Jesse" (11:1). This King from David's line would be empowered by the Spirit of God and establish a righteous reign (11:2–5). His kingdom would be so peaceful that it would even alter the nature of predatory animals (11:6–9). He would not just be the King of Israel, but

---

[29] Even C. L. Blomberg, who advocates a "double fulfillment" hermeneutic, recognizes that "the larger, eschatological context, especially of Isa. 9:1–7, depicted a son, never clearly distinguished from Isaiah's [Maher-Shalel-Hash-Baz according to Blomberg], who would be a divine, messianic king." That is, the canonical book of Isaiah itself clearly linked, in some way at least, the divine Messiah of Isa 9:1–7, 11:1–10, etc., with the prophecy of a virgin-born son in 7:14. "Matthew could indeed speak of Isaiah's prophecy as fulfilled in Christ. The canonical form of Isaiah was already pointing in this twofold direction" ("Matthew" in *Commentary of the New Testament Use of the Old Testament*, ed. G. K. Beale and D. A. Carson [Grand Rapids: Baker, 2007], 5).

[30] While some have objected to finding the deity of the Messiah in the Hebrew Bible, it appears that this is purely circular reasoning. It begins with the presumption that the Hebrew Scriptures do not reveal a divine Messiah. Then every passage that appears to indicate the deity of the future Messiah is dismissed because "the Hebrew Scriptures do not reveal a divine Messiah." The classic defense of taking Isa 9:6 as referring to Messiah as God is J. D. Davis. "The Child Whose Name is Wonderful," in *Biblical and Theological Studies* (New York: Scribner, 1912). For authoritative defense of the Messiah's deity in the Hebrew Scriptures, see B. B. Warfield. "The Divine Messiah in the Old Testament," in *Christology and Criticism* (New York: Oxford, 1921).

when He comes, all the nations will seek "the root of Jesse" (11:10). This description is an innertextual clarification of the King described in Isaiah 9, giving further details of His peaceful and righteous reign.

Robert Culver has conceded that perhaps Isa 7:13–15 is a difficult passage and hard to identify as messianic without careful reading. However, it becomes clearly messianic "when one continues to the final verses of the prophecy,"[31] referring to Isaiah 9 and 11. He adds that reading Isa 7:13–15 within the context of these other passages would cause a reader to "understand that a virgin was someday to bear a very human baby whose very character would be divine."[32] Certainly, the prophet has included these passages in the book of Immanuel, as Isaiah 7–12 is frequently called, to clarify on whom the house of David should pin their hopes. It was the child written about in Isa 7:13–15, namely, the future Davidic Messiah who would be "God With Us."[33]

Micah 5:3

The prophet Micah, a contemporary of Isaiah, provides an intertextual confirmation of the messianic reading of Isa 7:13–15. Located in the well-known prophecy of the Messiah's birth in Bethlehem (Mic 5:2–5), this prophecy is clearly related to Messiah's birth. It identifies His human origin ("Bethlehem Ephrathah . . . One will come from you to be ruler over Israel for Me"), His eternal source ("from antiquity, from eternity"), and the time of His coming ("when she who is in labor has given birth"). This last phrase has long been recognized as an intertextual reference to the virgin birth in Isa 7:13–15.[34]

The passage indicates that Israel will be abandoned (referring to the captivity and exile) until "she who is in labor has given birth" to the

---

[31] R. D. Culver, "Were the Old Testament Prophecies Really Prophetic?" in *Can I Trust My Bible?* ed. H. Vos (Chicago: Moody, 1963), 104.

[32] Ibid.

[33] Moreover, the author also provides an innertextual reference between the Messiah of Isaiah 11 and the Suffering Servant of Isa 52:13–53:12. Just as the Messiah, "the *root* of Jesse will stand as a banner for the peoples" (Isa 11:10) and would also be compared to "a *root* out of dry ground" (Isa 53:2). When all the innerbiblical dots are connected in Isaiah, it serves to inform the reader that (a) the future son of David would be the virgin-born Immanuel (Isa 7:13–15); (b) He would be God in the flesh (Isa 9:6); (c) He would reign over a righteous and peaceful, eternal Kingdom (Isa 9:7; 11:1–10); and (d) He would only accomplish this after His substitutionary death and resurrection (Isa 52:13–53:12).

[34] N. Snaith, while denying the messianic interpretation of both Isa 7:13–15 and Mic 5:2–5, has recognized that Micah is indeed referring to the Isaiah passage (*Amos, Hosea, and Micah* [London: Epworth, 1960], 95. Snaith admits that Micah 5 is referring to the birth of a great king who, as heir to the Davidic throne, would be endowed with remarkable qualities.

Son of David. Only after this birth will the remnant of Messiah's brethren reunite as a nation (they will "return to the people of Israel"). The reason they will be able to return is the glorious reign of the Messiah, of whom it says, "He [this One] will be their peace" (5:5).

Micah 5:2–5 has multiple allusions and references to the Book of Immanuel. Both Micah 5 and Isaiah 7 refer to the Messiah's birth; both refer to the pregnant woman giving birth; both allude to His divine nature (Micah saying He comes from long ago and the days of eternity, and Isaiah calling Him Immanuel, Mighty God, and Eternal Father); both Micah ("He will stand and shepherd them in the strength of Yahweh," 5:4) and Isaiah (9:7; 11:1–10) refer to the glorious reign of the Messiah; both point out that Messiah will be the source of peace for Israel ("He will be their peace," Mic 5:5; "He will be named . . . Prince of Peace," Isa 9:6).

These many intertextual references are significant. If a plainly messianic passage like Mic 5:2–5[35] cites Isa 7:13–15, it shows that the earliest interpretation of Isa 7:14 (and no less, an inspired interpretation) recognizes the messianic prophecy of the virgin birth.

Matthew 1:23

Matthew's use of Isa 7:14 in his narrative of the virgin birth has been regarded in a variety of ways: a double fulfillment or *sensus plenior*; an example of typical fulfillment; a pesher interpretation;[36] or even a misuse of Isaiah, who was not referring to the virgin birth in any way at all. However, it appears that Matthew was following a careful and close reading of Isaiah[37] and recognized that the prediction given to

---

[35] Certainly some have disputed that Mic 5:2–5 is messianic and have regarded it as nothing more than hope for the restoration of a Davidic king. Nevertheless, the messianic interpretation is ancient and well established. It is only those interpreters with a presumption that the Old Testament has no messianic hope at all that seem to reject the messianic interpretation of Mic 5:2–5. Cf. K. L. Barker, "Micah" in *Micah, Nahum, Habakkuk, Zephaniah*, NAC 20 (Nashville: B&H, 1998), 95–103.

[36] Evangelicals who hold this view would consider this rabbinic-style, creative exegesis under the inspiration of the Holy Spirit.

[37] Some might object that the careful reading available to Matthew was not understandable to Ahaz, who might be considered "the original audience" of this prophecy. This objection fails to understand the nature of the Bible as a text. While Ahaz did receive this prophecy in a particular time and place, all we have is a textual record of that event in the composition known as the book of Isaiah. Thus, Ahaz is not the original audience of the book of Isaiah but a character in the inspired narrative written in the book. The audience of the book is eighth century BC Judah, to whom a careful reading of the visible compositional strategies were available. They could read it in context with Isaiah 9 and 11 just as any reader of the book of Isaiah can after

the house of David had found its fulfillment in the virgin birth of Jesus of Nazareth. Immanuel had come just as prophesied eight centuries earlier. God was with Israel. The inspired words of the apostle Matthew in 1:22 (lit, "Now all this happened *in order that* what was spoken by the Lord through the prophet might be fulfilled") make it clear that God's words to Isaiah in 7:14 had made the particular nature of the Messiah's birth to the virgin as inevitable as thunder that follows the lightening. Furthermore, to remove the intentionality of this connection is to deny the truthfulness of Matthew's words.

The Virgin Birth in Proclamation

We end where we began. What if Jesus did indeed have a human father named Larry? What if the gospel writers were merely mythologizing to make their message more palatable to pagans? What if Isaiah's prediction referred to a young woman giving birth to a child via natural means in eighth century BC Judah? According to some evangelicals, these are insignificant questions. Their approach says that faith in Jesus is still the truth even if the virgin birth is questioned or if Isaiah's prediction of it is explained away as exegetically untenable. But truth is foundational to faith. According to Bell, and others, we must believe in Jesus because "it works," not because it is true. In fact, Jesus' claim is just the opposite. According to Him, faith in Him only works because it is a true faith. Moreover, He is the truth.

It appears that according to prophecy, the Messiah's virgin birth was an essential to be believed for two reasons. First, the virgin birth was to be a major sign to confirm Messiah Jesus' position as the messianic Son of David. If Jesus of Nazareth had a human father named Larry or Joseph, it would prove that He really was not the Messiah. No matter how good a life one could lead by believing in Jesus, it would be a sham. Following Jesus changes our lives because He truly is the Messiah.

Second, the virgin birth is in some way related to the deity of Jesus. The prediction foretells that the Messiah would be Immanuel or "God with us." Luke, when recording the virgin birth, records the angel's message to Mary: "The Holy Spirit will come upon you and the power of the Most High will overshadow you. Therefore, the holy One to be

---

them. In other words, what was available and understandable to Matthew was also available and understandable to the original readers.

born will be called the Son of God" (Luke 1:35). Just as Isaiah related the virgin birth to Messiah being God with us, so Luke regards the virgin birth as the basis for Jesus' being the Son of God, that is, Deity. Foundational to our faith is that God became a man in order to redeem us. Without the virgin birth, we deny the doctrine of Messiah's deity and lose the truth of His atonement.

Philip Roth's short story, *The Conversion of the Jews*, relates the tale of a young Jewish boy, Ozzie, who asked his rabbi about the virgin birth. Relating his question to his friend, young Ozzie says,

> I asked the question about God, how if He could create the heaven and earth in six days, and make all the animals, and the fish and the light in six days . . . if he could make all that in six days, and He could *pick* the six days he wanted right out of nowhere, why couldn't He let a woman have a baby without having intercourse?[38]

Ozzie's point about the possibility of a supernatural birth makes perfect sense. I would go one step further to affirm supernatural revelation. If God could create the world and miraculously enable a young Jewish virgin to have a baby, certainly He could have allowed an eighth-century BC Jewish prophet to predict the first-century virgin birth of the Jewish Messiah.

---

[38] P. Roth, "The Conversion of the Jews," in *Goodbye Columbus and Five Short Stories* (New York: Vintage Books, 1987), 140–41.

Chapter 11

AN EXAMPLE FROM THE WRITINGS: INTERPRETING PSALM 110 AS A MESSIANIC PROPHECY

Psalm 110 has long been understood as a direct prediction of the Messiah. Even Franz Delitzsch, who generally viewed the messianic character of the Psalms to be merely typical, recognized Psalm 110 as a direct messianic prophecy. In his commentary on the Psalms, he wrote that in Psalm 110 David "looks forth into the future of his seed and has the Messiah definitely before his mind."[1] Also, according to Delitzsch, "the Messiah stands objectively before the mind of David."[2] For reasons derived from the text of the psalm itself, even among interpreters who, like Delitzsch, did not interpret any other psalm messianically, Psalm 110 has been consistently interpreted as directly prophetic of the Messiah.

But this is no longer the case. For example, Tremper Longman III states of the Psalms in general, "Some people believe that a few psalms are messianic in the narrow sense. That is, some psalms are prophetic and have no direct message of significance for the Old Testament period. They only predict the coming Messiah." Longman rejects this possibility, writing, "no psalm is messianic in the narrow sense."[3]

Speaking specifically of Psalm 110, evangelical scholar Herbert W. Bateman IV rejects the messianic interpretation and instead affirms that Psalm 110 is directed to David's son Solomon, stating, "Thus it seems reasonable that Psalm 110 refers to Solomon's second coronation in 971 B.C. when David abdicated his throne to his son Solomon" and "that David did not speak the psalm to the Messiah, the divine Lord."[4] Eugene Merrill is another evangelical scholar that rejects

---

[1] F. Delitzsch, "Psalms," in *Commentary on the Old Testament*, by C. F. Keil and F. Delitzsch, trans. J. Martin (Grand Rapids: Eerdmans, 1980), 1:66.

[2] Ibid., 3:184.

[3] T. Longman III, *How to Read the Psalms* (Downers Grove, IL: InterVarsity, 1988), 67–68. Longman does say the Psalms ultimately speak of Messiah Jesus but only in a secondary sense, not in a directly predictive way. His argument is that direct messianic psalms remove the significance of a psalm from its Old Testament context. According to him, the psalmist's intended meaning must not be eschatological and future oriented but rather must refer to events in the writer's own day.

[4] H. W. Bateman IV, "Psalm 110:1 and the New Testament," *BSac* 149 (1992): 452–53.

reading Psalm 110 as speaking directly of the Messiah. While affirming that David is indeed the author of the psalm, Merrill maintains that in Ps 110:1, David is calling himself "my lord." According to him, David is merely establishing a motif of royal priesthood for all Davidic kings, and the psalm was only generally fulfilled by the Messiah Jesus.[5]

Is it possible to view Psalm 110 as a direct messianic prediction while still practicing sound exegesis? In this chapter, I will attempt to demonstrate that the most reasonable interpretation of Psalm 110 is to view it as a direct messianic prediction. To do so, I will begin by examining the presuppositions that should guide the interpretation of Psalm 110. Having done that, I will present a careful exegesis of the psalm, examining its location in the Psalter, analyzing the exegesis of the text itself, and then noting the psalm's innertextual and intertextual relationship with other passages in the Hebrew Scriptures. The conclusion will emphasize the messianic significance of the psalm.

Interpretive Presuppositions

Much of the interpretation of Psalm 110 depends on the interpreter's presuppositions. If one presupposes that there are no direct messianic predictions or any concept of a Messiah in the Hebrew Bible, then certainly it would be necessary to look for alternative interpretations of Psalm 110. However, if there is good reason to presuppose that the Psalms are indeed messianic, then this will yield a messianic explanation of the psalm. Hence, these preliminary considerations will attempt to establish the presuppositions that provide a foundation for interpreting Psalm 110 as a direct prediction of the Messiah.

Davidic Authorship of Psalm 110

The first of the interpretive presuppositions pertains to the authorship of the psalm. If David is not the author of the psalm, it is more likely that the subject of the psalm is David himself or the Davidic king. If he did write the psalm, it allows for the likelihood that the Messiah is the subject of the psalm. H. H. Rowley suggested that the author of Psalm 110 was David and Zadok together,[6] while others

---

[5] E. H. Merrill, "Royal Priesthood: An Old Testament Messianic Motif" *BSac* 150 (1993): 50–61.

[6] H. H. Rowley, "Melchizedek and Zadok (Ge 14 and Ps 110)," in *Festschrift: Alfred Bertholet zum 80. Geburtstag*, ed. W. Baumgartner (Tübingen: J. C. B. Mohr, 1950), 461–72.

have proposed that it was some unnamed author.[7] Yet some interpreters still take the superscription *lĕdāwid* ("of David") at face value, ascribing authorship to David.[8]

The first reason for accepting Davidic authorship is that this is the plain meaning of the superscription. The Hebrew preposition can indeed mean "[dedicated] to David," or "about David." Alternatively, it can mean "of David," showing that David was the author. Of course, critical scholars frequently reject Davidic authorship of any of the psalms. Yet evangelicals tend to accept that David was the author of many of them.[9] As such, most of the Davidic psalms have the identical superscription *lĕdāwid*. It would be inconsistent to accept other psalms as written by David but to reject Davidic authorship of Psalm 110 merely to avoid taking a messianic interpretation. David L. Cooper makes the case well, noting that the many usages of this superscription generally indicate David as the author of a given psalm. "Hence, the remaining possibility, unless there is unmistakable proof to the contrary, it must be accepted as the only plausible one, namely, that this preposition indicates authorship. Since in this case negative proof is lacking, we must accept David as the inspired writer."[10]

A second reason to maintain Davidic authorship of Psalm 110 is that Jesus Himself asserted it.[11] In a controversy with the Pharisees, Jesus quoted Psalm 110 and asked them, "How it is then that David, inspired by the Spirit, calls Him [i.e., the Son of David] 'Lord' . . . If

---

[7] C. A. Briggs and E. G. Briggs, *A Critical and Exegetical Commentary on the Book of Psalms*, ICC (Edinburgh: T&T Clark, 1986), 2:375; M. Dahood, *Psalms*, AB (Garden City, NY: Doubleday, 1970), 3:113; J. Goldingay, *Psalms* (Grand Rapids: Baker, 2008), 3:291.

[8] Bateman, "Psalm 110:1 and the New Testament," 444–45; Merrill, "Royal Priesthood: An Old Testament Messianic Motif," 54–55; J. J. S. Perowne, *The Book of Psalms* (Grand Rapids: Zondervan, 1966), 2:295–98. H. C. Leupold, *Exposition of the Psalms* (Grand Rapids: Baker, 1969), 770–75.

[9] Although the term לְדָוִד is capable of several interpretations, W. A. VanGemeren explains, "The Bible clearly teaches that David was a poet of extraordinary abilities (2 Sam 23:1) and a musician (Amos 6:5; cf. 1 Sam 16:15–23; 18:10; 2 Sam 1:17–27; 3:33–34; 23:1–7) and that he created the temple guilds of singers and musicians (1 Chronicles 6:31–32; 15:16,27; 25:1–31; 2 Chronicles 29:25–26; cf. Neh 12:45–47). The NT writers likewise assumed that David was the author of many psalms (cf. Matt 22:43–45; Acts 2:25–28; 4:25–26; Heb 4:7) and even spoke of the Book of Psalms as being David's (Luke 20:42)." See *EBC* 5:34.

[10] D. L. Cooper, *Messiah: His Redemptive Career* (Los Angeles: Biblical Research Society, 1963), 64.

[11] D. Kidner has remarked that most contemporary scholarship views the author of the psalm as "an anonymous cultic official" writing for "either David or one of his successors." He bitingly comments, "Our Lord and the apostles, it is understood, were denied this insight." *Psalms 73–150* (Downers Grove, IL: InterVarsity, 1975), 392.

David calls Him 'Lord,' how then can the Messiah be his Son?" (Matt 22:41,46; cf. also Mark 12:35–37; Luke 20:41–44). Delitzsch correctly asserts that if David were not the author of this psalm, then Jesus' question to the Pharisees concerning this psalm "would lack . . . cogency as an argument."[12] Some might object that Jesus, in His humanity or self-limitation, did not know that David was not actually the author of the psalm. Others might suggest that He was merely repeating, not actually affirming, the common contemporary Jewish understanding of the psalm's authorship. But if either of these possibilities is true, then Jesus' argument is invalid—a conclusion I am not willing to accept. Therefore, since there is no compelling reason to doubt the credibility of the superscription, we may assume that David wrote Psalm 110.

Nevertheless, even if David was the author, it may not be automatic that his subject was the future royal Messiah. For example, Merrill maintains Davidic authorship but argues that David was writing of himself. In his view, the word *'ădōnî* (my lord) "became so formulaic that a king could use it even of himself. That is, 'my lord' came to mean nothing more than 'I' or 'me' when employed by the royal speaker." Yet, Merrill also demonstrates the grave weakness of his own assertion when he states, "There is no other clear reference in the Old Testament to an individual addressing himself in this manner."[13] So if this is what David is doing here, it is the only place a king speaks of himself like this in the Old Testament.

Similarly, Bateman maintains Davidic authorship but identifies Solomon as the subject of the psalm. In his view, David wrote Psalm 110 after he had abdicated kingship and given the crown to Solomon. Since Solomon had become king, David could refer to him as "my lord." Bateman bases his view on the word *'ădōnî*, as pointed in the Masoretic Text (as opposed to the term *'ădōnay*, so often used of God), asserting that 94 percent of its 168 uses refer to a human king.[14] Barry C. Davis responds that in two cases (Josh 5:14 and Judg 6:13), the word *'ădōnî* is used of the Lord God appearing as the angel of the Lord. Thus he concludes, "There is nothing to preclude the possibility that the referent of David's use of *'ădōnî* is the Messiah."[15] Further

---

[12] F. Delitzsch, *Psalms* in *Commentary on the Old Testament* Volume V (Three Volumes in One), V:III:184.

[13] Merrill, "Royal Priesthood: An Old Testament Messianic Motif," 55.

[14] Bateman, "Psalm 110:1 and the New Testament," 448–49.

[15] B. C. Davis, "Is Psalm 110 a Messianic Psalm?" *BSac* 157 (2000): 162–63.

evidence for David's addressing one far more eminent that himself or his son Solomon will be seen in David's last words (2 Sam 23:1, considered below), which provides David's own authorial explanation of his psalms.

Authorial Intent of Psalm 110

A second interpretive presupposition for understanding Psalm 110 as messianic is that David himself in his last words (2 Sam 23:1–5) identified the Messiah as his favorite subject in the Psalms. In this paragraph, much like an author interview in the *Paris Review*,[16] David reveals his own authorial intent, that his psalms refer to the Messiah. As explained in chapter 3, this interpretation of David's last words is not as evident in the Masoretic Text of 2 Sam 23:1 as it is if the Masoretic *ʿāl*, "on high," is read as *ʿal*, "concerning," based on the Septuagint, yielding (my translation),

> These are the last words of David:
> the declaration of David son of Jesse,
> the declaration of the man raised up *concerning*
> the Messiah [Anointed One] of the God of Jacob,
> and the Delightful One of the songs of Israel.

In his last words David has said that the future Messiah was his favorite subject in the Psalms. This passage gives a crucial interpretive clue to reading Davidic psalms in general and Psalm 110 in particular. David, by his own assertion, claims he frequently wrote about "the Messiah, the Delightful One of the songs of Israel," indicating that the Psalms have a messianic focus and that Psalm 110 has the Messiah as its subject.

Postexilic Redaction of the Psalms

Yet a third interpretive presupposition for interpreting Psalm 110 as a messianic prediction is to view the entire book of Psalms as a postexilic redaction. Although it is normal for contemporary interpreters to view the psalms as individual texts gathered with little regard for structure or theme, in recent years this trend has begun to shift. There is considerable movement to understanding the book of

---

[16] The *Paris Review* is an English language literary magazine most known for its interviews of authors in which they explain their work.

Psalms as the product of a purposeful redaction in the postexilic period with an identifiable theme.[17]

By recognizing the Psalms as a coherent collection of the postexilic period, the message of the entire book becomes clearer. That is not to say that the later redaction altered the original meaning of the book of Psalms.[18] Rather, as Bruce Waltke maintains, such a redaction of the Psalms did not change the "original authorial intention" but rather "deepened and clarified" it.[19]

The clarification of the message of the Psalms came about because there no longer was a "son of David sitting on Yahweh's throne."[20] In light of this reality, Brevard Childs insightfully asks, "Indeed, at the time of the final redaction, when the institution of kingship had long since been destroyed, what earthly king would have come to mind other than God's Messiah?"[21] In fact, as Mitchell states,

> The very inclusion of the royal psalms in the Psalter suggests that the redactor understood them to refer to a future *mashiah*-king. For otherwise, their presence in a collection for use in second temple times, when the house of David was in eclipse, would have made little sense.[22]

Since the book of Psalms was a postexilic redaction, then its message looks forward to the restoration of the Davidic dynasty in fulfillment

---

[17] G. H. Wilson has effectively made the case for viewing the Psalms as having a purposeful postexilic redaction with an identifiable theme (*The Editing of the Hebrew Psalter* [Chico, CA: Scholars Press, 1985], 9–10, 182–99. However, according to Wilson, that theme looks backward historically, focusing on the failure of the Davidic dynasty. In his view, the Psalms do not look forward to a restored Davidic dynasty under the Messiah but a return to the premonarchic days when the Lord alone was Israel's king (pp. 214–15). Treating the Psalms as a postexilic redaction is not merely a current approach. J. Forbes, in the late nineteenth century, made the case that the Psalms were a coherent postexilic collection with a messianic intent (*Studies on the Book of Psalms* [Edinburgh: T & T Clark, 1888]).

[18] B. K. Waltke's article, "A Canonical Process Approach to the Psalms," in *Tradition and Testament*, ed. J. Feinberg and P. Feinberg (Chicago: Moody, 1981), 3–18, is a masterful explanation of the nature of the book of Psalms and the way the Psalms should be read as a messianic text.

[19] Ibid., 8.

[20] Ibid., 15.

[21] B. S. Childs, *Introduction to the Old Testament as Scripture* (Philadelphia: Fortress, 1979), 516.

[22] D. C. Mitchell, *The Message of the Psalter: An Eschatological Programme in the Book of Psalms* (Sheffield, England: Sheffield Academic Press, 1997), 86. Mitchell, much like Forbes a century before, has persuasively argued for interpreting the Psalms as a coherent postexilic redaction with an eschatological/messianic theme throughout the Psalter. D. M. Howard has recognized the importance of Mitchell's thesis, writing, "The overall force and logic of his argument is impressive, however, and his work will surely occupy a pivotal position in future discussions of the Psalter's composition and message" ("Recent Trends in Psalm Study," *The Face of Old Testament Studies*, ed. D. W. Baker and B. T. Arnold [Grand Rapids: Baker, 1999], 338).

of the Davidic covenant. Thus, Mitchell accurately states, "the messianic theme is central to the purpose of the collection."[23] In the context of the whole book and not just individual songs, the Psalms should be read as referring to the future king, namely, the Messiah. And in Psalm 110, the king described as seated at the right hand of God is not David, Solomon, or any other historical king—it is the royal Messiah. Having established that the Psalms in general and Psalm 110 in particular should be read messianically, the issue arises as to whether the details of the psalm allow for this approach. Therefore, it is necessary to evaluate the details of the psalm itself.

Exegetical Considerations

A careful reading of Psalm 110 will show that the most natural interpretation is that it describes the future Messiah, the eschatological Son of David. This will become evident by an examination of the literary context of Psalm 110, a close intextual reading of the psalm, and evaluation of the innertextual and intertextual references, all serving to confirm the messianic interpretation of Psalm 110.

Contextual Analysis

Book Five of the Psalter comprises Psalms 107–150. The first seven psalms of Book Five contain a discernible unit of thought, with Psalm 110 forming their focal point. As Davis says, Psalm 110 is the "thematic unifier of Psalm 107–13."[24] (See Figure 11.1.) In this section of the Psalms, Psalms 107–109 each contain a plea for deliverance, while each of Psalms 111–113 expresses praise for deliverance. Psalm 110 is central to the thoughts of these psalms since it reveals the Messiah as King, Priest, and Warrior—He is the answer to God's people's supplications for rescue (Psalms 107–109) and the reason for their praises to God (Psalms 111–113). The point of Psalm 110's location in the Psalter is that Israel is to find the answer to their pleas for deliverance from oppression in the future Messiah and is to offer praise to God for the messianic redemption He provides.

[23] Ibid., 87.
[24] Davis, "Is Psalm 1110 a Messianic Psalm?" 168.

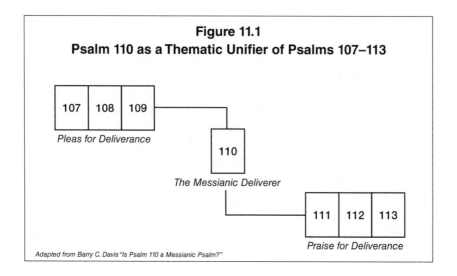

Figure 11.1
Psalm 110 as a Thematic Unifier of Psalms 107–113

| 107 | 108 | 109 |

Pleas for Deliverance

| 110 |

The Messianic Deliverer

| 111 | 112 | 113 |

Praise for Deliverance

Adapted from Barry C. Davis "Is Psalm 110 a Messianic Psalm?"

Intertextual Interpretation

At the outset, the superscription begins by ascribing authorship to David. To those who have denied Davidic authorship and argued that this is merely a royal psalm describing David, Kidner has responded, "Therefore those who deny David's authorship of the psalm on the ground that the psalm reads like an enthronement oracle, curiously miss the point. It is just such an oracle. What is unique is the royal speaker, addressing this more-than-royal person."[25]

The psalm can be divided into three units of thought, each describing the messianic Son of David. The first three verses show Him to be the Divine King (110:1–3), the central verse identifies Him as an eternal priest (110:4), and the final three verses reveal Him as a victorious warrior (110:5–7).[26] The central verse, in its brevity, forms the literary focal point of the psalm. The theme of the psalm is that the Lord has granted universal dominion to the messianic Priest-King.

I. *Messiah, the Divine King (110:1–3).* The first stanza of the psalm emphasizes the royalty of the Messiah, describing Him in a variety of his kingly roles.

A. *The Messiah is Lord (110:1a).* The psalm opens with the Hebrew phrase *nĕʾum yhwh* (lit., "declaration/proclamation/oracle of the

---

[25] Kidner, *Psalms 73–150*, 392.
[26] This structure is adapted from Kidner, *Psalms 73–150*, 393–96.

Lord"), an oracular expression frequently used in the Prophets to emphasize that the pronouncement comes from God Himself. Hence, at the outset of the psalm, the usage of prophetic imagery casts the sense that this psalm is a prophetic oracle.[27]

This oracle is addressed to "my lord" (*'ădōnî*), using a word that is generally used of a human superior, not deity. Yet as explained above, the word is used of the angel of the Lord in Josh 5:14 and Judg 6:13, where He is then identified with the Lord Himself. Furthermore, as Robert Alden observes, the psalm was originally written with consonants alone, with the Masoretic vowels added much later (between the eighth and tenth centuries AD).[28] One must be careful, then, not to base one's interpretation (i.e., whether the addressee is human or divine) solely on a single Hebrew vowel. There are, in fact, strong reasons to conclude that the original author of the psalm intended to speak of a divine Lord. David, Israel's most exalted king, was looking forward to the coming of a future ruler even more exalted than himself.

B. Messiah Is at God's Right Hand (110:1b). The Lord directs the exalted king to sit at His right hand. This appears to be a special place of honor (Ps 45:9[Hb. 10]) as indicated by Solomon setting up a throne for his mother Bathsheba so that she could sit at his right hand (1 Kgs 2:19). Leupold states that the location of the throne at God's right hand indicated "that the Lord God of Israel Himself ('Yahweh') had designated for the Messiah a position at his own right hand, making Him coequal in rank and authority with Himself, and so virtually declaring His divine character."[29] This may very well overstate the significance of the right hand, as Solomon merely exalted Bathsheba but did not necessarily present her as equal to himself. It seems safer to surmise that the right hand is merely a place of exaltation and honor. However, it still does not disallow viewing the exalted one seated at the right hand as being divine.

---

[27] The HCSB translation "This is the declaration of the Lord" and the NET Bible's "Here is the Lord's proclamation" are based on the recognition that the phrase's common function is not to identify the speaker but to insist that Yahweh is the source of the speech (cf. Jer 23:41; 9:21[Eng. 22]; Ezek 13:7). Cf. T. L. Wilt, "'Oracle of Yahweh': Translating a Highly Marked Expression," *Bible Translator* 50.3 (1999): 301–4; S. A. Meier, *Speaking of Speaking: Marking Direct Discourse in the Hebrew Bible* (Leiden: Brill, 1992), 298–314.

[28] R. L. Alden, *Psalms: Songs of Discipleship* (Chicago: Moody, 1976), 3:31–32. I am not suggesting that only the consonantal text is reliable and authoritative, but only that the body of evidence for the original reading must be carefully evaluated. The relationship between the oral and written traditions is complex and beyond the scope of this study.

[29] Leupold, *Exposition of the Psalms,* 771.

Some have speculated that the right hand of God refers to the placement of the royal palace in close proximity to the ark[30] or the king's enthronement on the side of the Holy of Holies at the outset of the fall festival.[31] More likely, being seated at the right hand of God refers to the bestowal of authority and dominion in God's own heavenly throne room.[32]

C. *The Messiah Awaits Victory (110:1c).* The royal Messiah is seated at the right hand of God, awaiting the day that God makes the King's enemies a footstool for His feet. The phrase "your enemies" (*ʾōyĕbeykā*) used in Psalm 110 (in vv. 1,2) is commonly used of God's enemies in the book of Psalms (8:2; 21:8; 66:3; 74:23; 89:10,51; 92:9).[33] The only exception might be Ps 21:8, but Dahood maintains that even in this verse, the opponents are the enemies of the divine King, not the human ruler.[34]

The image of the footstool is that of triumph. Just as the victor subdues the defeated underfoot (cf. Ps 47:3; Josh 10:24, Isa 49:23), so this divine Ruler awaits the day when His feet will rest on His enemies. Moreover, the word "footstool" (*hădōm*) is used as belonging to God (1 Chr 28:2; Pss 99:5; 132:7; Isa 66:1; Lam 2:1).[35] To summarize, Ps 110:1 describes an exalted Ruler, in a supreme place of honor in the throne room of God, awaiting victory over the enemies of God, who will become a divine footstool. This could not describe anyone other than an exalted, eschatological messianic figure.

D. *The Messiah Will Rule (110:2–3).* Although the King initially awaits victory in God's heavenly throne room, vv. 2–3 indicate a descent from heaven to earth, where He receives dominion over His enemies and leads His servants into battle. Thus, Messiah will rule over both His enemies (v. 2) and His willing servants (v. 3).

The Messiah's rule is described as the Lord extending the King's scepter from Zion (v. 2), a figure for His reign from earthly Jerusalem.[36] The implication of the King's dominion issuing forth from Zion

---

[30] A. F. Kirkpatrick, *The Book of Psalms* (Cambridge: Cambridge University Press, 1902), 666.

[31] H.-J. Kraus, *Psalms 60–150*, trans. H. C. Oswald (Minneapolis: Fortress, 1993), 348.

[32] D. C. Mitchell argues for this interpretation based on this understanding in Dan 7:13–14, 11QMelch, the New Testament, and the *Testament of Job* (*The Message of the Psalter: An Eschatological Programme in the Book of Psalms*, 259–60).

[33] Davis, "Is Psalm 110 a Messianic Psalm?" 164.

[34] M. Dahood, *Psalms*, AB (Garden City, NY: Doubleday, 1970), 1:131.

[35] Davis, "Is Psalm 110 a Messianic Psalm?" 164.

[36] Mitchell suggests that there may be further evidence for the King's descent from the heavenly heights. He notes that the word often translated "rule" may, in fact, be a further reference

and the King's role in the final earthly battle (v. 5) shows that He will descend from the heavenly heights to the earth. Thus, the King will descend upon His enemies[37] and rule over them.

Not only will the future King have dominion over His enemies. According to v. 3, the King will also lead His faithful servants in war. His people are described as voluntary warriors on the day of battle (see also Judg 5:2). The text of this depiction of an eschatological army volunteering to fight for the Messiah has two possible Hebrew readings, both of which make good sense. According to the more well-attested reading, the warriors are dressed "in holy splendor" (*běhadrê qōdeš*). In a significant variant reading (*běharrê qōdeš*),[38] their battlefield is "on holy mountains." In the former reading, the soldiers of the messianic Priest-King are wearing priestly garments for the "sacrificial feast" of slaughter on the mountains of Israel during the great eschatological war (Ezek 39:17). The latter reading describes the battlefield as the "holy hills" of the great eschatological war that will take place on the mountains of Israel (Ezek 38:21). Either reading fits the messianic presentation of the eschatological warrior-King in Psalm 110.[39]

David M. Hay correctly notes that the last phrase of 110:3 is "virtually unintelligible."[40] The MT reads "from the womb of the dawn, your youth [*yalduteykā*] are to you as dew" (or "the dew of your youth belongs to you," as in the HCSB), leading to a variety of strained and unlikely interpretations since these words make virtually no sense. Booj describes the phrase as "especially problematic and indeed . . . meaningless." He concludes that "some deformation must have crept in."[41]

Although a canon of textual criticism is that the harder reading is to be preferred, there is a difference between a harder reading and an

---

to a descent from the heavenly throne room. Of this imperative, Mitchell writes, "Might רְדֵה of v. 2 at some time have been understood, possibly by ancient aural ambiguity, as רְדָה: *Descend among your enemies?* There is no textual evidence for it, although descent (ירד) upon the earth, albeit metaphorical, is attributed to the superhero-king of Ps. 72:6" (D. C. Mitchell, *The Message of the Psalter*, 260).

[37] Note the comment on v. 1 that the word for enemies is generally used in the psalm of God's enemies, once again hinting that this King is more than royal, even divine.

[38] So in 83 Masoretic manuscripts, Symmachus, and Jerome; see Th. Booj, "Psalm 110: Rule in the Midst of Your Foes," *VT* 41 (1991): 398.

[39] Mitchell, *The Message of the Psalter*, 261.

[40] D. M. Hay, *Glory at the Right Hand: Psalm 110 in Early Christianity* (Nashville: Abingdon, 1973), 21.

[41] Booj, "Psalm 110: Rule in the Midst of Your Foes," 398.

incoherent, impossible one. For this reason, Sigmund Mowinckel and other scholars prefer the LXX, which reads, "from the womb of the dawn, I have begotten you," a translation based on the same Hebrew consonants but with different vowel pointings (*yĕlidtîkā*).[42] Additionally, Bentzen has suggested that the corruption of the MT resulted from deliberate scribal efforts to obfuscate the meaning and its plain allusion to Ps 2:7.[43]

Since the LXX reading is preferable,[44] it leads to a strongly messianic interpretation, describing in Hay's words "the birth of a divine child" as King. The King is said to be begotten "from the womb of the dawn," a phrase Kraus links to the coming of the messianic king described in Num 24:17 as a star that comes forth from Jacob. Furthermore, Kraus sees "the place and procedure of the begetting" as belonging "to the heavenly sphere. The 'divine king' comes from the superworldly heights, from God's world." Linking the phrase "from the womb of the dawn I have begotten you" to Ps 2:7, Kraus rightly concludes that it is "a reference to the heavenly divine origin of the king."[45] McCaul adds that it not only indicates origin from heaven but One eternally begotten "before conception of the morning light" or "before creation."[46]

Thus, the first stanza of Psalm 110 presents a divine King, seated at the right hand of God and awaiting future victory. On that eschatological day of triumph, He will descend from God's heavenly throne room as the begotten one and establish His dominion from Zion over the whole world. In that great last battle, the King will establish his rule, destroying His enemies while leading His willing servants to victory.

---

[42] S. Mowinckel, *He That Cometh*, trans. G. W. Anderson (Nashville: Abingdon, 1956), 67; A. McCaul, *The Messiahship of Jesus* (London: Parker, 1852), 172, 174. This reading is also supported by a number of Masoretic manuscripts and the Syriac (cf. A. Y. Collins and J. J. Collins, *King and Messiah as Son of God* [Grand Rapids: Eerdmans, 2008], 17).

[43] A. Bentzen, *Introduction to the Old Testament* (Copenhagen: Gad, 1952), 100.

[44] One problem with adopting the variant reading is that the LXX drops the Hebrew phrase לְךָ טַל ("to you the dew"), while the Syriac reads *talya*, "child," in its place. The volume by Collins and Collins suggests that both of these readings reflect "either difficulty of comprehension or theological discomfort" (Collins and Collins, *King and Messiah as Son of God*, 18). W. P. Brown has suggested the reading לְךָ כְּטַל, "go forth as the dew," proposing that one kaph dropped out by haplography ("A Royal Performance: Critical Notes on Psalm 110:3ag," *JBL* 117 [1998]: 95). Kraus accepts the LXX reading, proposing that perhaps the original text read כְּטַל, yielding the translation "Like dew, I have begotten you" (Kraus, *Psalm 60–150*, 350). S. R. A. Starbuck's view is similar, interpreting the phrase, "Just as Yahweh gives birth to the dew every morning" even so the Lord has begotten the King (*Court Oracles in the Psalms: The So-Called Royal Psalms in Their Ancient Near Eastern Context* [Atlanta: SBL, 1996], 148, 150).

[45] Kraus, *Psalm 60–150*, 350.

[46] McCaul, *The Messiahship of Jesus*, 172, 174.

II. Messiah, The Priest-King (110:4). A major break occurs at this juncture in the psalm. The shorter but more surprising description of the King in v. 4 draws attention to this verse as the focal point of the psalm.

A. The Promise of God (110:4a). Providing a second oracle in the psalm, the writer focuses on the certainty of God's promise to His chosen King. Since the Lord swore it, He will cause it to happen and He will not be sorry.[47] This "assures us that Yahweh's statement is guaranteed by a declaration that is irrevocable and sworn."[48] Yahweh's promise to the Messiah is absolute and certain to occur because of His strong oath.

B. The Office of Messiah (110:4). God's strong oath was required because of the unusual promise that the Messiah would be a priest. There are three unique features of the Messiah's priesthood, the first of which is that God would unite the offices of priest and king in the Messiah. This is special in that these offices were always separate in Israel. Some interpreters who see David or an Israelite king as the subject of the psalm maintain that the office of priest-king was common in Israel.[49] Merrill supports this by citing several biblical passages. For example, in 2 Sam 8:18 David's sons are called "priests" (*kōhănîm*), although in the parallel passage (1 Chr 18:17) they are called "chief officials" (*ri'šōnîm*). Merrill writes, "Despite various efforts to explain *kōhănîm* as something other than priests, it seems best to view these sons as priests in the same sense in which David was."[50] In direct contradiction to this statement, Merrill writes in another work, "The Hebrew word, usually rendered 'priests,' is explained in 1 Chronicles 18:17 as "chief officials" (cf. 2 Sam. 20:26). This no doubt is the better meaning since David's sons, as Judeans, were ineligible to serve as priests."[51]

---

[47] BDB identifies the verb יִנָּחֵם ("He will not take it back") as a Niphal imperfect, 3rd person singular with a negative particle, with the translation, "he will not be sorry."

[48] Kraus, *Psalm 60–150*, 350.

[49] J. G. Gammie, "A New Setting for Psalm 110," *AThR* 51 (1969): 4–17; J. L. Mays, *Psalms*, IBC (Louisville: John Knox, 1994), 350–55; Merrill, "Royal Priesthood: An Old Testament Messianic Motif," 59–61.

[50] Merrill, "Royal Priesthood: An Old Testament Messianic Motif," 60.

[51] E. H. Merrill, "2 Samuel," *The Bible Knowledge Commentary: Old Testament*, ed. J. F. Walvoord and R. B. Zuck (Wheaton, IL: Victor Books, 1985), 464. C. F. Keil and F. Delitzsch make a good case for translating כֹּהֲנִים as royal officials in 2 Sam 8:18 and not "priests," demonstrating that the word is explained as "the king's friend" in 1 Kgs 4:5 (*Biblical Commentary on the Books of Samuel* [Grand Rapids: Eerdmans, n.d.], 368–69). Note also that the LXX translates כֹּהֲנִים as αὐλάρχαι ("court rulers") and not priests.

Merrill also argues that in 2 Samuel 6 David is described as wearing priestly attire (v. 14, "a linen ephod"), offering sacrifice (vv. 17–18), and issuing priestly benedictions (v. 18). The linen ephod was indeed priestly attire, but as Keil and Delitzsch point out, it was not the clothing required to be worn when performing priestly duties. Rather, it denoted the character of the wearer.[52] Furthermore, David did not offer the sacrifices himself but rather *through* the Levitical priests present.[53] He also blessed the people as their king and leader, not as their priest. In ancient Israel, David was not, nor were any of his royal descendants, priest-kings. The Law made it clear that there was "a clear distinction between Israel's three theocratic officers, king, prophet, and priest."[54]

The point is that the Lord's oath to the messianic King promises Him a unique office—not merely as royalty but as a Priest-King, who would both rule and represent His people before God. Yet a second aspect of the King's unique priesthood is that he would not serve as a Levitical priest but as a "priest like Melchizedek."[55] Melchizedek, described in Genesis 14, served as a priest-king of God Most High. From him, Abram received bread and wine for a meal of sacral worship (Gen 14:18) and a blessing from God Most High (Gen 14:19–20). To him Abram also offered a tenth of all the spoils he had just taken in his war with the four kings (Gen 14:20). Just as Melchizedek shared the office of priest and king, so the messianic figure of Psalm 110 will likewise be a priest-king, in the manner of Melchizedek.

Yet a third unique facet of the Messiah's royal priesthood is that it is "forever." Kidner remarks that "this is the most significant clause of

---

[55] Ibid., 336.

[53] A. McCaul notes various scriptural references where people are said to offer sacrifice without themselves being priests (cf. Josh 8:31; Judg 20:26). His point is that "There were, according to the traditions of the Jews, certain operations in the act of sacrifice performed by the laity, and others peculiar to the priest. The owner of the victim laid his hands on it, killed, flayed, cut it up, and washed the inwards. The priest received the blood and sprinkled it, put fire on the altar, arranged the wood on the fire, and the sacrifice on the wood. The expressions referred to do not prove that either David or Solomon was a priest." *The Messiahship of Jesus*, 174.

[54] W. A. VanGemeren, "Psalms," *EBC* 5:699.

[55] Mitchell suggests the strained interpretation that this passage should view the name Melchizedek as a vocative. Then it would be translated, "You are priest forever according to my promise, Melchizedek." He speculates that 11QMelch derives its understanding of Melchizedek as an eschatological figure from this passage (D. C. Mitchell, *The Message of the Psalter*, 259–60).

all" in that it shows the eternal work of this Priest-King "in contrast to the ephemeral priests whose labours were manifestly inconclusive."[56]

The point of v. 4, in the center of the psalm, is to emphasize the priesthood of the coming King. This is significant in that both the verses before and those after v. 4 describe the King at war. Thus, the priesthood of the messianic King is one in which He offers up God's enemies in a great "sacrificial feast" (Ezek 39:17–20) to the Lord in the end of days.

III. *Messiah, the Victorious King (110:5–7).* The final stanza of the psalm emphasizes Messiah's victory over the nations in the great eschatological battle He will fight. In this description of Messiah's triumph at war, vv. 5–6 identify those whom He will defeat, while v. 7 reveals the refreshment He will experience after the battle.

A. *The Defeated Nations (110:5–6).* This stanza begins with the statement: "The Lord [*ʾădōnāy*] is at your right hand." Unlike v. 1, where the vowels used generally (although not exclusively) indicate a human master (*ʾădōnî*) rather than God, in v. 5 the vowels indicate that it is certainly a Divine Master being described. This has led many commentators to assume that this is not the King at Yahweh's right hand but instead Yahweh at the King's right hand.[57]

Yet it is better to view this as the King at the right hand of God. First, grammatically, all the third-person singular pronouns in vv. 5–7 refer back to the Lord (*ʾădōnāy*).

> The Lord [*ʾădōnāy,* the messianic king] is at Your right hand;
> *He* will crush kings on the day of *His* anger.
> *He* will judge the nations, heaping up corpses;
> *He* will crush leaders over the entire world.
> *He* will drink from the brook by the road;
> therefore, *He* will lift up His head.

Plainly, it is the King who battles and drinks. Since there is no change in subject, it is the King who is called the Divine Lord (*ʾădōnāy*) in v. 5. Edward J. Kissane notes the error of understanding *ʾădōnāy* as Yahweh while taking the third singular pronouns that follow as referring to the King: "This introduces a change of subject of which there

---

[56] Kidner, *Psalm 73–150,* 395.

[57] VanGemeren, "Psalms," *EBC* 5:699; Kidner, *Psalms 73–150,* 396; Kraus, *Psalm 60–150,* 351–52; Mitchell, *The Message of the Psalter,* 262.

is no indication in the text. If the Messiah is the subject of v. 7, he must also be the subject of the preceding verses."[58]

Secondly, just as it is the Lord (*'ădōnî*) who is seated at the right hand of God in v. 1, so He is once again described in v. 5 as the one who is on the right hand of God. As Perowne says, "It is hardly probable that in so short a Psalm the King should first be said (ver. 1) to be at the right hand of Jehovah, and then that in ver. 5 Jehovah, on the contrary, should be said to be at the right hand of the King."[59] The logical conclusion is that the King is called "the Lord" (*'ădōnāy*), a title reserved for God alone. While it is possible to object that the King would not have been granted a divine title, there are implications of the King's deity throughout the psalm. In light of Ps 45:6 saying to the King "Your throne, God, is forever and ever," therein calling Him "God" (*'ĕlōhîm*), why is it so objectionable, apart from dogmatic presupposition, for Him to be called "Lord" (*'ădōnāy*) in this one?

Thus, in 110:5–6 the victorious divine Messiah is graphically depicted defeating all those who have rebelled against God. He crushes kings and rulers, judges the people (nations), and heaps up corpses, indicating that no rebels will escape. The violence of the imagery recalls Isa 63:1–6, where the messianic King tramples through the winepress of the nations, staining His garments with blood and crushing nations in His anger.[60] The psalmist says all this will occur on "the day of His anger," with the pronoun "His" referring to the King. Since the phrase "day of anger" *(yôm 'ap)* occurs in only six verses in Scripture[61] and in each case it refers to God's wrath, this would imply that the triumphant King is indeed a divine King.[62]

---

[58] E. J. Kissane, *The Book of Psalms* (Dublin: Browne and Nolan, 1954), 2:194.

[59] Perowne, *The Book of Psalms*, 2:309.

[60] Perowne has objected to the messianic interpretation of this section, wondering how it can describe the Messiah as "literally reigning in Zion" and engaging "in fierce and bloody war with his enemies." (*The Book of Psalms*, 2:296). This sort of objection stems from a false image of Jesus as the meek and mild one. Although at present "He will not break a bruised reed" (Isa 42:3), in the Hebrew Bible there are many wrathful images of the Messiah executing justice against the nations, such as Psalm 2 and Isaiah 63. There will one day be a literal last battle in which the Messiah will crush all rebellion against the true God. D. Sayers' observation is helpful: "We have very efficiently pared the claws of the Lion of Judah, certified Him 'meek and mild,' and recommended Him as a fitting household pet for pale curates and pious old ladies" (*The Whimsical Christian: Eighteen Essays* [New York: Macmillan, 1978], 14).

[61] Job 20:28; Lam 2:1,21–22; Zeph 2:2–3.

[62] Davis, "Is Psalm 110 a Messianic Psalm?" 166.

B. *The Refreshed King (110:7)*. The last verse of the psalm "forms an anticlimax to the gore of the preceding lines."[63] Using a refreshment metaphor, the messianic King is pictured drinking from the brook after His last battle. In contrast to 110:1, where He sits, awaiting the day when His enemies become a footstool, in 110:7, having vanquished the rebels, "He will lift up His head." Psalm 110 as a whole paints a picture of the divine Priest-King of Israel who will rule over all from Zion when He crushes all rebellion against Himself and then brings peace to the world.

Innertextual Interpretation

Much could be said about the links between Psalm 110 and other parts of the Psalter. Yet, it seems that the most basic interaction is with Psalm 2, which describes the King as "the Anointed One" (*māšîaḥ*) and has been viewed as a messianic psalm in both Jewish and Christian tradition. Based on its location in the Psalter, in a sense, Psalm 110 can be viewed as an innertextual reference back to Psalm 2, using a variety of verbal and thematic associations.

The first link from Psalm 110 to Psalm 2 is that in both psalms God promises the King dominion over rebellious enemy nations. In Psalm 110, God tells the King to sit at His right hand until He makes all enemy nations His "footstool" and tells Him to "rule over" the surrounding enemy nations (110:2–3). Psalm 2 describes the nations as rebellious, whose leaders "take their stand . . . against the Lord and His Anointed One" (2:2). God then promises the king that He will give Him "the nations" as an "inheritance" and "the ends of the earth" as a "possession" (2:8).

A second link between Psalm 110 and Psalm 2 is that the King acts with righteous wrath. In Ps 110:5 the King "will crush kings on the day of His anger [*běyōm ʾappô*]," while in Ps 2:5 God "speaks to them in His anger [*beʾappô*]." Moreover, the nations are warned that if they fail to "pay homage" to the King, "He will be angry" (*ʾnp*) and they "will perish" (2:12). Not only does 2:5 use the same word for anger as 110:5, but it also uses two synonyms: "wrath" (or "burning anger," *ḥārôn*) and the verb "be angry" (*ʾnp*), heightening the thematic links between the two psalms.

---

[63] J. P. Sterk, "An Attempt at Translating a Psalm," *BT* 42 (1991): 441.

A third innertextual link between Psalm 110 and Psalm 2 is in the description of the King's victorious battle. In Ps 110:2 God promises to extend the King's "mighty scepter [*maṭṭeh*] from Zion" over all the nations. Similarly, in Ps 2:9 the King is promised the nations as an inheritance, noting that He "will break them with a rod [*šebeṭ*] of iron," using the synonyms *maṭṭeh* and *šebeṭ*. Both psalms depict the King's victory in graphic terms: Ps 110:5–6 describes Him as crushing kings, piling corpses, and crushing leaders; similarly, Ps 2:9 portrays Him as shattering earthly kings and nations into pottery shards.

Yet another link between the two psalms is that the King is to reign from Zion. In Ps 110:2, the Lord stretches forth the King's scepter "from Zion." Accordingly, Ps 2:6 presents the King as enthroned on "Zion," God's "holy mountain."

A final but significant innertextual link between the two psalms is derived from the variant reading for 110:3.[64] There, God declares to the King, "from the womb of the dawn, *I have begotten You* [*yelidtikā*]," the same word used in God's oracle to the King in 2:7: "You are my Son, today *I have begotten you* [*yelidtikā*]." Although Psalms 2 and 110 are clearly linked in the New Testament (Heb 1:3–5,13; 5:5–6), the phrases about the Begotten One were not associated (as far as we know) until Justin Martyr in the second century. Hay proposes that the New Testament authors neglected to do so "because they knew that its meaning (and form) were disputed and because they could find other scriptural texts to support ideas of Jesus' divine sonship."[65] Another possible explanation for the New Testament omission of this link is that perhaps the association of this word was so obvious that it was unnecessary for the New Testament authors even to cite it. With or without the association of the phrase "I have begotten you," plainly Psalm 2 and 110 use verbal and thematic links to present a fully orbed picture of the eschatological messianic King.

Intertextual Interpretation

A number of later biblical authors refer to Psalm 110 and interpret it in an eschatological, messianic way. Three of these intertextual associations are especially significant.

---

[64] See exegesis of Ps 110:3 above.
[65] Hay, *Glory at the Right Hand*, 22.

The first, Daniel 7, with its glorious vision of the Ancient of Days and the Son of Man, appears to be a reference to the seating of the messianic King at the right hand of God (Ps 110:1). Daniel 7:9 states, "thrones were set in place, and the Ancient of Days took His seat." Further on in the passage, "One like a son of man" approaches "the Ancient of Days" and receives "authority to rule, and glory, and a kingdom." The Son of Man is also given "an everlasting dominion that will not pass away" and a kingdom "that will not be destroyed" (Dan 7:13–14).

In light of the plural use of "thrones," it seems that this Son of Man will take His seat next to the Ancient of Days, a vivid reminder of Ps 110:1, where the Lord takes His seat at the right hand of God.[66] A possible link between the two passages is Ps 80:18 [Eng. 17]: "Let Your hand be with the man at Your right hand, with the son of man You have made strong for Yourself."[67] Rabbi Akiba made the connection between Daniel 7 and Psalm 110. When explaining the plural "thrones" used in Dan 7:9, he said, "One [throne] was for Himself and one for David," that is, for the Messiah.[68] As Hay points out, "It seems distinctly possible that both Akiba and the writer of Daniel 7 were thinking of Ps 110:1."[69]

Yet a second important intertextual reference to Ps 110:4 is Zech 6:9–15. There it describes the eschatological unification of the royal and priestly offices with a role play by Joshua the high priest. A composite crown, representing kingship and priesthood, is placed on Joshua's head, and he is called by the messianic title, "Branch" (6:12). This Priest-King will build the eschatological Temple and "sit and rule on His throne . . . He will be a priest on His throne, and the counsel of peace will be between the two offices" (Zech 6:12–13 NASB). Clearly this is a reference to the King described in Ps 110:4, who is a priest like Melchizedek, uniting the offices of king and priest. Delitzsch aptly writes of the relationship between Zechariah 6 and Ps 110:4:

> Zechariah removes the fulfillment of the Psalm out of the Old Testament present, with its blunt separation between the monarchial and hierarchical dignity, into the domain of the future, and refers it to Jahve's Branch (צֶמַח

---

[66] Ibid., 26; Mowinckel, *He That Cometh*, 352.

[67] Hay cites this verse as a link and credits N. A. Dahl with the suggestion (*Glory at the Right Hand*, 26).

[68] *b. Sanh.* 38b.

[69] Hay, *Glory at the Right Hand*, 26.

[ṣemaḥ]) that is to come. He who will build the true temple of God, satisfac-
torily unites in his one person the priestly with the kingly office. . . . Thus
this Psalm was understood by the later prophecy.[70]

Delitzsch concludes by rhetorically asking how Ps 110:4 could have
been understood in light of Zechariah's reference to it other "than in
the eschatological Messianic sense?"[71]

The third crucial intertextual link is also with Zechariah 14. There
the Lord is said to "go out to fight against those nations as He fights
on a day of battle" so that "His feet will stand on the Mount of Olives"
which "will be split in half from east to west" (Zech 14:3–5). This
certainly refers to the coming of the messianic deliverer as representative of the Lord. Mitchell points out that "it would be a high degree of
anthropomorphism indeed to regard Yhwh as physically touching the
earth with his feet so that it split."[72]

The imagery of Zechariah 14 relies on Psalm 110 in several ways.
Both passages depict a descent from heaven—Psalm 110 from the
right hand of God to the battlefield (110:1,5–6) and Zech 14:3–5 from
the heights of heaven to Jerusalem in defense of God's people. Both
passages describe a deliverer coming to the battle accompanied by a
holy army. Psalm 110:3 states, "Your people will volunteer on Your
day of battle in holy splendor," while Zech 14:5 proclaims, "Then
the Lord my God will come and the holy ones with Him." Finally,
Ps 110:5–6 graphically portrays the King destroying the rebellious
nations, crushing them and "heaping up corpses." Similarly, Zech
14:12–14 graphically displays the plague and panic that will seize enemy armies in their defeat.

The point of what has been discussed in this section is this: in the
postexilic era, the books of Daniel and Zechariah provide a clear messianic hope by relying on the words and images contained in Psalm
110. Plainly, these later writers understood Psalm 110 to refer to the
Messiah of Israel.

It is not the intertextual references alone that point to a messianic
interpretation. By placing the psalm in context of the whole Psalter
and performing careful intextual and innertextual readings, it appears
that Psalm 110 presents the glorious Messiah Priest-King, seated at

---

[70] Delitzsch, "Psalms" in *Commentary on the Old Testament*, 3:194.
[71] Ibid.
[72] Mitchell, *The Message of the Psalter*, 264.

the right hand of God and returning in power to establish His dominion over all the earth.

Conclusion

This chapter began by asking if Psalm 110 should be read as a messianic text? The case has been made that Psalm 110 does indeed picture the divine Priest-King, now seated at the right hand of God but who will descend from heaven at the end of days to save Israel and extend His rule over all the earth. This is none other than the Messiah.

Likely that is why both Jewish and Christian sources have long held that Psalm 110 is about the Messiah.[73] It is not necessary to blame their messianic interpretations on their historical circumstances or exegetical predispositions. It seems better to say that they derived their views from the text of Scripture. That is why Jesus, speaking to some of his Jewish contemporaries about Psalm 110, pointedly asked how David could call the son of David, Lord (Matt 22:41–46)? Their failure to answer Jesus' question demonstrated that they must certainly have agreed with the messianic interpretation of Psalm 110[74] but could not explain how the psalm could present the Messiah as deity (Lord). Although Jesus does not add any further commentary to this text, it is obvious that He too interpreted Psalm 110 as speaking of a divine Messiah.

What Alexander McCaul wrote of Psalm 110 in the middle of the nineteenth century in response to the growing critical denial of messianic prediction in his day is as valid today: "The words of the psalm, taken in their ordinary sense, admit of no other interpretation. The subject of the psalm is the king in Zion, exalted to heaven, as Dan. vii.13; in verse 5 is called אֲדֹנָי [*’ădōnāy*], The LORD, and is described as judge of kings and nations. The description can apply only to him who is David's son and David's Lord."[75]

---

[73] For a discussion of the messianic interpretation of Psalm 110 in Jewish and Christian sources, see Hay, *Glory at the Right Hand*, 19–51. Although some Jewish sources identify Abraham as the subject of Psalm 110, *Midr. Tehillim* 18:29 provides the clearest messianic interpretation: "R. Yudan said in the name of R. Hama: In the time to come when the Holy One, blessed be He, seats the Lord Messiah at His right hand, as is said *The Lord saith unto my lord: 'Sit thou at My right hand'* and seats Abraham at His left, Abraham's face will pale, and he will say to the Lord: 'My son's son sits at the right, and I at the left!'" According to these sages, Abraham will be shocked at his descendant's greater glory.

[74] According to Hay, "Having reviewed the evidence, Billerbeck concluded that the messianic interpretation was the norm for rabbis of the first century." *Glory at the Right Hand*, 29.

[75] McCaul, *The Messiahship of Jesus*, 175.

Chapter 12

CONCLUSION: A CALL TO RETURN TO THE MESSIANIC HOPE

My mouth was dry, my hands were clammy, and I felt foolish, but I was trying my best to defend my faith in Yeshua (Jesus) the Messiah in front of the Hebrew Club at my High School. The year was 1973. I was 16 years old, and I had become a follower of Yeshua the previous year. It was an astonishing time—an amazing number of Jewish young people were coming to believe in Yeshua. In fact, Jewish people all over America were making decisions to follow Him in numbers that had not been seen since the first century. There were about 30 messianic Jews in my public high school in Brooklyn, New York, and I was a ring leader. In fact, there were so many Jewish students interested in what we messianic Jews were saying about Yeshua that a student group, the Hebrew Club, decided to counter our message.

One student in the Hebrew Club, a girl who had been particularly distressed about so many of her fellow Jewish students believing in Yeshua, discussed the issue with the youth leader at her synagogue. Let's call him David. An Orthodox Jew, David knew Rabbinics, Talmud, and the Bible. Additionally, he was a brilliant graduate student at one of the great universities in the world. Above all, he was a terrific speaker—glib, charming, persuasive, and knowledgeable. So they came up with a plan—David, the synagogue youth leader, would come to a Hebrew Club event and speak on the subject: "Jews and Jesus: Why We Don't Believe in Him!"

When word spread of the upcoming Hebrew Club meeting, we messianic Jewish students on campus saw it as an opportunity. So, designated as the group spokesman, I went to visit our high school principal with a request. I asked if we could arrange for someone from a messianic Jewish organization or a leader of a messianic congregation to speak as well. The principal, an open-minded Jewish man, told me he was sorry, but he could not require the Hebrew Club to invite a messianic speaker. He said that the Hebrew Club alone could decide who would speak to them, and he could not tell them to include "both sides" of the issue.

I was disappointed and distressed, but our band of messianic students still felt we could not let this occasion pass. Most of us belonged
to the Hebrew Club, and for those who did not, the meeting was still
open to any interested student. So we decided we would go and speak
up during the question and answer time. And since I was raised in an
orthodox Jewish home and had engaged in several discussions with
rabbis in the past year, I was chosen as the spokesman for our group.
It was my job to make the case that Yeshua was indeed the Messiah
promised in the Hebrew Scriptures, and as such Jewish people should
believe in Him. Frankly, I did not feel too intimidated at the prospect
of challenging David—I had never heard of him before and did not
know too much about him. Moreover, when I had met with those
rabbis in the previous year, they seemed incapable of answering the
biblical passages I had shown them. Little did I know how poorly this
upcoming interaction would go.

The day of the afterschool event was exciting as we messianic Jewish students met in the back of an art room between classes to pray.
We did not know what to expect, but we anticipated that many Jewish
students would hear how credible it was to believe in Yeshua. Some of
us thought that maybe a revival would break out at our school! David
came and spoke for 45 minutes in front of a packed room of about 100
(mostly Jewish) students. His presentation was clear and compelling,
focusing on the history of Christian anti-Semitism. It broke my heart
since, unfortunately, his talk was factually true. Still, when the question and answer time arrived, I stood up and identified myself as a
Jewish follower of Yeshua. I said that although the Church's history of
anti-Semitism was indeed horrific, the issue really was whether or not
Yeshua had fulfilled the messianic predictions of the Hebrew Bible.
And that was when it all came apart.

David challenged me to come up with one, just one, messianic prediction that Yeshua had indeed fulfilled. I took out my Bible and began. I started with Gen 3:15, but David adeptly pointed out that the
passage was merely a "just so story" about how snakes and humans
came to attack each other and had nothing to do with the Messiah.
It went downhill from there. I brought up passage after passage, prediction after prediction, and David would spin each passage to show
that it, without doubt, could not be about the Messiah. He took literal
words figuratively and figurative words literally. He was fast and he

was funny. I had never before encountered a speaker as capable as David. And worse, even though I knew I was right, I could not speak as smoothly or skillfully as David. I started to sweat, I became tongue-tied, my hands turned to ice, but I did not quit. Every time he shot me down, I came up with another passage, only to have him shoot me down again. It was awful. Finally, mercifully, the meeting ended, but only then did my real misery begin.

As I reflected on my interaction with David, I became angry and disappointed, not at him but at myself. Here I had been given such an opportunity to represent my Messiah Yeshua in a very public way, but because of my own lack of preparation, overconfidence, and poor communication skills, I had failed Him. I had let Him down. My sorrow was indescribable. When I considered all those whom I could have influenced for Yeshua that day, I was crushed, because all they saw and heard was a fumbling, flummoxed high school kid. How would they ever believe in Yeshua if that was the best I could do to present His truth? I feared that God would never again give me the opportunity to speak for Yeshua.

As the years passed, I pursued Jewish Studies and Bible as an undergraduate, went to a terrific seminary for four years for my master's degree, and even completed a doctorate. Having studied much more, gratefully I was given many chances to represent Yeshua publicly again. In fact, much to my amazement, I saw a significant number of Jewish people come to faith in Yeshua through my speaking and teaching. But my high school encounter with David still bothered me like a bone in my throat. I just could not clear the thought of it. I was still disappointed that I had let Yeshua down.

But what became of David? He finished graduate school and began writing books. Then he hosted a local radio talk show. Before too long, he was hosting a TV talk show. And now, he is a nationally syndicated radio talk show host and commentator on popular culture. David today is a well-known and well-respected radio personality, author, and lecturer. In fact, I listen to him often and enjoy his still persuasive speaking ability.

Through the years, from time to time, I have been asked to debate Jewish leaders about the Messiahship of Yeshua, and I generally say no because I find such debates to be unproductive. But I have always wanted to have another opportunity with David. I have wanted a chance at redemption—to engage David once again, now that I am more prepared. Three or four different times, radio and television talk shows have attempted to arrange a discussion about Yeshua between David and me, and each time he refuses. I am certain that he does not remember me, and he is certainly not intimidated by me; it is only that, as a public figure, he does not want to offend his Christian audience. So I remained in my disappointment, without any chance at redemption, for more than 30 years. Then a most surprising interaction changed my perspective.

Fast-forward 32 years from my high school encounter with David. I had just published a book on the Arab-Israeli conflict, so a messianic congregation in Southern California had asked if I would do an all-day seminar on that topic. As I set up my computer with the data projector that morning, a messianic Jewish man, about 60 years old, with a thick Brooklyn accent just kept talking and talking to me. He seemed familiar, and I assumed I had met him the previous year when I had spoken at this congregation. So he kept talking and, frankly, it was a little annoying because I was having a hard time getting the technology to obey me. Finally, when everything was working and I was less distracted, I had a few minutes before teaching, so we began to chat together in earnest.

I asked him how he got that Brooklyn accent, and we both laughed when he said he came by it honestly, by living there. He said he had left Brooklyn for Southern California 10 years earlier. Fairly soon, I learned that he had been a high school teacher in Brooklyn. In fact, he had taught at my high school! After learning that fact, it dawned on me—he seemed familiar not because I had met him the previous year but because he had been my very own high school music teacher. My eyes widened in surprise and I burst out, "You're Vince Saltzman—you were my guitar teacher in high school!" We were both so surprised and happy, thumping and hugging each other, even as the rest of the seminar students began to roll into the classroom. I just could not believe it—my Jewish music teacher from high school had become a follower of Yeshua. Class started a minute after I made this discovery, but I could not wait for the break to hear how Vince had come to faith.

An hour later, I listened to Vince's story. It seems that more than 30 years before, one of Vince's Jewish colleagues, my former history teacher at the high school, had become a follower of Yeshua and had spoken to Vince about his faith. Vince had been intrigued and began to consider whether Yeshua was indeed the Messiah. Then, Vince related, he heard that someone was coming to speak at the Hebrew Club about Jews and Jesus. Thinking this might be interesting, Vince decided to attend. At this point, Vince looked at me and said, "You probably have heard of the guy who spoke—now he's on the radio all over the country," and he told me David's name. "Yes," I said, "I remember when he spoke at the high school." Vince tells the rest of his story this way:

> Well, I really don't remember what the speaker said, but I do remember that there was some kid there with a Bible. And he stood up and said he was Jewish and believed in Jesus and began to quote messianic prophecies. The funny thing is that this guy, the speaker, had an answer for every passage the kid cited. No matter what verse the kid showed, this smart guy knocked it down, showing why it absolutely couldn't be speaking of the Messiah. He had an answer for everything. But this kid wouldn't stop. Every time a verse got shot down, he'd bring up some other verse. Finally, when the whole thing was over, I got to thinking that those verses sounded pretty messianic to me. So, I decided to get a Bible and read them for myself. And, as I read the Old Testament, I began to see that it really was all about Yeshua. So, it took a couple of years of reading the Bible and studying the prophecies, but then I became a believer in Yeshua.

Having told me his story, Vince asked simply, "Hey, do you know who that kid was?" to which I replied, "Yes, I do—it was me." And I was awed by God's grace. Thirty-two years after my horrible failure, I learned that God used it to help someone along the way to faith in Yeshua. Clearly, it was not my unrealistic self-confidence, my persuasive arguments, or my skillful handling of the Scriptures that helped Vince. Rather, it was the power of God's Word alone, just as the Lord said through the prophet Isaiah so long ago: "My word that comes from My mouth will not return to Me empty, but it will accomplish what I please and will prosper in what I send it to do" (Isa 55:11).

So what does this long, convoluted story have to do with a book about messianic hope? First, this story underscores the power of God's Word in communicating truth. It is not the vessel proclaiming the Word but the Scriptures themselves that have power. Moreover, messianic prophecy has the power to convince people that God's Word is true and that Jesus is indeed the Messiah.

Second, Vince's story demonstrates that a simple literary reading of the text of Scripture in its final form reveals that it is about the Messiah. Pulling the Bible out of its literary context in order to emphasize the historical events behind the text yields a historical interpretation that fails to see the messianic message in the text. But if, like Vince, we read the Old Testament in its final form for its plain meaning, the messianic hope shines out like a clear beam of light.

Third, messianic prophecy is an essential element for proving that Jesus is the Messiah. In fact, Jesus identified Himself as the Messiah, the fulfillment of all messianic prophecy, by directing His followers to the Law, the Prophets, and the Psalms (Luke 24:44–46). The apostles, in turn, used messianic predictions to convince their listeners to believe that Jesus was the true Messiah. The power of messianic prophecy continues today. It would be supremely regrettable for evangelicals to abandon messianic prediction for the sake of respectability in the academy or acceptance among critical scholars. Of course, we want to interpret the Bible correctly, but it is not necessary to adopt the naturalistic presuppositions to which critical scholarship subscribes. The Bible is inspired, and the authors of the Scriptures could indeed write a supernatural prophetic message that pointed to a Messiah who would come many hundreds of years later. Abandoning this conviction will bring the loss of one of the most potent arrows in our apologetic quiver.

Here is my point, not just in this chapter but in the whole book: beginning with Jesus, moving to the apostolic period, and continuing until today, the message of Messiah has been proclaimed by using messianic prophecy. It is a foundational element for identifying Jesus as the true Messiah. As has been shown, the views of the modern academy have made their way into evangelical scholarship, leading to a minimization or even a denial of messianic prediction. Evangelical scholarship must rethink this trend because, as Jacob Jocz has noted, messianic prophecy is "the infallible guide leading in a straight line from Moses and the Prophets to Jesus and the Apostles." Without it, "The Messiahship of Jesus becomes a purely subjective conviction without anchorage in historical revelation."[1]

---

[1] J. Jocz, *The Jewish People and Jesus Christ* (Grand Rapids: Baker Books, 1979), 208–9.

SELECT BIBLIOGRAPHY

Books

Abegg, M., Jr., P. Flint, E. Ulrich. *The Dead Sea Scrolls Bible*. New York: HarperSanFrancisco, 1999.

Alexander, T. D. *The Servant King*. Vancouver, British Columbia: Regent College, 1998.

Anderson, F. I. *The Sentence in Biblical Hebrew*. The Hague: Moulton, 1974.

Archer, G. L. *A Survey of Old Testament Introduction*. Chicago: Moody, 1964.

——— and G. C. Chirichigno. *Old Testament Quotations in the New Testament: A Complete Survey*. Chicago: Moody, 1983.

Ashley, T. R. *The Book of Numbers*. NICOT. Grand Rapids: Eerdmans, 1993.

Baron, D. *Rays of Messiah's Glory*. London: Wheeler & Wheeler, 1886.

Beale, G. K., ed. *The Right Doctrine from the Wrong Texts?* Grand Rapids: Baker, 1994.

——— and D. A. Carson, eds. *Commentary on the New Testament Use of the Old Testament*. Grand Rapids: Baker, 2007.

Becker, J. *Expectation in the Old Testament*. Translated by D. E. Green. Philadelphia: Fortress, 1977.

Beecher, W. J. *The Prophets and the Promise*. New York: Crowell, 1905.

Bentzen, A. *King and Messiah*. London: Lutterworth, 1955.

Briggs, C. A. *Messianic Prophecy: The Prediction of the Fulfillment of Redemption Through the Messiah*. New York: Scribner, 1886.

——— and E. G. Briggs. *A Critical and Exegetical Commentary on the Book of Psalms*. ICC. Edinburgh: T&T Clark, 1986.

Bruce, F. F. *The Defense of the Gospel in the New Testament*. Grand Rapids: Eerdmans, 1959.

Bullock, C. H. *An Introduction to the Old Testament Prophetic Books*. Chicago: Moody, 1986.

Bultema, H. *Commentary on Isaiah*. Translated by D. Bultema. Grand Rapids: Kregel, 1981.

Cassuto, U. *A Commentary on the Book of Genesis*. Translated by I. Abrahams. Jerusalem: Magnes, 1989.

Charlesworth, J., ed. *The Messiah*. Philadelphia: Fortress, 1988.

Chazan, R. *In the Year 1096*. Philadelphia: Jewish Publication Society, 1996.

Childs, B. S. *Introduction to the Old Testament as Scripture*. Philadelphia: Fortress, 1979.

Collins, A. Y., and J. J. Collins. *King and Messiah as Son of God*. Grand Rapids: Eerdmans, 2008.

Collins, C. J. *Genesis 1-4: A Linguistic, Literary, and Theological Commentary*. Phillipsburg, NJ: P&R, 2006.

Cooper, D. L. *Messiah: His Historical Appearance*. Lost Angeles: Biblical Research Society, 1958.

———. *Messiah: His Nature and Person*. Los Angeles: Biblical Research Society, 1933.

———. *Messiah: His Redemptive Career*. Los Angeles: Biblical Research Society, 1963.

Craigie, P. C. *The Book of Deuteronomy*. NICOT. Grand Rapids: Eerdmans, 1976.

Dahood, M. *Psalms*. AB. Garden City, NY: Doubleday, 1970.

Davies, W. D., and D. C. Allison. *A Critical and Exegetical Commentary on the Gospel according to Saint Matthew*. ICC. Edinburgh: T&T Clark, 1988.

Delitzsch, F. *Biblical Commentary on the Book of Psalms*. Translated by F. Bolton. Commentary on the Old Testament, C. F. Keil and F. Delitzsch, eds. Vol. 5. Grand Rapids: Eerdmans, 1980.

———. *Messianic Prophecies in Historical Succession*. Translated by S. I. Curtiss. Edinburgh: T&T Clark, 1891.

Dewart, E. H. *Jesus the Messiah in Prophecy and Fulfillment: A Review and Refutation of the Negative Theory of Messianic Prophecy*. New York: Hunt & Eaton, 1891.

Edersheim, A. *Life and Times of Jesus the Messiah*. Repr., Grand Rapids: Eerdmans, 1971.

———. *Prophecy and History in Relation to the Messiah*. London: Longmans, 1901.

Ellis, E. E. *The Old Testament in Early Christianity: Canon and Interpretation in the Light of Modern Research*. Grand Rapids: Baker, 1992.

Ellison, H. L. *The Centrality of the Messianic Idea in the Old Testament*. London: Tyndale, 1957.

Engnell, I. *Studies in Divine Kingship in the Near East*. Oxford: Blackwell, 1943.

Feinberg, J., and P. Feinberg, eds. *Tradition and Testament*. Chicago: Moody, 1981.

Forbes, J. *Studies on the Book of Psalms*. Edinburgh: T&T Clark, 1888.

France, R.T. *The Gospel according to Matthew*. TNTC. Grand Rapids: Eerdmans, 1985.

———. *The Gospel of Matthew*. NICNT. Grand Rapids: Eerdmans: 2007.

———. *Jesus and the Old Testament: His Application of Old Testament Passages to Himself and His Mission*. London: Tyndale, 1971.

Fruchtenbaum, A. *Messianic Christology*. Tustin, CA: Ariel Press, 1998.

Gloag, P. J. *Messianic Prophecies*. Edinburgh: T&T Clark, 1879.

Goldingay, J. *Isaiah*. NIBC. Peabody, MA: Hendrickson, 2001.

Goodspeed, G. S. *Israel's Messianic Hope to the Time of Jesus*. New York: MacMillan, 1900.

Gressman, H. *Der Messias*. Gottingen: Vandenhoeck & Ruprecht, 1929.

Hailperin, H. *Rashi and the Christian Scholars*. Pittsburgh: University of Pittsburgh Press, 1963.

Hamilton, V. P. *The Book of Genesis: Chapters 1–17*. NICOT. Grand Rapids: Eerdmans, 1990.

Hay, D. M. *Glory at the Right Hand: Psalm 110 in Early Christianity*. Nashville: Abingdon, 1973.

Hengstenberg, E. W. *Christology of the Old Testament*. Translated by Reuel Keith. London: Francis and John Rivington, 1847; repr., Grand Rapids: Kregel, 1970.

Hess, R. S., and M. D. Carroll, eds. *Israel's Messiah in the Bible and the Dead Sea Scrolls*. Grand Rapids: Baker, 2003.

Hindson, E. E. *Isaiah's Immanuel*. Phillipsburg, NJ: P&R, 1978.

Horbury, W. *Jewish Messianism and the Cult of Christ*. London: SCM, 1998.

Instone-Brewer, D. *Techniques and Assumptions in Jewish Exegesis before 70 CE*. Tübingen: J. C. B. Mohr, 1992.

Johnson, S. L. *The Old Testament in the New*. Grand Rapids: Zondervan, 1980.

Juel, D. *Messianic Exegesis: Christological Interpretation of the Old Testament in Early Christianity*. Philadelphia: Fortress, 1988.

Kaiser, W. C., Jr. *The Messiah in the Old Testament*. Grand Rapids: Zondervan, 1995.

————. *The Uses of the Old Testament in the New*. Chicago: Moody, 1985.

Kelly, W. *An Exposition of the Book of Isaiah*. London: Paternoster, 1897.

Kidner, D. *Genesis: An Introduction and Commentary*. TOTC. Downers Grove, IL: InterVarsity, 1967.

————. *Psalms 73–150*. Downers Grove, IL: InterVarsity, 1975.

Kirkpatrick, A. F. *The Book of Psalms*. Cambridge: Cambridge University Press, 1902.

Kissane, E. J. *The Book of Psalms*. Dublin: Browne and Nolan, 1954.

Kline, M. G. *Treaty of the Great King: The Covenant Structure of Deuteronomy: Studies and Commentary*. Grand Rapids: Eerdmans, 1963.

Kraus, H. J. *Psalms 60–150: A Continental Commentary*. Translated by H. C. Oswald. Minneapolis: Fortress, 1993.

Laato, A. *A Star Is Rising: The Historical Development of the Old Testament Royal Ideology and the Rise of the Jewish Messianic Expectations*. Atlanta: Scholars Press, 1997.

Leupold, H. C. *Exposition of the Psalms*. Grand Rapids: Baker, 1969.

Levey, S. H. *The Messiah: An Aramaic Interpretation*. Cincinnati: Hebrew Union College—Jewish Institute of Religion, 1974.

Longenecker, R. N. *Biblical Exegesis in the Apostolic Period*. Grand Rapids: Eerdmans, 1975.

Longman, T., III. *How to Read the Psalms*. Downers Grove, IL: InterVarsity, 1988.

McCaul, A. *The Messiahship of Jesus*. London: Unwin, 1852.

Merrill, E. H. *An Exegetical Commentary: Haggai, Zechariah, Malachi*. Chicago: Moody Press, 1994.

Mitchell, D. C. *The Message of the Psalter: An Eschatological Programme in the Book of Psalms*. JSOTSup 252. Sheffield, England: Sheffield Academic Pres, 1997.

Moore, G. F. *Judaism in the First Centuries of the Christian Era*. Repr., New York: Schocken, 1971.

Motyer, J. A. *The Prophecy of Isaiah: An Introduction and Commentary*. Downers Grove, IL: InterVarsity, 1993.

Mowinckel, S. *He That Cometh: The Messiah Concept in the Old Testament and Later Judaism*. Translated by G. W. Anderson. Oxford: Blackwell, 1959.

Muraoka, T. *A Greek-English Lexicon of the Septuagint*. Leuven: Peeters, 2009.

Murphy, R. E. *The Song of Songs*. Minneapolis: Fortress, 1990.

———. *A Study of Psalm 72*. Washington, DC: The Catholic University of America, 1948.

Oesterley, W. O. E. *The Evolution of the Messianic Idea: A Study in Comparative Religion*. London: Pitman, 1908.

Oswalt, J. *The Book of Isaiah: Chapters 1–39*. NICOT. Grand Rapids: Eerdmans, 1986.

Payne, J. B. *Encyclopedia of Biblical Prophecy*. Grand Rapids: Baker, 1973.

Perowne, J. J. S. *The Book of Psalms*. Grand Rapids: Zondervan, 1966.

Porter, S. E., ed. *The Messiah in the Old and New Testaments*. Grand Rapids: Eerdmans, 2007.

Reich, M. *The Messianic Hope of Israel*. 2nd ed. Chicago: Moody, 1945.

Reymond, R. L. *Jesus, Divine Messiah: The Old Testament Witness*. Ross-Shire, Scotland: Christian Focus, 1990.

Rhiem, E. *Messianic Prophecy: Its Origin, Historical Growth, and Relation to New Testament Fulfillment*. Translated by L. A. Muirhead. 2nd ed. Edinburgh: T&T Clark, 1891.

Ringgren, H. *The Messiah in the Old Testament*. Chicago: Allenson, 1956.

Ryle, H. E. *The Canon of the Old Testament*. 2nd ed. London: Macmillan, 1914.

Sailhamer, J. H. *Introduction to Old Testament Theology: A Canonical Approach*. Grand Rapids: Zondervan, 1995.

———. *The Meaning of the Pentateuch: Revelation, Composition and Interpretation*. Downers Grove, IL: InterVarsity Press, 2009.

———. *The Pentateuch as Narrative*. Grand Rapids: Zondervan, 1992.

Satterthwaite, P. E., R. S. Hess, and G. J. Wenham, eds. *The Lord's Anointed: Interpretation of Old Testament Messianic Texts*. Grand Rapids: Baker, 1995.

Shereshevsky, E. *Rashi: The Man and His World*. Northvale: Aronson, 1996.

Sigal, G. *The Jew and the Christian Missionary: A Jewish Response to Missionary Christianity*. New York: KTAV, 1981.

Smalley, B. *The Study of the Bible in the Middle Ages*. Oxford: Blackwell, 1952.

Smith, J. *What the Bible Teaches about the Promised Messiah*. Nashville: Thomas Nelson, 1993.

Starbuck, R. A. *Court Oracles in the Psalms: The So-Called Royal Psalms in Their Ancient Near Eastern Context*. Atlanta: SBL, 1996.

Tate, M. E. *Psalms 51–100*. WBC 20. Dallas: Word, 1990.

Tov, E. *Textual Criticism of the Hebrew Bible*. Minneapolis: Fortress, 1992.

VanGemeren, W. A. *Psalms*. EBC. Grand Rapids: Zondervan, 1991.

Van Groningen, G. *Messianic Revelation in the Old Testament*. Grand Rapids: Baker, 1990.

von Orelli, C. *The Old Testament Prophecy of the Consummation of God's Kingdom, Traced in Its Historical Development*. Translated by J. S. Banks. Edinburgh: T&T Clark, 1889.

Von Rad, G. *Old Testament Theology*. New York: Harper and Row, 1965.

Waltke, B. K., and M. O'Connor. *An Introduction to Biblical Hebrew Syntax*. Winona Lake: Eisenbrauns, 1990.

Walton, J. H. *Genesis*. NIVAC. Grand Rapids: Zondervan, 2001.

Watts, J. D. W. *Isaiah 34–66*. WBC Nashville: Nelson, 1987.

———. *Isaiah 1–33*. 2nd ed. WBC. Nashville: Nelson, 2002.

Wenham, G. J. *Genesis 1–15*. WBC. Waco, TX: Word Books, 1987.

Westermann, C. *Genesis*. Translated by J. J. Scullion. CC. Minneapolis, MN: Fortress, 1994.

Wilson, G. H. *The Editing of the Hebrew Psalter*. Chico, CA: Scholars Press, 1985.

Wright, C. J. H. *Knowing Jesus Through the Old Testament*. London: Marshall Pickering, 1992.

Wurthwein, E. *The Text of the Old Testament*. Translated by E. F. Rhodes. Grand Rapids: Eerdmans, 1979.

Young, E. J. *Studies in Isaiah*. Grand Rapids: Eerdmans, 1954.

———. *Genesis 3: A Devotional and Expository Study*. Edinburgh: Banner of Truth, 1983.

Articles

Alexander, T. D. "Messianic Ideology in Genesis." In *The Lord's Anointed: Interpretation of Old Testament Messianic Texts*, ed. P. E. Satterthwaite, R. S. Hess, and G. J. Wenham, 19–32. Grand Rapids: Baker, 1995.

———. "Further Observations on the Term 'Seed' in Genesis." *TynBul* 48 (1997): 363–67.

Bateman, H. W., IV. "Psalm 110:1 and the New Testament." *BSac* 149 (1992): 438–54.

Beale, G. K. "Did Jesus and His Followers Preach the Right Doctrine from the Wrong Texts?" *Them* 14 (1989): 89–96.

Beckwith, R. T. "Formation of the Hebrew Bible." In *Mikra: Text, Translation, Reading and Interpretation of the Hebrew Bible in Ancient Judaism and Early Christianity*, ed. M. J. Mulder. CRINT, 39–86. Minneapolis: Fortress, 1990.

Booj, Th. "Psalm 110: Rule in the Midst of Your Foes." *VT* 41 (1991): 396–407.

Brown, W. P. "A Royal Performance: Critical Notes on Psalm 110:3ag." *JBL* 117 (1998): 93-96.

Broyles, C. C. "The Redeeming King: Psalm 72's Contribution to the Messianic Ideal." In *Eschatology, Messianism, and the Dead Sea Scrolls*, ed. C. A. Evans and P. W. Flint, 23–40. Grand Rapids: Eerdmans, 1997.

Clements, R. E. "Messianic Prophecy or Messianic History?" *HBT* 1 (1979): 87–104.

Collins, C. J. "Galatians 3:16: What Kind of Exegete Was Paul?" *TynBul* 54 (2003): 75–86.

———. "A Syntactical Note on Genesis 3:15: Is the Woman's Seed Singular or Plural?" *Tynbul* 48 (1997): 139–48.

Culver, R. D. "The Old Testament as Messianic Prophecy." *BETS* 7 (1964): 91–97.

Davis, B. C. "Is Psalm 110 a Messianic Psalm?" *Bsac* 157 (2000): 160–73.

Davis, J. D. "The Child Whose Name Is Wonderful." In *Biblical and Theological Studies*. New York: Scribner, 1912.

Gese, H. "Wisdom, Son of Man, and the Origins of Christology: The Consistent Development of Biblical Theology." *HBT* 3 (1981): 23–57.

Gordon, C. H. "*Almah* in Isaiah 7:14." *JBR* 1 (1953): 106.

Greenstein, E. L. "Medieval Bible Commentaries." In *Back to the Sources*, ed. B. W. Holtz, 213–60. New York: Simon and Schuster, 1984.

Gren, C. R. "Piercing the Ambiguities of Psalm 22:16 and the Messiah's Mission." *JETS* 48 (2005): 283–99.

Hamilton, J. "The Skull Crushing Seed of the Woman: Inner-Biblical Interpretation of Genesis 3:15." *SBJT* 10 (2006): 30–54.

Hamilton, J. M., Jr. "The Messianic Music of the Song of Songs: A Non-Allegorical Interpretation." *WTJ* 68 (2006): 331–46.

Kaiser, W. C., Jr. "The Single Intent of Scripture." In *Evangelical Roots*, ed. K. Kantzer, 123–41. Nashville: Thomas Nelson, 1978.

Kim, Y.-H. "The Prophet like Moses': Deut. 18:15-22 Reexamined within the Context of the Pentateuch and in Light of the Final Shape of the TaNak." Ph.D. diss., Trinity Evangelical Divinity School, 1995.

Lai, C. K. "Jacob's Blessing on Judah (Genesis 49:8–12) with the Hebrew Old Testament: A Study of In-Textual, Inner-Textual, and Inter-Textual Interpretation." Ph.D. diss., Trinity Evangelical Divinity School, 1993.

LaSor, W. L. "Prophecy, Inspiration, and *Seneus Plenior.*" *TynBul* 29 (1978): 49–60.

Longenecker, R. N. "'Who Is the Prophet Talking About?' Some Reflections on the New Testament's Use of the Old." In *The Right Doctrine from the Wrong Texts?*, ed. G. K. Beale, 375–87. Grand Rapids: Baker, 1994.

Martin, R. A. " The Earliest Messianic Interpretation of Genesis 3:15." *JBL* 84 (1965): 425–27.

McConville, J. G. "Messianic Interpretation in Modern Context." In *The Lord's Anointed: Interpretation of Old Testament Messianic Texts*, ed. P. E. Satterthwaite, R. S. Hess, and G. J. Wenham, 1–17. Grand Rapids: Baker, 1995.

Merrill, E. H. "Rashi, Nicholas de Lyra, and Christian Exegesis." *WTJ* 38 (1975): 66–80.

———. "Royal Priesthood: An Old Testament Messianic Motif." *Bsac* 150 (1993): 50–61.

Moran, W. L. "Gen. 49–10 and Its Use in Ez. 21:32." *Bib* 39 (1958): 405–25.

Perrin, N. "Messianism in the Narrative Frame of Ecclesiastes." *RB* 108 (2001): 37–60.

Rosenthal, E. I. J. "Anti-Christian Polemic in Medieval Bible Commentaries." *JJS* 11 (1960): 115–35.

———. "Medieval Jewish Exegesis: Its Character and Significance." *JSS* 9 (1964): 265–81.

———. "The Study of the Bible in Medieval Judaism." In *The Cambridge History of the Bible*, ed. G. H. Lampe, 252–79. Cambridge: Cambridge University Press, 1969.

Sailhamer, J. H. "The Messiah and the Hebrew Bible." *JETS* 44 (2001): 5–23.

Shepherd, M. B. "Targums, New Testament, and Biblical Theology of the Messiah." *JETS* 51 (2008): 45–58.

Silva, M. "The New Testament Use of the Old Testament." In *Scripture and Truth*, ed. D. A. Carson and J. D. Woodbridge, 143–65. Grand Rapids: Zondervan, 1983.

Snodgrass, K. "The Use of the Old Testament in the New." In *The Right Doctrine from the Wrong Texts?*, ed. G. K. Beale, 29–54. Grand Rapids: Baker, 1994.

Vasholz, R. "Isaiah and Ahaz: A Brief History of Crisis in Isaiah 7 and 8." *Presb* 13 (1987): 79–84.

Waltke, B. K. "A Canonical Process Approach to the Psalms." In *Tradition and Testament*, ed. J. Feinberg and P. Feinberg, 3–18. Chicago: Moody, 1981.

Walton, J. H. "Isa. 7:14: What's in a Name?" *JETS* 30 (1987): 289–306.

Warfield, B. B. "The Divine Messiah of the Old Testament." In *Christology and Criticism*, 3–49. New York: Oxford, 1921.

Wegner, P. D. "A Re-examination of Isaiah IX 1–6." *VT* 42 (1992): 103–12.

Wenham, G. J. "*Betûlâ*: A Girl of Marriageable Age." *VT* 22 (1972): 326–48.

Wifall, W. "Gen, 3:15—A Protoevangelium?" *CBQ* 36 (1974): 361–65.

Wood, A. S. "Nicholas of Lyra." *EvQ* 33 (1961): 196–206.

NAME INDEX

SUBJECT INDEX

SCRIPTURE INDEX